# Agricultural reform in China

# AGRICULTURAL REFORM
# IN CHINA:
## FROM COMMUNES
## TO COMMODITY ECONOMY 1978–1990

**Simon G Powell**

STUDIES ON EAST ASIA

## MANCHESTER
## UNIVERSITY PRESS
Manchester and New York

distributed exclusively in the USA and Canada
by St. Martin's Press

First published in 1992 in Great Britain by
Manchester University Press, Oxford Road, Manchester M13 9PL, England
and Room 400, 175 Fifth Avenue, New York, NY 10010, USA

Editorial responsibility for *Studies on East Asia* rests with the Northumbrian
Universities East Asia Centre, University of Newcastle upon Tyne and University
of Durham, England, which promotes publications on the individual countries
and cultures of East Asia, as well as on the region as a whole.

*British Library Cataloguing in Publication Data*
A catalogue record of this book is available
from the British Library

*Library of Congress Cataloguing-in-Publication Data applied for*

ISBN 0–7190–3382–9

Printed in Great Britain
by Billing & Sons Limited, Worcester

# Contents

# Map of the People's Republic of China

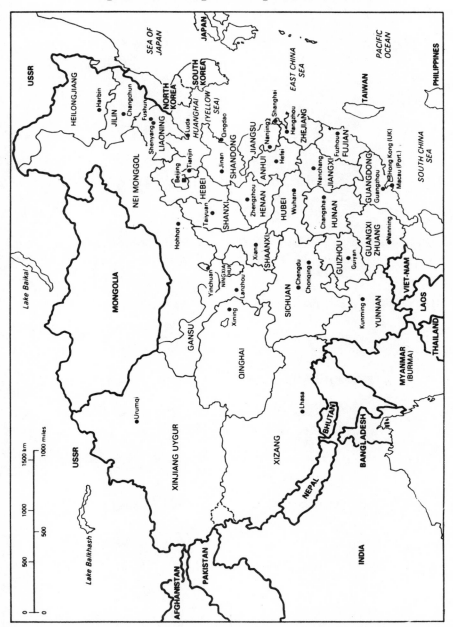

Source: *The Far East and Australasia 1990*, 21st edition, Europa Publications Ltd, London

## Abbreviations used in References

FBIS/DR/PRC    Foreign Broadcast Information Service/Daily Report/ People's Republic of China

FBIS/CR/A      Foreign Broadcast Information Service/China Report/ Agriculture

JPRS/CR/RF     Joint Publications Research Service/China Report/Red Flag

SCMM           Selections from China Mainland Magazines (Title changed to Selections from People's Republic of China Magazines (SPRCM) in 1973

SCMP           Selections from China Mainland Press (Title changed to Selections from People's Republic of China Press (SPRCP) in 1973

SWB/FE/DR      Summary of World Broadcasts/Far East/Daily Report

Xinhua         Xinhua (New China) News Agency

## Chinese Weights and Measures

*Mu*           Chinese unit for measuring land areas. One acre equals 6.07 *mu*; one hectare, 15 *mu*.

*Jin*          Chinese unit for measuring weight. One kilogram equals just under 2 *jin*.

*Yuan*         Chinese currency. US$1 equals c 5.3 *yuan*.

# China: Regional Diversity

Geographically, China is a land of vast size, rich in rural resources and with a range of development opportunities at the local level. It varies East to West: from the Eastern Coastal plains and hinterlands which extend far inland to the mountains and plateaux of Central Asia; and North to South: the harsh winters which dominate the landscapes of the north contrasting with the milder climates of the south.

The land use systems map (Figure 1) distinguishes this regional diversity and also the food production systems which dominate the landscapes. These regions are detailed elsewhere, but some general points can be made.[1] An immediate distinction is drawn between the Central Asian half of China and the Pacific half (area 1 on the map). The Asian portion, with its weak agricultural resource base, supports only a sparse population, and even these numbers are barely sustainable. Herding - the traditional livelihood of the area - is still strong, though less nomadic than in former times.

By contrast, much of south, southeast and eastern coastal China (areas 2 and 3) is extremely rich in agricultural resources. Double- and triple-cropping is found. Rural population densities are high, reaching 2000 per square kilometre and beyond. Agricultural production is intensive, using large amounts of inputs and yielding high outputs. These are the richest rural areas of China.

The southwest (area 4) is a mixed area with varied agricultural landscape. The valley bottoms may be intensively cultivated, but the mountain slopes represent more difficult production conditions. Populations are less dense than those found further south and east; production levels are similarly lower.

The North China Plain (area 5), is one of the traditional Chinese granaries. However, the short summer period limits cropping schedules to three crops in two years compared to the double-cropping common to the south. This weaker productivity is, however, coupled with high rural population densities which the resource base struggles to feed. Opportunities beyond grain are less abundant than those provided by the more fertile and varied conditions to the south.

Immediately to the west of the North China Plain is the Loess plateau (area 6). This is an environment which has long suffered from drought and desiccation. Soil erosion - thin soils washed away by much-needed but concentrated rainfall - is a major concern. Cultivation is limited to one crop per year, barely adequate to sustain population levels.

Finally, to the north and northeast, are the plateau of Inner Mongolia and the plains of the northeast - Manchuria (area 7). The Inner Mongolian plateau is a barren area, ravaged by harsh winters, with serious erosion and desertification problems. The plains of the northeast, while not exempt from similar problems, are relatively fertile, with adequate water supplies and good soils. Population densities are low; land relatively abundant. It is here that some of China's most mechanised agricultural production can be found.

1

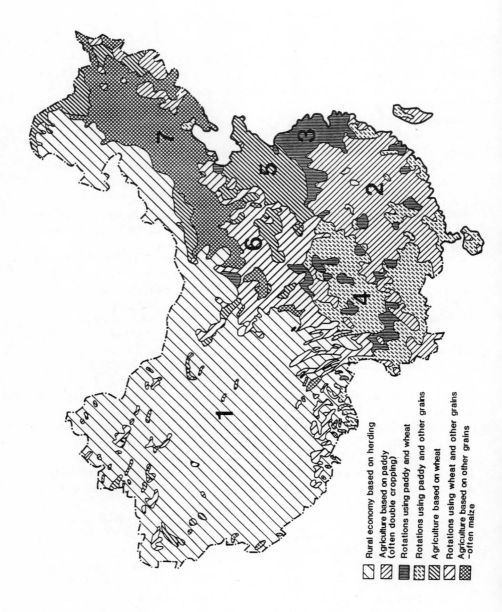

**Figure 1  China - Land-use systems**

With this level of diversity, it must be expected that different localities confront different problems and will develop in different ways. This is important in the current phase of development in rural China. The emphasis of rural policy is commercialisation of agriculture and the rural sector. However, the ability of local units to develop commodity production and increase rural trade depends upon the potential they have to finance such a policy direction - that is, upon their capacity to establish income-generating undertakings.

Regionally, physical limitations - evident even in the brief sketches of rural landscapes given above - are a key determinant of what a locality can and cannot do to generate wealth. Political limitations are another. The need for areas to grow grain not only for themselves (a practical consideration given difficulties in commerce beyond the locality) and for the non-productive urban population is still a basic production goal. Substantial grain outputs are expected from most areas before they engage in commodity production and enter the commercial system with more than just poorly-rewarded grain. Areas with a sophisticated production organisation intended to seize on the opportunity to move beyond grain farming, must still answer the grain question - either by finding ways to produce sufficient grain at minimum cost, or through political manoeuvring.

Political considerations then, serve to reemphasise physical limitations. Those areas which can meet basic grain needs while developing commodity production will prosper ahead of localities which must invest so much in grain that commodity production is limited for lack of land, labour and capital.

It is not, however, simply a case of physical limitations curtailing local development potential. For sure in the western half of China and on the Mongolian plateau for example, the resource base is very weak. Production levels are low. Production potential is scant. However, in the North China plain, agricultural output is relatively high but the peasants' return for this output is low because of demands for grain (both to feed the dense local population levels and for sales elsewhere), low grain prices and high production costs. In addition, little diversified production is possible after grain demands are met. Wealth is elusive.

The kind of production conditions exhibited by the North China plain, where output is relatively high but remuneration remains low, is known in the Chinese material as the 'high-output-poor' trap.[2] First noted in 1979 in a discussion of the North China plain county of Gaocheng, the high-output-poor trap is an important contradiction in the Chinese countryside, falling between the two poles of 'low-output-poor' (the peripheries) and 'high-output-rich' (much of the south and southeast).

The development problem thus becomes how to break out of the high-output-poor trap - or how to stay out. The state has argued that rural units can break out of the high-output-poor trap by first, modernising agriculture in order to increase per-unit yields, freeing resources for commodity production and thereby entering rural trade with cash crops; and secondly, by rearranging

3

production management to promote specialisation in grain production, again freeing resources to develop the commodity economy.

However, Chapters 2 and 3 demonstrate that the effectiveness of the post-1978 rural economic reforms depends on a complex web of interacting variables. The weakness of some of these variables - rural commerce for example has been strongly criticised - can severely curtail the impact that these reforms might have. This in turn limits the wealth creation necessary to finance agricultural modernisation and production specialisation.

The regional chapters that form the bulk of this study further discuss the effectiveness of post-1978 reforms using local materials. They are intended also to exemplify the diversity of development, and detailed development paths, which are identifiable throughout rural China as rural production units attempt to break free of the high-output-poor (or low-output-poor) trap.

Given this diversity of environment within the Chinese setting, it seems necessary and important to go beyond the national or even provincial level so often adopted for research on China. At the same time, over-emphasis on rural administrative units at the county level and below, is also unrealistic. Local characteristics - both human and physical - may be so specific as to render it impractical to adopt such materials as being representative of rural economic development at any higher level. Thus, it is the meso-level - prefecture or group of counties - which has been adopted for the present research.

A meso-level approach has the advantage of being able to draw upon trends from macro-level data sources and at the same time to find a place for local materials. In this way a more realistic assessment of economic development can be made; much of the over-generalisation of macro-level statistics avoided; and important local characteristics which influence rural economic development used positively to identify the wide range of experiences within a given geographical region.

Meso-level research is, however, not without problems. One such problem is that while meso-level spatial areas may be better identified with natural geographic regions and with trends in the real world, data for such areas are rarely readily available. The six regional areas chosen for this research include three which are administrative units - Nenjiang prefecture, Heilongjiang; Yanbei prefecture, Shanxi; and Nanjing municipality, Jiangsu. The others - Taihu and Xuhuai agricultural districts in Jiangsu; and the Northern Guangdong mountain region - are identified as such in the literature but are not administrative units. In all the regions, no wide data base was available and so had effectively to be constructed (although the same is true for work at virtually any level in China).

Choice of region was dictated at one level by the need for contrast, but more specifically by the availability of substantial materials which identified the various regions as distinct geographical entities. A more comprehensive picture of that region was sought by adding materials mainly drawn from Chinese provincial newspapers concerning rural production units within the given research region. Again, availability of such provincial newspapers narrowed the choice of region. Furthermore, potentially more fruitful sources of information such as county/prefectural newspapers were unavailable.

The six regions demonstrate a variety of development paths, illustrating the diversity of natural environment and economic opportunity within rural China. They are also intended to showcase the new organisational forms in the countryside. The chapters on Nanjing and Taihu represent areas of rural wealth; Nanjing's suburban counties benefiting greatly from the proximity of the urban centre; Taihu being a traditionally rich agricultural region in which diversified production and rural industry play a significant role.

By contrast, Xuhuai in northern Jiangsu, represents the southernmost reaches of the North China plain. Climatic and environmental conditions contrast quite sharply with those of Taihu and the Nanjing suburbs in the south of the province, and offer a different development question. Similarly, material from Nenjiang, Heilongjiang, is of a different climate and environment again. Here, mechanisation is a basic requirement for development and imposes a heavy financial burden on unit resources.

The material for Yanbei prefecture, Shanxi, is different again because it is very much concerned with the solution to the grain question offered by grain specialists. The material is more 'theoretical' than practical, but nevertheless offers an insight into the potential conflicts confronting localities in their attempts to utilise the production forms now available to them.

Finally, there is a discussion of development problems in China's mountain areas. Material is more difficult to collect, the Chinese media still preferring to detail striking success rather than the everyday struggle which typifies so many of the mountain areas. But, the significance of these environments within China and their development problems and possibilities need to be briefly outlined.

The available data are incomplete and in parts no more than sketchy. However, it remains possible to gather enough information to make qualitative judgments about regions as a whole. Such qualitative judgments are based not only upon the kind and amount of the available qualitative and quantitative data, but also on its depth and versatility. For example, materials which concentrate only on successes of individual households may be symptomatic of a lack of anything better to report. Data which comment upon progress at county level, though necessarily hiding backward units within it, probably indicate more widespread development. To be sure, local examples of economic development can be found quoted throughout China especially at the brigade level. Yet, what is important, is the extent to which such examples are typical of more widespread development within the area or field of interest.

In this way, absolute assessments and comparisons remain largely impossible - income and production figures telling only a partial truth and masking real barriers to rural development which continue in spite of observed gains. However, only by identifying the range of alternative regional development possibilities as well as barriers, can the reader become aware of the complexity of the Chinese rural situation and the diversity of local needs.

## Notes to Introduction

1   Leeming and Powell, 'Rural China: Old Problems and New Solutions', in Cannon and Jenkins (eds), *The Geography of Contemporary China: the Impact of the Deng Xiaoping Decade*, (Routledge, 1990).
2   Wang Guihai and Hou Zhiyi, 'How to change Gaocheng's "high-output-poor" condition', *People's Daily*, 7.8.1979, p 2.  For a further discussion see Leeming, op cit.

# Chapter One

## Rural China in 1978

In general, however, our agricultural development over the past twenty years has not been rapid enough. Thus, there is a very sharp contradiction between agricultural development on the one hand and the needs of the people and the requirements of the four modernisations on the other. Between 1957 and 1978 the country's population increased by 300 million, 40 million of whom were non-agricultural people, while the total area under cultivation decreased because of land used for capital construction and other purposes. Therefore, although there were increases in both yields per unit area and total grain output, per capita grain output in 1978 was only equivalent to that in 1957. The average per capita income for the agricultural population was only a little over 70 *yuan*, and that of a commune member in nearly one-fourth of the production teams was less than 50 *yuan*. On the average, the collective fund accumulation of each production brigade was less than 10,000 *yuan*, and some production brigades could not even carry out simple reproduction. Industry and all other undertakings just cannot advance without speeding-up agricultural development. In that case the four modernisations will be out of the question. The seriousness and urgency of our country's agricultural question must draw the full attention of all comrades throughout the party.[1]

The period following the Cultural Revolution and the power struggle which resulted in the removal of the so-called 'Gang of Four' has been an important one in determining China's future economic progress. In December 1978 the third plenary session of the 11th Chinese Communist Party Central Committee (CCPCC) decided that the key to future economic progress lay in the rapid development of the agricultural sector and to this end two important documents were approved: 'Decisions of the Central Committee of the Communist Party of China on some questions concerning the acceleration of agricultural development (Draft)' and 'Regulations on the work of the rural people's communes (Draft for trial use)'. Collectively they were issued under the title 'Zhongfa (1979) No 4' on 14 January 1979 and distributed to state organs for discussion and implementation on a trial basis.[2]

The fourth plenary session of the 11th CCPCC subsequently approved the 'Decisions' document but deferred judgment on 'Regulations'.[3] However, most commentators recognise the third plenum as marking an important shift in the agricultural policy of China and it will be used as the starting-point for this discussion on contemporary developments in the Chinese rural economy.[4]

The most striking feature of post-1978 policy statements was the stark assessment made of China's agricultural sector. In the Cultural Revolution - or

'10 years of internal disorder' from 1967 to 1976[5] - the Chinese media gave the impression that Chinese agriculture was in a healthy condition and coping well with the burden imposed upon it by the huge peasant population.

The Cultural Revolution was the culmination of a long effort by Mao Zedong and his supporters to socialise Chinese agriculture. Change has characterised rural China since Liberation. First came radical land reform in 1951. Completed by 1953, this reform transferred 40% of China's arable land from the ownership of landlords to peasant smallholders. In 1954 and 1955, following a largely unsuccessful call for the voluntary association of peasants into mutual-aid teams, a campaign for the widespread creation of rural cooperatives took place.

Cooperatives involved the management of collected peasant landholdings by committee. However, in 1956 the movement towards cooperatives was abruptly replaced by a call for universal collectivisation. Ownership of landholdings reverted to the collective. In the Great Leap Forward (1958-1961), these collectives were the basis for the commune system. Communes, units of local government directly responsible to the state, were to be the driving-force towards complete socialisation of rural family life even to the point of communal dining-halls.

The famine of 1960 brought the Great Leap Forward to a resounding halt, but communes remained a standard rural feature. In the Cultural Revolution they formed the cornerstone of what proved to be Mao's final bid to enforce socialism throughout every aspect of rural life. Communes, typically 3000 households in 50 villages (and their subordinate brigades, 500 households in eight villages or teams), exercised control and management over all aspects of rural production. The planning system was completed by county-level authorities above the communes, who communicated details of the state plan from provincial and state bureaucracies.

In this system, almost all that took place in localities, in terms of resource allocation (land, labour and capital inputs) and production, was officially sanctioned. The seeming success of this system in stimulating economic growth was forcefully illustrated by examples of model communes and brigades, the most used being Dazhai brigade, Xiyang county, Shanxi, adopted by the Maoists as a model for agricultural development in the 'learn from Dazhai' campaign.[6]

The reality of conditions in the Chinese countryside according to post-1978 statements was far removed from the impressions given by the Maoists. Basic peasant living conditions showed little improvement between 1949 and 1978, the periods of the Great Leap Forward and the Cultural Revolution in particular revealing the stark failure of rural policy. Some indication of this is illustrated by the fact that between 1952 and 1978 average annual per capita consumption of grain fell by some 20%. According to Ch'en Po-wen, a speech delivered by Chen Yun at the CCPCC 'work conference' of April 1979 noted that many people had starved to death every year since the Great Leap Forward.[7]

In addition to poor living conditions, agricultural production remained dominated by manual operation. Labour productivity was low and little improvement was being shown in any agricultural sector. Commodity production was small, both in quantity and in the variety of marketable products offered for sale.[8]

Other Maoist claims for rural improvement were laid bare. As noted above for example, the amount of cultivable land had decreased significantly in spite of Maoist claims for huge construction and reclamation projects.[9] Between 1957 and 1977 it is estimated that there was a net reduction of 180 million *mu* in the amount of cultivable land.[10]

The burden of blame for China's depressing rural economic performance in the '10 years of internal disorder' has been, not surprisingly, placed upon the principal characters and policies of the previous regime:

> During the 10 years of the Great Cultural Revolution, the ultraleftist line pushed by the conspiratorial cliques of Lin Biao and the 'Gang of Four' seriously undermined party organisations at various levels, the party policies and fine traditions and the work-style in the countryside. This ultraleftist line undermined the collective economy and the worker-peasant alliance and most seriously dampened the enthusiasm of the peasants and cadres.[11]

Certainly, in many ways the agricultural policies of the Cultural Revolution were blinkered and had a serious negative effect on peasant enthusiasm for agricultural production and general agricultural development. In this period what mattered was not economic argument but political ideology and policy statements were shaped accordingly.

The kinds of problems which arose from the agricultural policies of the Cultural Revolution are perhaps best illustrated by the grain policy of the period. Grain production, and by inference the ability to feed the population, has been the yardstick by which all Chinese rulers, ancient and modern, have been judged. The Maoist attempts to stimulate grain production were encapsulated in the 'Take grain as the key link' policy.

The 'Take grain as the key link' slogan continued 'and promote all-round development in the rural economy'.[12] However, all too often cadres used this policy to emphasise grain at the expense of other economic crops. Indeed, during that time grain production statistics were likely to influence personal political standing and inevitably local cadres sought to promote personal political ambitions through increased grain production - as well as falsifying grain statistics.[13] Grain-planting often occurred with little regard to natural conditions and local suitability to grain production. In many places this indiscriminate expansion had resulted in the destruction of forests and cash crops, increased soil erosion, and an undermining of the ecological balance.[14]

The irony of this situation is that the Maoists placed great stress on the need to increase the extent of high and stable-yield land and the level of advanced techniques in farming so as to improve the natural resource base and increase agricultural output.[15] The 'Eight-point charter' was one such example of Maoist policy in this field - that is, deep ploughing and soil improvement, rational application of fertiliser, irrigation, seed selection, close planting, plant protection, field management and improvement of tools.[16] Indeed, the growth of modern inputs into farming between 1965 and 1976 was striking in comparison to earlier years.

**Table 1  Inputs to farming**

|  | 1952 | 1957 | 1965 | 1976 |
|---|---|---|---|---|
| Tractors (excluding small tractors - 1000s) | 1 | 1 | 17 | 40 |
| Powered irrigation (mn hp) | 0.1 | 0.6 | 9 | 54 |
| Artificial fertilisers (jin/mu of arable) | 0.1 | 0.4 | 3 | 8 |
| Output of artificial fertilisers (mn tons) | neg | 0.2 | 2 | 5 |
| Farm inputs sold at retail (100 mn yuan) | 14 | 33 | 80 | 240 |

Source: Leeming, Table 2.1, p 16, see note 19.

However, the impact of these modern inputs to farming was restricted. First, they were most commonly applied in grain production, for which the peasants had little enthusiasm. This in turn reduced peasant enthusiasm to implement advanced agricultural techniques fully and properly. The same emphasis upon grain saw the extension of grain production to the margin of its production possibility and beyond, both in terms of triple-cropping and planting on unsuitable terrain, further reducing the potential impact of such modern inputs. All this took place at a time when technical skills, training and state financial support were very much in short supply.

Furthermore, much of the equipment involved was of poor quality and often unsuited to local conditions. In addition, the introduction of modern inputs was poorly managed, some areas over-extending their resources for example, in order to mechanise agricultural production. Thus, peasants found themselves with machines they could not use because supplies of electricity and diesel oil needed to power them were inadequate. When the machines broke down, the available repair services were often too costly.[17]

It is true that the Maoist emphasis upon grain production did in fact prompt some increases in per-unit yields and in multi-cropping levels which combined to increase grain outputs. However, the costs - ecological, economic, and to rural vitality - were enormous. Crucially, population increases, made ever more dramatic by improving standards of medical treatment under the collective structure and Maoist ambivalence towards population control, quickly overtook the nominal gains made in grain output and served to increase pressure on limited agricultural resources.

Rural China in 1978

**Table 2  Cultivable land resources. Population. Grain statistics**

| | Popn mn | Sown area mn *mu* | Sown area/ rural popn *mu*/cap | Sown area/ total popn *mu*/cap | Grain O bn *jin* | Unit yield *jin/mu* | O/ head *jin*/cap | C rate % |
|---|---|---|---|---|---|---|---|---|
| 1952 | 574.8 | 2119 | 4.21 | 3.68 | 327.8 | 176.2 | 570.0 | 23.8 |
| 1957 | 646.5 | 2359 | 4.31 | 3.64 | 390.1 | 195.1 | 602.9 | 23.6 |
| 1965 | 725.4 | 2149 | 3.61 | 2.96 | 389.1 | 217.4 | 536.7 | 20.2 |
| 1970 | 829.9 | 2152 | 3.13 | 2.59 | 479.9 | 268.1 | 578.9 | 19.4 |
| 1978 | 962.6 | 2251 | 2.84 | 2.33 | 609.5 | 336.7 | 632.9 | 16.7 |

Key: O = Output; C = Commodity.  Some figures deduced.  Compiled from materials in *Statistical Yearbook of China*, 1981.

Clearly, before 1978, population increase negated the increases in grain production.  In many rural areas, as the commodity rate of grain fell, so lack of grain became a key concern.[18]

To sum up, it must be said that despite the attempts made by the Maoists to improve the natural agricultural resource base and increase the efficiency of farming, a combination of factors - amongst which their own agricultural policies featured strongly - undermined these attempts.  Indeed, Maoist policies like 'Take grain as the key link' in terms of the rigidity of crop schedules and irrational land-use which it encouraged, did much to exacerbate what have always been major flaws in Chinese agriculture: the continuing severe environmental degradation of the agricultural resource base closely linked with agricultural vulnerability to the elements.

Thus, in 1978 Chinese policy-makers, inheriting a situation largely created by their predecessors, were faced with a countryside which can best be described as stagnant.  Peasant enthusiasm for agricultural production was low, a result of such past policies as egalitarian distribution - 'eating from the same big pot'; a reduction in private plots; and an over-emphasis upon grain production combined with low state grain prices.

Those advanced agricultural techniques which were available, tended to be poorly utilised.  In addition, supplies of other modern agricultural inputs - inorganic fertiliser for example[19] - remained inadequate.  The over-emphasis on grain farming had also curtailed the extent of alternative employment opportunities in the Chinese countryside, further exacerbating the problem of surplus labour.  The official commercial system remained hopelessly inefficient.  Finally, the agricultural resource base was weak, subject to excessive degradation and vulnerable to natural disasters.

Important and immediate reforms were necessary to change this situation.  The Dengist regime responded to these problems in the Chinese countryside with a set of 25 policies and measures, clarified and modified in subsequent policy statements.[20]  Indeed, clarification is ongoing as irregularities and

11

tensions within the earlier policies emerge and demand action. Such revisions can be expected to continue for some considerable time with the pace and direction of those revisions determined by the prevailing political climate.

The original policy statement can best be summarised under two headings: increasing peasant incentive for production; and commercialisation of agriculture. Of course, these headings and the policies discussed under each one overlap. However, they have been adopted here for ease of discussion.

Increasing peasant incentive and enthusiasm for production represents the immediate response of the current regime to repair the damage done to peasant enthusiasm by Maoist excesses in rural policy.[21] To this end, measures such as those outlined in Chapter Two were adopted, including the core policy in the rural economic reforms - *baogan daohu*, essentially a return to family farming. The *baogan daohu* system is a bold step by the current regime. It has sought - with some considerable success - to stimulate short-term rural growth, but the potential long-term ramifications are significant and need closer inspection.

The move towards commercialisation of agriculture is interpreted as the long-term policy goal of the Dengist faction; it is discussed in Chapter Three. A number of rural production management forms which are thought to form the heart of the state's desire to commercialise rural production are detailed. Some are practical economic entities; others remain, at least at present, bureaucratic creations whose impact upon rural performancce is difficult to judge.

Together, the combination of short- and long-term policy measures represent what must be considered the core economic policies in place in rural China today. The two chapters provide the necessary backdrop for what is the main offering of this study: the regional development chapters.

Drawing on material from a cross-section of environments, the regional chapters demonstrate the variety of development emphases and experiences which have emerged within the rural sector. Differences in environment serve to ensure that each region has different needs and priorities in its efforts to generate wealth. The regions have reacted to their own set of economic possibilities in a variety of ways, utilising different organisational forms and development strategies to capitalise on the advantages offered by their environment.

This regional study is by no means complete. Given China's vastness, diversity of rural experience is inevitably great. What is being offered here, is an insight into the kind of diverse rural possibilities and experience which characterises China. This represents a distinct move away from a 'uniform' national level approach to Chinese rural economic development. By placing rural experiences in a regional context, the materials and ideas in Chapters Four to Nine, necessarily represent the foundation of Chinese rural geography at the present time and for the forthcoming decade. For the geographer - as well as those in other disciplines - this focus on the rural condition at a level below that commonly offered (that is, the state, and to a lesser extent the province), is crucial.

# Notes to Chapter One

1   *Xinhua Radio*, 'CCPCC's decision on agricultural development', 5.10.1979 tr FBIS/DR/PRC 25.10.1979 supplement 032, pp 1-18. An alternative translation appears in *Issues and Studies*, 1979 15 (7) pp 102-19; (8) pp 92-112; (9) pp 104-15.
2   *Issues and Studies*, 1979 (7) (8) (9) op cit. *Xinhua Radio*, 5.10.1979 op cit. *Beijing Review*, 'The agricultural development programme', 24.3.1980 23 (12) pp 14-20.
3   Lin Chen, 'The commerce system: survival or extinction', *Issues and Studies*, 1982 18 (2) pp 18-30.
4   Du Runsheng (a) 'The modernisation of agriculture and the comprehensive development of the countryside', *Red Flag*, 16.2.1980 tr JPRS/CR/RF No 4, pp 2-17. Zhan Wu & Liu Wenpu (c) 'The 3rd plenary session of the 11th CCPCC creates the new path for agricultural development in our country', *Red Flag*, 1.9.1982 tr JPRS/CR/RF No 17, pp 29-38. Huang Daoxia, 'The practice and development of the theories of scientific socialism in China's countryside', *Guangming Ribao*, 28.5.1984 tr FBIS/CR/PRC 14.6.1984, K18-23.
5   Li Chengrui, 'An analysis of China's economic situation during the period of 10 years of internal disorder - and a look at reliability of statistics from this period', *Jingji Yanjiu* (*Economic Research*), 1984 (1) pp 23-33 tr FBIS/DR/PRC 7.4.1984, K2-15.
6   P Steidlmayer, *The Dazhai model in Chinese agriculture 1964-1974*, (University microfilms international, 1975).
7   Ch'en Po-wen, 'Agriculture in mainland China as revealed in CCP documents: an analysis', *Issues and Studies*, 1979 (11) pp 46-58.
8   *People's Daily*, 'Effectively protect ownership by people's communes and their right of decision', 24.1.1979 tr FBIS/DR/PRC 26.1.1979, E9-13.
9   *Xinhua Radio*, 5.10.1979, op cit.
10  Wang Jialiang, Zhang Yuerong & Zhang Qiaolong, 'We must give serious attention to the study of the land problems', *People's Daily*, 9.4.1982 tr FBIS/DR/PRC, K3-5.
11  *Xinhua Radio*, 5.10.1979, op cit.
12  Anhui provincial revolutionary committee, 'Taking grain as the key link, vigorously develop economic crops', *People's Daily*, 7.4.1971 tr SCMP 1971 (17) pp 16-21. *Red Flag*, 'Conscientiously carry out the three-in-one combination in the development of agriculture, forestry and animal husbandry - an investigation report on Qianan county, Hebei', 1.1.1972 tr SCMM 1972 (1) pp 65-74.
13  B Stone, 'The use of agricultural statistics: some national aggregate examples and current state of the art', in Barker, Sinha & Rose, eds, *The Chinese agricultural economy*, (Westview, 1982).

14   *People's Daily*, 'Correct understanding and all-round development of agriculture', 28.2.1979 tr FBIS/DR/PRC 6.3.1979, E11-15.

15   *People's Daily*, 'Use revolution to lead mechanization - investigation of the state of agricultural mechanization in Jiading county, Shanghai municipality', 4.2.1970 tr SCMP 1970 (07) pp 194-203. Nong Jibing, 'Our agricultural mechanization advancing by leaps and bounds', *Guangming Ribao*, 25.9.1970 tr SCMP 1970 (40) pp 13-19. Siyong country CCPC, 'We must rely on the masses in breeding fine-seed strains - A criticism of the "line of reliance on specialists" pursued by renegade, hidden traitor and scab Liu Shaoqi in seed research', *People's Daily*, 23.11.1971 tr SCMP 1971 (49) pp 8-14. First ministry of machine building, 'Advance along the road of agricultural mechanization shown by Chairman Mao', *People's Daily*, 17.7.1971 tr SCMP 1971 (40) pp 54-65. Li Feng, 'Strive for the realisation of agricultural mechanisation', *Red Flag*, 1.3.1972 tr SCMM 1972 (3) pp 99-104.

16   Lu Xiang, 'Conscientiously implement the "Eight-point charter" for agriculture', *Red Flag*, 1.3.1972 tr SCMM 1972 (3) pp 119-27.

17   Xue Muqiao (b), *China's socialist economy*, (Beijing, 1981).

18   *Issues and Studies*, op cit.

19   F A Leeming, *Rural China Today*, (Longmans: London, 1985).

20   *Xinhua Radio*, 5.10.1979, op cit. *Beijing Review*, 24.3.1980, op cit.

21   Wu Shuo, 'A talk on the second major reform of the rural economic structure', *Liaowang*, 21.1.1985 tr FBIS/DR/PRC 7.2.1985, K19-22. *Liaowang*, 'Help peasants learn this well', 20.5.1985 tr FBIS/DR/PRC 6.6.1985, K1-2.

# Chapter Two

# Increasing Peasant Incentive and Enthusiasm for Rural Production

A number of measures may reasonably be included under this heading: the popularisation of production responsibility systems; an increase in the state purchase price of certain key agricultural products; the status of private plots; and a reemphasis upon diversification and rural industry within the rural economy.

## Production responsibility systems

The key item of rural policy in China since 1978 has been production responsibility systems. Such systems are not a wholly new social form having been used during the late 1950s and early 1960s, to be abandoned with the Cultural Revolution.[1]

The 3rd plenum decisions reestablish production responsibility systems as a key measure in stimulating the rural economy. The broad aims of these systems in agriculture are: to increase agricultural production and income; to consolidate and expand the collective economy; to put into effect the principle of equal pay for equal work; and to enable the broad mass of the peasants to prosper.[2]

The content of the systems themselves varies from place to place. It is argued that this is an inevitable result of the state respecting the autonomy of the production brigades in their choice of detail, enabling them to structure production responsibility systems to suit local conditions and needs.[3] Indeed, one advantage claimed for such systems is that they establish a management framework within which it is possible to avoid the arbitrary decisions which had previously caused so much dislocation in the Chinese countryside.[4]

Nevertheless, it must also be said that variety of detail within responsibility systems also reflects the somewhat flawed nature of the Chinese planning system, whereby complex policies are disseminated from the centre to the localities and at the same time become subject to local interpretation. In the current phase of development, the state is willing to allow this flexibility if it serves to fulfil goals of increased rural production.

The wide variety of production responsibility systems in the Chinese countryside has been documented by numerous authors.[5] Lin Zili, a noted Chinese commentator, distinguishes three broad categories: first, that which is not linked to output. Within this system, responsibility is allocated for the fulfilment of certain production tasks but is not linked to output.[6] Secondly, that which is linked to output and retains the use of workpoints. The important point here is the linkage of responsibility with output. Responsibility for tilling

15

or using the land or other means of production is passed to the peasants, and the workpoints are determined by contracted output targets. Payment is based on workpoints after certain deductions have been made by the collective.[7]

The final type of responsibility system is that which is linked to output and has abolished the use of workpoints.[8] This form is referred to as the 'all-round contract system'. Commonly responsibility is allotted to each household - *baogan daohu*. The basic characteristic of this system is that incomes are directly determined by the contracted output targets. Remuneration is directly linked to output without the need to use workpoints.

In the period since the 3rd plenum, it has been possible to distinguish distinct changes in the dominant form of responsibility system. This is well illustrated by material from Hubei province. At first, 80% of production teams adopted a system which linked responsibility to output and retained workpoints. However, by 1982 only 2.8% of the production teams retained this system. At this point, the *baogan daohu* system of production responsibility had emerged as the most popular form of responsibility system within Hubei and throughout China.[9] By 1983, 94.5% of China's rural brigades had adopted *baogan daohu*.

## *Baogan daohu*

Initially the state was concerned not to allow the *baogan daohu* system to develop widely. The fixing of output quotas by individual households was intended only for 'poor and backward areas' where 'the level of productive forces is low'.[10] The state was explicit that:

> Except for those with special requirements to develop sideline production and the few individual households in remote hilly areas with poor communications, the fixing of output quotas based on the household should not be practised.[11]

However, despite these pronouncements, the *baogan daohu* system has been developed as the basic management form in the Chinese countryside with the household emerging as the basic production unit.[12]

Various explanations have been offered to account for this. It is argued that such a system links labour more closely with output, encouraging peasants to work harder and produce more.[13] At the same time this closer relationship between labour and output has encouraged individual peasants to utilise their skills and experience to cut production costs while increasing economic benefits.[14] Perhaps most significantly, by linking labour and output with rewards the principle of 'distribution according to work' is more directly implemented.[15] This may be the argument which carries most weight among the country people themselves, because it leaves no opportunities for egalitarian distribution at the grassroots level through the use of workpoints.

Furthermore, there is little doubt that after the Maoist excesses of 'eating from the same big pot' most Chinese peasants were keen to seize the chance to work for themselves, relying on their own skills and reaping the benefits of their own efforts without having to worry about the work-attitude of fellow collective members.  In reality, many peasants are embarking on a system of family farming.  Whereas in 1978 only one-quarter of rural household income originated from household-based occupations, by the end of the 1980s, virtually all such income (83%) came from household-based occupations.[16]

It is probably of no great significance that the *baogan daohu* system emerged so swiftly throughout the Chinese countryside despite the CCPCC's stated intention that it should not do so.  Though the post-1978 Dengist regime may have felt constrained in the immediate official dismantling of Maoist rural economic forms, unofficially it would appear that from the first they were quite willing to see the *baogan daohu* system develop throughout rural China.  Certainly, by 1982 articles were appearing which accepted the *baogan daohu* system as being widespread throughout the Chinese countryside.  Material from 1981 for maize production in the three production teams of Zhangshen brigade, Ling county, Dezhou prefecture in Northwest Shandong for example, point out the system's superiority.  This example merits a little further consideration.[17]

Zhangshen brigade is an advanced rural production unit.  Most ploughing and sowing are mechanised.  Zhangshen has 43.5 hp/100 *mu* of farm machinery which compares well to the 21 hp/100 *mu* for Shandong and 15.2 hp/100 *mu* for China as a whole.  The cultivable land resources of 1200 *mu* are fully irrigated. In the cultivation of maize, each of the three production teams used different management forms.  The number one team adopted a contract system with responsibility to work-groups, the number three team utilised a *baogan daohu* system while the number two team used no form of responsibility system.  Soil fertility, labour skill and expertise, fertiliser applications and so forth were said to be basically similar.  Production figures however, reveal striking differences.

**Table 1  Zhangshen production brigade, Shandong. Maize production characteristics. 1981**

| Prodn team | Cultiv- able land (*mu*) | Contract figure (*jin/mu*) | Per-unit yields (*jin/mu*) | Total output (1000 jin) | Above contract production (*jin/mu*) | (1000 jin) |
|---|---|---|---|---|---|---|
| 1 | 200 | 500 | 700 | 140 | 200 | 40 |
| 2 | 200 | 500 | 580 | 116 | 80 | 16 |
| 3 | 200 | 500 | 750 | 150 | 250 | 50 |

Source: Guo Ming *et al*, op cit, (slightly adapted).

This example was used to demonstrate that contract responsibility systems in general, and the *baogan daohu* system in particular, are more effective in generating peasant enthusiasm for production.

## The contract in the *'baogan daohu'* system

> The core of the system of contracted responsibilities with payment linked to output is 'contract'.[18]

Simply defined, individual households through a contract have at their disposal a specific parcel of 'responsibility' land on which they may farm. In return for use of the land the household must fulfil contracted output targets for both state procurements and collective retentions. It must also provide for subsistence of the contracting family. Once these demands are met, the individual household is entitled to any output from that land. Some of this output will be contracted as above-target at the appropriate above-quota prices. Alternatively, it can be sold privately. Contracts should stipulate such things as the amount of labour days to be contributed by a household to the collective unit, the amount of accumulation funds and so forth. (For a full account of a model *baogan daohu* contract from Gongtong county, Shanxi see Crook quoting a Shanxi Ribao article.[19])

In 1985 it was announced that peasants were, in theory, allowed to decide either to accept or reject state sales targets in contracts offered by the state. Rejection of contracts would leave the peasants free to sell all their output privately - while still fulfilling other contractual obligations such as collective investment contributions. However, in many areas, there was effectively little choice for peasants when signing contracts and they were required to accept state sales targets. On the one hand, local authorities are still reluctant to let production move so completely beyond their control. On the other hand, many areas are unable to take advantage of the option offered to them of selling their produce on private markets, because commercial accessibility remains poor. In essence, it still remains to be seen if this further reform will become established in the countryside. Recent grain production figures indicate that the state may not be able to trust grain production to the market as it would like.

In the official press the standard rationalisation is that the contract has the key function of linking peasant agricultural output with the state plan.[20] That is to say, the contract is a guide to producers and binds the production relationship between the state, the collective, and the individual peasant.[21]

It is also standard policy that once state and collective demands have been met, peasants can then sign further contracts with other departments, production units, individuals and so forth for the sale of surplus agricultural produce, thereby gaining entry into the wider commodity economy.[22] Through the use of 'legal and binding contracts' it is argued that the interests of all parties can be safeguarded, the peasants able to enthusiastically develop agricultural production without the risk of being unable to sell surplus produce.

Inevitably there will be some convergence and divergence (potential and real) between state ideals and needs and peasant actions and needs. However, in the current phase, the state is apparently willing to be flexible for the sake of economic development. At some point however, left-wing ideological concerns may return to the fore and curtail such flexibility.

## Land allocation and procurement quotas

The two key measures within the contract are land allocation and the level of contracted sales to the state. Perhaps the most important consideration is how responsibility land should be allocated within rural production units. Four methods of allocating responsibility land can be identified: first, to assign responsibility land on the basis of the total number of people within that unit.[23] Secondly, to assign responsibility land on the basis of the available labour-force of individual households within that unit.[24] Thirdly, a mixture of the above, whereby a fixed proportion of responsibility land is assigned according to the total population while the remainder is allotted on the basis of available labour.[25] Finally, the assignment of land can be done purely on the basis of ability, that is specialised contracts, where the grain ration of those households who receive little land is guaranteed through collective retention of grain.[26]

The first three practices have given rise to numerous contradictions. Within a production unit there is often a disparity in the quantity and skill of labour between households as well as a disparity in the means of production available to them. Per capita distribution of land will result in some households with a large potential production capacity but only limited land resources. Conversely, other households will find it impossible to till all the land assigned to them.[27]

Further, agricultural land is graded according to its quality - soil fertility, irrigation conditions, accessibility from the village and so forth - with each household receiving the appropriate amount of a variety of graded pieces of land. Invariably, the process of proportionate land division leads to excessive dispersal of farmland which is unfavourable for tillage. Hongkouqiao brigade, Bishi commune, Hubei for example has 1602 *mu* of cultivable land divided into 4871 pieces of varying quality. The average size of such plots works out at 15 square metres. Such a dispersal of farmland is inconvenient for cultivation, irrigation and drainage as well as management. Such inconvenience will be very much exacerbated in those units where intensive and mechanised cultivation is carried out.[28]

Distribution of land on such a *pro rata* basis could give the state certain ideological and policy difficulties. Some households with responsibility land but without labour power either engage others to till or ask others to till for them

19

(on commission).[29] The state is very unwilling for such wage-labour relationships to develop.

Similarly, allocating land on a per capita basis or according to available labour power only serves to advertise the viability of large households, something the state is vigorously trying to counter with its current population policies, whereby couples are encouraged to have only one child.

Nevertheless, there are two reasons why assigning land on a *pro rata* basis is inevitable. First, Chinese peasants associate their land with their means of subsistence. It is difficult to change their desire to collect as much land as they can possibly obtain from the collective, and not just what they might be able to cultivate. This argument relates to reliance on land in a general way.

A similar argument is used for grain specifically. Because grain supply is still a problem in many rural areas, in implementing production contracts peasants tend to distribute land equally in the belief that if they do not have land they have no guaranteed grain supply. This is especially true in areas where agricultural production is backward and the commodity rate of grain is low. Memories of hard times are still fresh for too many peasants.[30]

Assigning land on the basis of household ability in specialised contracts is an attractive alternative. For the moment, however, specialised contracts, though undoubtedly on the increase, will remain concentrated in commodity production areas (bases) and those rural areas of relative economic wealth where conditions - physical, infrastructural, human and so forth - facilitate specialised production. (Specialised production is discussed at greater length below).

The second key consideration when contracts are made is the level of produce sales required to be made to the state in return for land allocations. Ideally, these levels should be rationally set, relating to the interaction of various physical and human resources available to any particular household. The question remains however, of how to achieve this. Those explanations that are offered in the materials tend to revert to political posturing, with little clear indication of how a rational mechanism for the setting of sales targets would actually work.[31]

Not surprisingly it would appear that production units opt for average allocation of sales targets. Average allocation might take the form of apportioning targets according to average crop acreage; according to household size; household labour capacity; a ratio of household size to labour capacity; or some temporary combination of the above.[32]

These methods of average allocation of quotas ignore non-labour factors such as price differentials between agricultural methods, relative investment costs, relative productivity rates and so forth. Under these circumstances, it is difficult for contract households to get reasonable remuneration after fulfilling their quotas. This is especially true for commodity grain households for whom low state grain prices in no way compensate for the cost of the agricultural inputs used in the production of grain (as discussed in detail below).

This problem is a serious one, and the necessity to perform the relevant calculations in several different units - cash, grain, working days and so forth - renders satisfactory solutions virtually impossible to find.

## Advantages and disadvantages of the 'baogan daohu'

The major advantage of *baogan daohu* is that it effectively implements the principle of 'to each according to his work'.[33] The peasant can see that hard work means in theory more reward and enthusiasm for work is encouraged. A clear attempt is being made to redress the absence of material incentives within the rural economy following the egalitarian policies which had previously prevailed and which had severely depressed enthusiasm for production.

Moreover, as already noted, it is argued that *baogan daohu* rids Chinese agriculture of the arbitrary decisions which had previously caused so much dislocation in the countryside. In theory, it is now possible to maintain flexibility and adopt the system to suit exploitation of local resources and meet local needs.[34] The ability to adapt *baogan daohu* to specialised production and commodity production remains an important benefit. This kind of adaptability is much welcomed after the uniformity of approach insisted upon in the 'learn from Dazhai' movement.

Other advantages include improved economic accounting; reduced production costs; increased labour productivity - both through better management in terms of specialisation and division of labour and also by raising the enthusiasm of the peasants by the removal of egalitarian management.[35]

We should not however, overlook the disadvantages - potential and actual - which *baogan daohu* contains within it. The most immediate set of problems are those associated with the contract itself. There are difficulties because contracts are not legally respected, sometimes by the authorities, sometimes by the people.[36] Quotas are arbitrarily raised and collective requirements increased. Alternatively, contracts are simply torn up. Again, some rural cadres have interfered with peasant production and thereby prevented them from fulfilling their contract terms.[37] Such contradictions, similar to those cited by Pfeffer when reviewing contracts in Chinese agriculture between 1949 and 1963, can seriously dampen peasant enthusiasm for production and slow potential rural economic growth.[38]

Another important concern is the possible breakdown of the collective structure, some localities believing that *baogan daohu* involves 'returning land to the owner', that is, the 'return of land to the farming household'.[39] The state has been quick to attack such viewpoints, emphasising that what has developed is a system of letting each individual household manage its own affairs and bear responsibility for its own profit or loss. This system remains part of the system of the public ownership of land in which peasant households and the collective maintain a contractual relationship, with the collective exercising unified control over the use of farmland, large farm machines and water conservation facilities and farmland capital construction.[40]

It must be doubted however, if all peasants can rationalise as effectively as the Chinese media and emphasis has been put on strengthening 'political and ideological work' to ensure that the 'peasants' private ownership mentality' does not grow further.[41] The state argues that it is the peasants themselves who are afraid of reverting back to a landscape dominated by small-scale farming under individual ownership. However, this argument carries little credence. Clearly the peasants are not afraid; the state, however, is.[42]

The weakening of the collective system has manifested itself in a number of ways. In a survey of Fujian, Jiangxi and Hunan for example, peasants were demanding the division of all communal property and the removal of any element of collective control, besides displaying an unwillingness to hand in grain to collective authorities and even indiscriminately appropriating collective property.[43] Similar problems are noted throughout China.[44]

The state has attempted to counter division of communal property for example, through illustration of the problems which can result. One such illustration was the case of Zuozhai and Huangkou brigades, Lankao County, in Jiangsu province. The water conditions in these two brigades were said to be virtually identical. After implementation of production responsibility systems, authorities in Huangkou brigade divided up the motor-pumped wells and the water channels. During a drought period in 1981, wheat production declined by 20,000 *jin* because fields were not sufficiently irrigated. By way of contrast, in Zuozhai brigade, where collective control of irrigation facilities was maintained, wheat output increased by 120,000 *jin* in spite of the drought.[45]

Nevertheless, despite such examples, it must be expected that throughout the Chinese countryside collective functions have been under attack. Wu Xiang, a noted Chinese commentator, for example records what he calls the 'ten disadvantages' of *baogan daohu*:

> disadvantage in the purchase, use, maintenance and repair, and management of large farm machines and tools; disadvantage in the unified and rational use of water resources; disadvantages in the care of draft cattle; disadvantage in the prevention of plant diseases and insect pests; disadvantages in the trial and popularisation of scientific farming; disadvantage for the unified guidance and the concentration of forces in combating natural disasters; disadvantage in the unified planning and the deployment of labour in agricultural capital construction; disadvantage in the development of enterprises run by communes and production brigades and teams and the development of the diversified economy; disadvantage in water and soil conservation; and disadvantage in the care of the four categories of dependants and of households enjoying the five guarantees.[46]

Such a list is an important one. Gray for example, comments that it reads 'like a denial of everything for which socialism has so far stood in rural China'.[47] To be fair, what it has stood for and what it has achieved are far removed.

Furthermore, the state admits that in many production units there is a problem of lax leadership by local officials. Too many local cadres are concentrating on developing their own income opportunities, neglecting their management responsibilities.[48]

Nevertheless, the state counters that *baogan daohu*, if properly implemented and linked to unified management, can overcome these weaknesses.[49] Also, in some areas so-called 'specialised service companies' are developing to provide those services which the household economy finds difficult to manage - pest control and irrigation and drainage for example. However, it is unclear as yet how effective and widespread such service companies will become.[50] (A fuller discussion follows in Chapter Four.)

The reduction in the influence of collective management over everyday peasant life has led to the continuing misuse of collective land.[51] Misuse of collective land can include: illegal building of houses by peasants upon good cultivable land; the illegal seizure and enclosure of land by commune- and brigade-run enterprises and other organisations; waste of cultivable land resulting from loopholes in contracts governing the acquisition of land; and finally, the illegal transaction, transfer and leasing of land.[52]

The state responded to the first problem, that of illegal building of houses on good farmland, in a series of housing construction regulations.[53] However, more recent reports indicate that there has been no change in the situation of indiscriminate occupation and random use of farmland in China. Indeed, according to one source, in recent years an annual average of five million *mu* of farmland has been occupied for non-agricultural purposes.[54] While some of these activities will be legitimate adjuncts of the rural economy, many will not. All this places increasing pressure on the available land resources.

Additionally, land used purportedly to improve basic rural infrastructure is often wasted because many projects are ill-conceived. In one report of highway construction in Henan for example, highway expansion occupied 33,500 *mu* of cultivable land. Furthermore, 31,400 houses were torn down and significant areas of forest were felled. Telecommunications facilities and water conservancy works were also destroyed.[55]

Again, the weakening of the collective structure is a root cause of birth control difficulties in the countryside at a time when the state is seeking to vigorously implement a 'one-child policy'. The role of population growth as a negative factor in Chinese rural economic well-being is widely argued and has been well illustrated in figures presented in Chapter One which indicated the burden placed upon agricultural resources by population growth.[56]

The state admits that the introduction of responsibility systems in general, and *baogan daohu* in particular, make birth control more difficult. Such difficulties are apparently widespread.[57] In Liaoning for example, problems arise because officials responsible for birth control are also responsible for the setting of output targets. They have tended to concentrate on production and neglect birth control.[58] The state has responded by widening the scope of production contracts to include some element of birth control.[59] Nevertheless, there is undoubtedly still widespread official concern over this issue.[60]

Another concern is the further creation of surplus labour in a rural economy where unemployment and underemployment are widespread. In some areas surplus labour may account for as much as 30% of the rural labour force and it is conceded that responsibility systems of all types add to this figure.[61] It is hoped that in time peasant enthusiasm for production will generate further employment opportunities - in commerce and processing industries for example - but how much employment can be generated remains open to question.

The final area of concern is the ability of collectives to accumulate the funds and labour needed to facilitate expanded rural production - a point which as discussion proceeds comes increasingly to the fore. State investment in agriculture is limited and is likely to remain so in the immediate and long-term future. Thus, collective retention of funds is crucial. Similarly, a collective role in rural labour accumulation is important. Households themselves have a labour capacity which is generally small in scale, limited in scope, and hardly feasible for undertaking large-scale farmland water conservancy capital construction and other major farmland improvements. In that contracts allow peasants to pay a cash sum in lieu of collective work-days, the collective has some means to hire labour on a casual basis.[62] Indeed, in view of the rural surplus labour reserves, this may be seen as desirable. Nevertheless, there is little doubt that *baogan daohu* has made collective retention of capital and labour more difficult to administer despite their inclusion in the contract.[63]

The main area of concern is that of accumulating capital. As responsibility systems were popularised, the amount of collective retention funds dropped considerably. In 1980 for example, collective retention funds fell by 15.2% on 1979 levels. Similarly, 1981 levels were a further 11.2% below those of 1980. By the mid-1980s, collective retention funds amounted to little more than 8% of net rural income, down from over 14% in 1978.

The primary reason for this decline was the partial shift in responsibility for accumulating capital from the collective to the household.[64] Under production responsibility systems, the peasant households are responsible for accumulating capital to invest in production, an undertaking previously managed exclusively by the collective. In other words, the peasants now have to purchase some amount of producer goods previously supplied by the collective. Thus, the collective accepts that a part of what was previously contributed to collective retention funds is now kept back by the households to purchase such goods. However, many peasants find it hard to differentiate between income which is used to purchase producer goods (in lieu of collective retention fund contributions) and that for consumer goods.[65]

In addition, it is also realistic to interpret this tendency towards consumption by the peasants as a reaction to two things. First, there is a grave lack of producer goods. Secondly, there is still a fear amongst peasants that the current income gains will be short-lived and followed by a return to egalitarian distribution. Not surprisingly many are more concerned to convert current gains into consumer goods.[66]

The state has tried to counter such fears through an emphasis upon stability in policy. It considers this approach is best served by an increased length of contracted time periods.[67] In 1984, state regulations allowed for a land contract period to be extended in order to encourage peasants to increase their investments, to develop soil fertility and to practise intensive farming. The land contract period was generally encouraged to be for 15 years or more. In addition, in the case of land contracted for development projects such as fruit growing, forestry work, and the development of barren hills and wasteland, the contract period could be extended up to 50 years.[68] Such long-term contracts may also be passed from one generation to the next.[69]

The 15 year time period seems to have been widely adopted.[70] However, such an extended period, while on the one hand encouraging stability in production relations, on the other hand sets up its own problems and rigidities, some of which (for instance, changes in the circumstances of households) may well prove intolerable to the state.

## 'Baogan daohu': a summary

Opinions as to the impact of baogan daohu and production responsibility systems in general remain varied. Gray feels the limitations of these systems represent a 'devastating case' against them.[71] In contrast, Wu Xiang, amongst others, feels the benefits - potential and real - outweigh the limitations. If production responsibility systems raise enthusiasm for production, and ensure peasants adequate supplies of food and clothing, it is believed that difficulties will be easier to solve. This belief is, however, simplistic.[72]

More realistically, it should be said that as a measure to promote immediate short-term growth baogan daohu works well. However, while baogan daohu may encourage peasant enthusiasm for production and promote some increases in per-unit yield and multi-cropping levels, inevitably natural constraints limit the extent to which enthusiasm for production can be a substitute for an improved agricultural resource base and advanced agricultural technical and managerial methods. It is important that such substantive improvement and advancement takes place. Until it does, the success of these production management systems in many areas will remain limited by natural resource capacity and subject to the vagaries of the weather.[73]

Furthermore, in the long-term, the limitations of these systems may take on greater significance. In the current phase the limitations are accepted as inevitable alongside a welcome growth in the rural economy, even though this growth may only be short-term. As natural constraints once more begin to curtail production possibilities, the limitations of these systems may be sufficient to engender policy change.

## Price reform

Clearly, the most important organisational change in the countryside since 1978 has been the emergence of *baogan daohu*, or family farming. However, peasant enthusiasm for grain production has been boosted by other reforms, less dramatic than *baogan daohu*, but nonetheless important. Some comment as to these reforms follows.

Before 1978 prices were irrational in two respects: first, in relation to production costs making the production of many items unprofitable; and secondly, relative agricultural prices were inconsistent with consumer demands of, and state expectations for, crop composition.[74] Thus, as part of the package of measures to improve peasant incentive and enthusiasm for production, important price rises for selected agricultural goods were announced.

The most important of these price rises were as follows.

**Table 2  Agricultural produce purchase price increases. 1979\***

|  | Quota price (as a % above previous prices) | Above-quota price (as a % above previous prices) |
|---|---|---|
| Grain | 20 | 50 |
| Cotton | 15 | 30 |
| Oil-bearing crops | 25 | 50 |
| Pigs | 26 | n/a |
| Cattle, goats, eggs, sugar, hides, silk and fish | 20 | 50 |

\*Klatt gives a more detailed assessment of price increases; see note 77.
Compiled from materials in *Xinhua*, 24.10.1979a, in FBIS/DR/PRC 25.10.1979, L12.

Undoubtedly, such price rises had some impact upon peasant income. Official state figures in 1979 noted that in Hubei province for example, rural per capita income could be expected to rise by 8.4 *yuan* as a direct result of the state price increases.[75] Across the nation peasants could expect an increase in incomes of some 7000 million *yuan* through increased purchase prices for farm products, that is by about 8.75 *yuan* per capita of rural population.[76]

While 8.75 *yuan* represents only about 5.6% of the average rural per capita income in 1979, it is about 34.9% of the total increase in average rural per capita incomes between 1978 and 1979.[77]

The scale of these price increases was considerable. Since 1979, the prices paid for agricultural produce have continued to increase, but much more steadily.

**Table 3  Index of farm and sideline produce prices (1978 = 100)**

| | | | |
|------|-------|------|-------|
| 1978 | 100   | 1982 | 141.6 |
| 1979 | 122.1 | 1983 | 147.8 |
| 1980 | 130.8 | 1984 | 153.8 |
| 1981 | 138.5 | 1985 | 166.9 |

Compiled from materials in *Statistical Yearbook of China*, 1986.

Realistically, the peasants can only expect these more moderate increases in purchase prices in the future. Such price increases (or conversely increased subsidies for production inputs) are a severe drain on the state treasury.

The state emphasises the point that peasants must increase their incomes through the expansion of production and a reduction in farming expenditures, that is, more efficient farming. They must not rely on large increases in the purchase price of farm and sideline products, or dramatic reductions in contracted production targets.[78]

This resistance to further price increases leaves many contradictions within the official pricing system. Although the price-scissors between agricultural and industrial goods has been reduced, it still exists. Furthermore, price differentials between grain and other farm produce remain large. Grain production continues to be a fundamental problem in the Chinese countryside because the income received in no way compensates for the expenditure of land, labour and capital involved in grain production. (The same is also true for cotton and other staples, but it is the problem of grain pricing which tends to dominate discussion of price differentials.)

The state has made attempts to more adequately reward grain production through the introduction of a '30/70' pricing system, for example.[79] The state will purchase as much as 150-160 billion *jin* of grain at this 30/70 price. That is to say, in any contractual agreement, 30% of the grain will be purchased at the state list price while the remainder, 70%, will be purchased at the state above-list price. While this represents an improvement for grain producers, grain prices still remain low in comparison to those of other crops. Again, qualitative differences between agricultural produce are not adequately reflected in the pricing structure.[80]

The need for reform in the pricing structure is recognised by the state. The problem remains how to finance it. For the state to increase market prices for grain in order to adequately reward grain producers would require a concomitant increase in urban wage supplements to offset the resultant increases in urban grain prices. Reductions in these supplements in certain cities has led to a disquiet amongst urban residents. The state cannot tolerate urban unrest, yet equally cannot afford the cost of such wage supplements. In the current phase, it seems to have adopted the attitude that the short-term gains offered by the rural reforms are sufficient to offset rural complaints about product prices. In the longer-term, this is clearly an issue which will continue to trouble policy-makers.

## Private plots

The use of private plots suffered considerably during the 'learn from Dazhai' movement. In Dazhai, the suppression of private plots was encouraged as 'cutting-off capitalism's tail'.[81] Many cadres blindly implemented similar measures to those taken by Dazhai, without reference to local experiences and the natural environment.[82]

The 1978 policy statements strongly repudiated the 'learn from Dazhai' line and firmly restored the private plot as an important element of the rural economy. Peasants were encouraged to use private plots to engage in domestic side occupations and thus increase their incomes.[83] The maximum amount of land which may be given over to private plots is set at 15% of the total cultivated area of a production team.[84] Interestingly the same report specifically excludes those areas where *baogan daohu* has been introduced from this 15% limit, presumably such areas were to retain the previous 5 to 7% limit. However, as the individual peasant now has more control over land resources - with the widespread use of *baogan daohu* - the need for private plots may be obsolete. They may effectively have been absorbed into household landholdings.

Whatever the precise details, the restoration of private plots, either as plots in their own right or as a part of *baogan daohu* holdings, will certainly do much to increase rural employment and income opportunities, and, it is hoped, utilise a significant amount of the existing surplus labour force.[85]

Animal husbandry for example, as a sideline occupation on private plots will not only increase livestock numbers, but also add to rural organic fertiliser supplies. Indeed, the importance of private livestock as a source of organic fertiliser should in no way be underestimated.[86] In the 1950s, for example, pigs kept on private plots supplied Chinese rural producers with the bulk of their organic fertiliser. In 1956, 70 million of 85 million pigs (83%) in China were estimated to be kept privately. By the mid-1970s, this figure had increased to 220 million (73%) despite the limitations on private ownership during the Cultural Revolution.[87]

Certainly, since 1978, from initial figures on the composition of per capita rural incomes, that part of per capita income made up from sideline production has increased at a much higher rate than total per capita rural incomes.[88] Much of this must be due to the widespread restoration of the private plot - and ultimately its incorporation within the *baogan daohu* holdings. This is a significant factor in the increased peasant enthusiasm for rural production and the improved rural condition.

## Diversification

> Planting the five cereals will provide us with sufficient food, whereas raising silkworms, planting hemp and rearing the six domestic animals will enrich the people.[89]

The immediate impact of a reemphasis upon diversification in farming - implicit in the *baogan daohu* through the granting of more overall control to the individual for the composition of agricultural production - and reinforced by agricultural price differentials, was a move towards an appropriate adjustment of the farming economy. Fields inappropriately claimed for the cultivation of grain at the height of the Maoist 'Take grain as the key link' period began to be reclaimed for their original use. This had important local ecological as well as economic benefits.[90] (For a further discussion see materials from a mountain district in Western Hunan, Chapter Nine).

The area sown with grain crops has shrunk significantly since the 1978 reforms. This area, which had usually been 1.8 billion *mu,* fell below 1.65 billion *mu* by the end of the 1980s. Conversely, the planting of industrial crops (including cotton and oil-bearing plants) rose from around 200 million *mu* in the pre-reform era to over 320 million *mu.*

However, this tendency to reduce grain farming may be due as much to peasant disinclination to grow poorly-rewarded grain crops as any rational restructuring of the farming economy. (For a further discussion of this issue see the material from Suzhou prefecture in Chapter Five).

Examples of diversification in the media invariably illustrate the absolute decline in sown area of grain crops coupled with an absolute increase in grain output. The reader is left in little doubt that grain, while not the dominant political concern it once was, remains the key crop within the Chinese countryside, and that grain outputs should not falter. Also, little mention is made of any increases in production costs which are usually involved in the raising of per-unit yields and multi-cropping levels necessary to support a decline in the area sown with grain. These concerns notwithstanding, it is clear however, that diversified production is an increasingly important element of the rural economy.

The standard illustrations of prosperity generated by diversified production also feature production responsibility systems prominently and favourably.

Concomitant to the emergence of diversified undertakings, rural industrial enterprises are also emphasised, in particular processing concerns. The state contends that rural industrialisation is a logical extension to diversification.[91]

One such illustration of a diversified economy is offered for Wanzai county in Yichun prefecture, Northwest Jiangxi. By Jiangxi standards, Wanzai is both densely-populated and well-developed. With a population approaching 400,000, the average cultivable land per capita is barely one *mu*. Traditionally, hand-made paper, ramie cloth and fireworks have been the key products in Wanzai's economy.[92] Fireworks in particular are a major source of employment and income and have been sold throughout China and Southeast Asia for over 600 years. Today, 80,000 people (21% of the county's population) are employed in over 100 fireworks factories and workshops. In addition, timber, ramie cloth, tea, castor oil, various medications, honey, rabbits, poultry and fish are important. During the Cultural Revolution, diversified production in Wanzai fell, but since the reforms its rich resource base - large areas of forest and woodland, as well as lakes and rivers - is again being fully exploited.[93] Certainly, diversification is playing its part in reinvigorating Wanzai's economy, with income from diversified production being as much as one-third of per capita income. However, it must be said that the role played by local industry appears more significant - a point not made by the materials. Peasant enthusiasm for production, apparently including grain production, has increased in the current phase with correspondingly better income and employment opportunities.

A commitment to a policy of diversification - undoubtedly alongside the development of rural industry - has a potentially more wide-ranging role in the Chinese countryside in the current phase: first, as the source of employment opportunities for increasing numbers of surplus labour;[94] and secondly, and more critically, as a source of wealth from which local collective accumulation funds might be raised and rural production - through the financing of appropriate capital construction projects - extended. Certainly, this has been true of Wanzai.[95] This more wide-ranging role for diversification - and rural industry - is made clearer in the regional examples discussed in Chapters Four to Nine.

## Rural industrialisation

In order to see that those who have been squeezed out of agriculture will not become jobless or that they will not be compelled to gather in cities, it is imperative to enable them to carry out industrial production in rural areas.[96]

After liberation in 1949, and especially in the period of collectivisation in the late 1950s, collective rural enterprises grew rapidly as a central theme in the Great Leap Forward. However, the truth of many of these enterprises was that they were poorly conceived, uneconomic, and soon closed down. In the mid-

1960s growth recommenced, receiving much attention from western commentators.[97] Of particular interest and importance were the so-called 'five small industries' of iron and steel, chemical fertiliser, farm machinery, cement and energy - coal and electricity.[98] Such industries were predominantly administered at the county level.

Since the 1978 reforms, rural industrial enterprises have burgeoned with particular emphasis on the development of small-scale commune- and brigade-run enterprises as well as individual undertakings. While individual enterprises and other cooperative forms of industrial ownership (that is, combinations of households and individuals pooling resources to establish enterprises) have bloomed significantly since 1978, they contribute much less to employment, production value, taxes and net profits. Additionally, they have tended to be much less stable than their collective counterparts. The relative importance of these types of enterprise is noted below.

**Table 4  Rural Industry by Ownership. 1985**

| Ownership*: | Township | Village | Other co-op | Individual | TOTAL |
|---|---|---|---|---|---|
| Number (mn) | 0.24 | 0.66 | 0.73 | 9.25 | 10.84 |
| (%) | 4.8 | 12.5 | 14.9 | 67.8 | 100.0 |
| Employment | | | | | |
| (mn) | 13.3 | 14.5 | 5.7 | 7.8 | 41.3 |
| (%) | 32.1 | 35.2 | 13.8 | 19.0 | 100.0 |
| Production value | | | | | |
| (bn *yuan*) | 79.9 | 66.0 | 19.1 | 17.7 | 182.8 |
| (%) | 43.7 | 36.2 | 10.5 | 9.7 | 100.0 |
| Taxes | | | | | |
| (bn *yuan*) | 4.0 | 2.6 | 0.4 | 0.4 | 7.5 |
| (%) | 52.0 | 34.7 | 7.7 | 5.6 | 100.0 |
| Net Profit | | | | | |
| (bn *yuan*) | 6.1 | 6.6 | 2.5 | 2.7 | 17.9 |
| (%) | 34.0 | 36.7 | 14.2 | 15.1 | 100.0 |

*Township enterprises and village enterprises correspond to the former commune- and brigade-run enterprises. A variety of other cooperative forms have emerged in the 1980s and these are combined in this table.
Compiled from materials in 'Statistics of China's agriculture, animal husbandry and fishery (1985)', Beijing 1986.

Since 1978, rural industry has sought to combine agriculture and industry through particular - though by no means exclusive - emphasis on agricultural produce processing industries.[99]

The potential contribution of these industrial enterprises to the rural economy, as demonstrated above in Wanzai county as part of the wider package of policies and measures intended to improve peasant enthusiasm and incentive, is large.[100] With the extension of output-related responsibility systems from farming production to such small-scale industrial enterprises, the state is clearly expecting much from rural industry.[101]

As with the diversification policy, the three most significant influences of rural industry upon local rural economic development appear to be as serving: first, as a source of peasant income;[102] secondly, as a source of peasant employment opportunities;[103] and finally, as a source of collective accumulation funds. (More detailed arguments are outlined in the regional materials, in particular that for Wuxi county, Chapter Five).

Of greatest significance in the context of this study is the contribution of rural industrial undertakings to collective accumulation funds which are subsequently used to expand rural production. Between 1979 and 1982 for example, eight billion *yuan* from the profits of commune- and brigade-run industries was reinvested in farmland construction and the purchase of farm machinery. This compares favourably to the eleven billion *yuan* invested by the state in agriculture, animal husbandry and water conservation projects in the same period.[104] By the end of the 1980s, these same industries were investing over 7 billion *yuan* annually in subsidising and developing agricultural production.[105]

Inevitably, the opportunities offered by rural industry must be tempered by the problems which they face. Some of these problems are old ones: low efficiency and high wastage of materials; difficulties in obtaining supplies of inputs; inadequate marketing skills; environmental and safety hazards; and a lack of technical and managerial knowledge. Others are emerging with the new economic reforms: chaotic enterprise development in the current economic environment which now results in bankruptcy and financial loss to the enterprise management; inefficient coordination between firms and the market-place because of insufficient market information; and tensions between management and the work-force because of the link between payment (especially of bonuses - as much as 40% of the average wage packet) and performance.

These are reservations which must be remembered. Yet, undoubtedly, rural industrial undertakings can, and do play a crucial role in rural economic development.

## Conclusions

The package of measures outlined in this chapter represents a distinct movement away from Maoist rural economic policies and has markedly altered the organisation of rural production within China.

By way of summary, the simple workings of the rural economy before 1978 are illustrated in Figure 2. Arable land was collectively tilled by the unit members and work-points allocated for time spent in the fields. Work points varied between men, women and children, but not by output. The same was true for work in collectively-run local industry or animal husbandry. Year-end income distribution within collective units was based upon the total number of work-points accumulated during the year.

The collective supplied the means of production and in return a certain amount of the produce from the collective arable - usually grain - was retained for subsistence, collective accumulation and to meet the needs of 'five guarantee' (social security) households. The remainder was sold to the state, the sales financing the purchase of producer goods and the year-end distribution. The state might also supply quantities of perennially scarce fertiliser to the collective. Often, such supplies were related to the amount of grain sold to the state.

The 'marginal links' in Figure 2 represent the part of the rural economy under the Maoists which was theoretically 'private', the 5-7% of collective land usually reserved as private plots. However, in many areas these plots were incorporated into the collective arable, significantly reducing cash-crop production and sideline occupations traditionally developed on this land. In this way, an important source of both foodstuffs and household income was curtailed.

By way of contrast, Figure 3 outlines the workings of the post-1978 rural economy. The collective arable is divided amongst individual households through production contracts. The household fulfils contracted output targets set by the collective and the state within the contract and also contributes to collective funds. All remaining produce may be sold to the state or privately. Workers in collectively-run local industry are also paid according to output.

The collective continues to supply some part of the means of production - either as part of the contract or at a price. However, households now have a bigger responsibility to purchase producer goods themselves from income generated by sales of their produce or skills. Households may contract jobs to individuals who specialise in agricultural services. The collective also continues agricultural capital construction. This is made possible by household contributions to the collective funds and - increasingly important - by contributions from local industry. Production is also increasingly diversified.

The 'blurred links' indicate a new development in the rural economy. In 1978, the status of private plots was reestablished within the rural economy. However, with the development of family farming, private plots have rapidly become merged into households' contracted resources, losing their distinctive identity and role. In many areas, this is also true of collective animal husbandry. There seems little doubt that the 1978 reforms in the rural sector have done much to increase peasant incentive and enthusiasm for rural production and prompt significant progress in the rural sector.

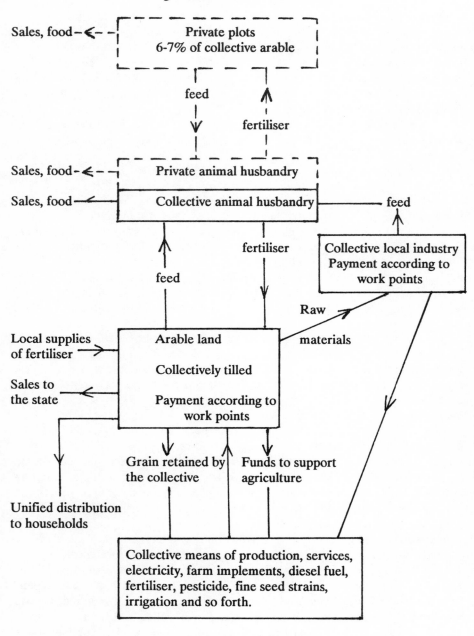

Sales, food $\leftarrow$ — —
Private plots
6-7% of collective arable

feed ↓  ↑ fertiliser

Sales, food $\leftarrow$ — — Private animal husbandry
Sales, food $\leftarrow$ — Collective animal husbandry — feed

feed ↑  fertiliser ↓

Collective local industry
Payment according to
work points

Local supplies
of fertiliser →
Arable land

Collectively tilled

Payment according to
work points

Raw materials →

Sales to
the state ←

Grain retained by
the collective

Funds to support
agriculture

Unified distribution
to households

Collective means of production, services,
electricity, farm implements, diesel fuel,
fertiliser, pesticide, fine seed strains,
irrigation and so forth.

— — — — 'Marginal' links (see text for full explanation)

**Figure 2  Collective Management**

34

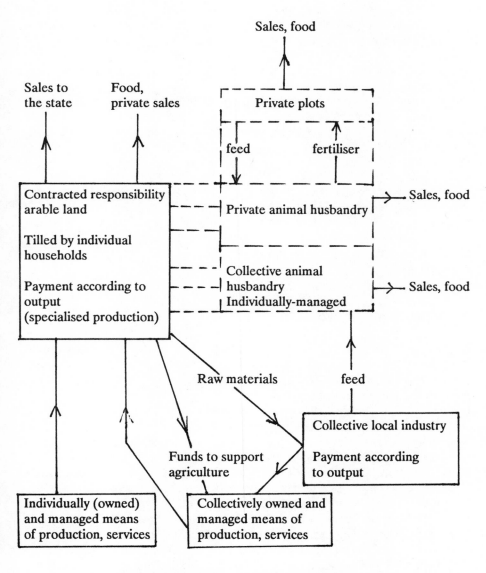

Figure 3 Family Management

**Table 5  China. Rural economic performance. Various Indicators**

|  | 1952 | 1965 | 1970 | 1978 | 1980 | 1982 | 1984 | 1986 | 1989 |
|---|---|---|---|---|---|---|---|---|---|
| **Grain crops:** | | | | | | | | | |
| Output (bn *jin*) | 327.8 | 389.1 | 479.9 | 609.5 | 641.1 | 709.0 | 814.6 | 783.0 | 815.0 |
| Yield (*jin/mu*) | 176.2 | 217.4 | 268.1 | 336.7 | 364.2 | 417.1 | 481.0 | 470.7 | 484.3 |
| Output (*jin*)/cap | 570.0 | 536.7 | 578.9 | 632.9 | 649.5 | 695.0 | 781.7 | 734.1 | 732.1 |
| **Cotton:** | | | | | | | | | |
| Output (bn *jin*) | 2.6 | 4.2 | 4.5 | 4.3 | 5.4 | 7.2 | 12.5 | 7.1 | 7.6 |
| Yield (*jin/mu*) | 30.9 | 56 | 60 | 58.9 | 72.9 | 82.8 | 121.4 | 109.9 | 97.4 |
| Output (*jin*)/cap | 4.6 | 5.8 | 5.4 | 4.8 | 5.5 | 7.1 | 12.1 | 6.6 | 6.8 |
| **Oil-bearing crops*:** | | | | | | | | | |
| Output (bn *jin*) | 7.5 | 6.5 | 6.8 | 9.1 | 12.5 | 19.8 | 18.8 | 24.6 | 22.1 |
| Yield (*jin/mu*) | 105.8 | 100 | 121.9 | 122.8 | 139.8 | 175.9 | 188.3 | 178.7 | 171.3 |
| Output (*jin*)/cap | 13.0 | 8.9 | 8.2 | 9.5 | 12.7 | 19.5 | 18.2 | 23.2 | 20.0 |
| **Sugar-cane:** | | | | | | | | | |
| Output (bn *jin*) | 14.2 | 26.8 | 26.9 | 42.2 | 45.6 | 73.8 | 79.0 | 100.4 | 97.6 |
| Yield (*jin/mu*) | 5182 | 5095 | 4629 | 5128 | 6342 | 7530 | 7238 | 7046 | 6507 |
| Output (*jin*)/cap | 24.7 | 36.9 | 32.4 | 43.8 | 46.2 | 72.7 | 75.8 | 94.1 | 87.7 |
| **Fruits:** | | | | | | | | | |
| Output (bn *jin*) | 4.9 | 6.5 | 10.8 | 13.0 | 13.6 | 15.4 | 19.7 | 27.0 | 36.6 |
| Output (*jin*)/cap | 8.5 | 8.9 | 13.0 | 13.5 | 13.8 | 15.2 | 18.9 | 25.3 | 32.9 |
| **Meat output - pork, beef, mutton:** | | | | | | | | | |
| (mn tons) | 3.4 | 5.5 | 5.9 | 8.6 | 12.1 | 13.5 | 15.4 | 19.2 | 23.3 |
| **Average per cap consumption of:** | | | | | | | | | |
| Grain (*jin*) | 398 | 365 | 375 | 319 | 427 | 451 | 531.3 | 516.2 | 483 |
| Edible Oils (*jin*) | 4.2 | 3.5 | 3.2 | 3.0 | 4.6 | 7.0 | 7.9 | 8.4 | 10.8 |
| Pork (*jin*) | 11.8 | 12.5 | 12.0 | 15.0 | 22.3 | 24.0 | 21.1 | 23.5 | 31.1 |
| Cloth (m$^2$) | 5.7 | 6.2 | 8.1 | 8.0 | 10.0 | 10.0 | 10.3 | 10.7¶ | 11.6 |
| **Average net per cap peasant incomes** | | | | | | | | | |
| (*yuan*) | n/a | n/a | n/a | 134§ | 191.3 | 270 | 310 | 397.6¶ | 601.5 |

*Oil-bearing crops here include only figures for peanuts, rape and sesame, or just over 85% of China's total oil-bearing crop output.

§This compares favourably with the figure of 70 *yuan* given by *Xinhua Radio*, 5.10.1979, and represents a survey figure as do all income figures.

¶Cloth and Income figures for 1986 are actually 1985.

Compiled from materials in *Statistical Yearbook of China*, 1981; 1986. *China Statistical Abstract, 1989 and 1990*. Some figures deduced.

   Similar examples of rural economic progress at the local level are also abundant.[106] Rural economic progress has also resulted in improved rural living standards and a narrowing of the gap between urban and rural residents. However, while the following tables demonstrate improved rural conditions, a distinction can still be made between urban and rural environments.

**Table 6  Per capita consumption levels (1989 prices)**

|      | Rural | Urban | Ratio rural:urban |
|------|-------|-------|-------------------|
| 1978 | 132   | 383   | 1:2.9 |
| 1979 | 152   | 406   | 1:2.7 |
| 1980 | 173   | 468   | 1:2.7 |
| 1981 | 194   | 487   | 1:2.5 |
| 1982 | 212   | 500   | 1:2.4 |
| 1983 | 234   | 531   | 1:2.3 |
| 1984 | 266   | 599   | 1:2.3 |
| 1985 | 324   | 747   | 1:2.3 |
| 1986 | 353   | 851   | 1:2.4 |
| 1987 | 393   | 997   | 1:2.5 |
| 1988 | 480   | 1288  | 1:2.6 |

*China Statistical Abstract, 1990*, (Praeger) 1990.

**Table 7  Ownership of durable consumer goods per 100 households**

|                  | 1980 R | 1981 U | 1985 R | 1985 U | 1986 R | 1986 U | 1987 R | 1987 U | 1988 R | 1988 U |
|------------------|------|------|------|------|------|------|------|------|------|------|
| Bicycles         | 37   | 136  | 81   | 152  | 90   | 163  | 98   | 176  | 107  | 177  |
| Sewing Machines  | 23   | 70   | 43   | 71   | 47   | 74   | 50   | 75   | 52   | 71   |
| Radios           | 33   | 100  | 54   | 74   | 54   | 69   | 53   | 67   | 52   | 49   |
| Wristwatches     | 38   | 241  | 126  | 275  | 145  | 299  | 161  | 315  | 169  | 294  |
| Black/white TVs  | 0.4  | 57   | 12   | 67   | 16   | 65   | 22   | 65   | 29   | 59   |
| Colour TVs       | n/a  | 0.6  | n/a  | 17   | 1.5  | 27   | 2.3  | 35   | 2.8  | 44   |

Key: R = Rural; U = Urban
Source: *China Statistical Abstract, 1988*, (Praeger) 1989.
The weakness of distribution channels to the rural areas remains a formidable barrier to major improvements in rural living standards. However, it can also be seen from Tables 5 and 6 that rural economic progress in the second half of the 1980s was much less vigorous than in the years immediately after the 1978 reforms.

Measures such as price reform and the restitution of private plots are short-term in nature and cannot be expected to have a long-term influence on rural economic growth. Similarly, *baogan daohu* while embodying extended contract periods to facilitate long-term stability, also contains contradictions (land transfer, compensatory payments and so forth) which could give rise to serious

37

problems and result in a shift of policy to the detriment of peasant enthusiasm for rural production. In other words, there is no guarantee that the success achieved in the years immediately after the 1978 reforms will be continued in the long term. Indeed, the data presented in Tables 5 and 6 indicate that rural economic performance both in terms of agricultural output and living standards seems to have stagnated in the late 1980s.

The state acknowledges the need for long term reform beyond concern for the immediate improvement of peasant livelihood. State encouragement of diversification and rural undertakings for example represents not only an attempt to improve the immediate rural economic environment, but also to secure long-term sources of income and employment opportunities to maintain the current momentum in the countryside. It is also an admission by the state that it is unwilling or unable to provide more directly for such opportunities through large injections of state investment capital. Indeed, state investment in agriculture reached a low of 3% of total state investment in 1988, (compared to 10.6% in 1978) before climbing to 4.6% in 1989 - still short of the levels of the early 1980s.

Thus, the question remains of how best to secure long-term rural growth.

# Notes to Chapter Two

1    Diu Qingqi & Yu Zhan, 'Study comrade Deng Zihui's viewpoint on the agricultural production responsibility system', *People's Daily*, 23.2.1982 tr FBIS/DR/PRC 5.3.1982, K16-20. Jin Wen, 'Grasp law and join in reforms - a talk commencing with the system of agricultural production responsibility', *Red Flag*, 1.5.1983 tr JPRS/DR/RF No 9, pp 29-36.

2    *Heilongjiang Radio*, 'Heilongjiang holds agricultural management forum', 29.1.1982 tr FBIS/DR/PRC 1.2.1982, S1-2.

3    Zeng Guoxiong, 'Properly implementing production responsibility systems is to manage the poor and deliver wealth and develop the fundamental path of agriculture', *Fujian Tribune*, 1981 (3) quoted by Guo Ming, 'A summary of discussions in the past year of the production responsibility system in agriculture', *Jingji Yanjiu*, 1982 (3) pp 75-9.

4    Diu Qingqi *et al*, op cit.

5    Leeming, op cit. J & M Gray, 'China's new agricultural revolution', in S Feuchtwang & A Hussain, *The Chinese economic reforms*, (Croom Helm: 1983).

6    Lin Zili (a), 'On the contract system of responsibility linked to output - a new form of cooperative economy in China's socialist agriculture', *Social Sciences in China*, 1983 (1) pp 53-104. Wang Guichen & Wei Daonan (a), 'Discussion of the fixing of farm output quotas for each household', *Jingji Yanjiu*, 1981 (1) quoted by Guo Ming, op cit.

7    Lin Zili (a), op cit.

8    Ibid. Du Runsheng (b), 'Good beginning for reform of rural economic system', *Beijing Review*, 30.11.1981 24 (48) pp 15-20.

9    Lin Zili (a), op cit.

10    Wu Xiang (a), 'The open road and the log bridge - a preliminary discussion on the origins, advantages and disadvantages, nature and future of the fixing of farm output quotas for each household', *People's Daily*, 5.11.1980 quoted by *Xinhua Radio*, 5.11.1980 tr FBIS/DR/PRC 7.11.1980, L21-29. *Sichuan Ribao (Sichuan Daily)*, 'It is necessary to stabilise, improve and perfect various forms of rural production responsibility systems', 20.12.1981 tr FBIS/DR/PRC 13.1.1982, Q1-4.

11    *Xinhua Radio*, 5.10.1979, op cit.

12    Tang Mingxi, 'The rising of new types of household economy in the Chinese countryside', *Jingji Yanjiu*, 1983 (12) pp 42-7.

13    Feng Zibiao, 'The integration of agriculture and output responsibility systems and production relations must suit the natural laws of production', *Jingji Yanjiu*, 1981 (4) quoted by Guo Ming, op cit.

14    Li Hongsi, 'Seeing production responsibility systems from the three labour forms', *Shanxi Ribao (Shanxi Daily)*, 16.9.1981 quoted by Guo Ming, op cit.

15    Wang Songpei, 'China's agricultural-industrial-commercial integrated enterprises', *Jingji Yanjiu*, 1980 (7) pp 42-7.

16   *China Statistical Abstract, 1989*, (Praeger: New York).
17   Guo Ming & Wang Shuwen, 'An investigation into the implementation of various kinds of production responsibility systems by a production brigade', *Jingji Yanjiu*, 1982 (9) pp 70-4.
18   Wan Li (a), 'Further develop the new phase of agriculture which has already opened up', *People's Daily*, 23.12.1982 tr FBIS/DR/PRC 4.1.1983, K2-20.
19   F W Crook, 'The *Baogan Daohu* incentive system. Translation and analysis of a model contract', *China Quarterly*, 1985 (102) pp 291-303.
20   *People's Daily*, 'Pay close attention to contracts', 23.8.1982 tr FBIS/DR/PRC 2.9.1982, K24-26. *People's Daily*, 'An important task in perfecting the responsibility system in agricultural production - on instituting and strengthening the economic contract system in agriculture', 18.9.1982 tr FBIS/DR/PRC 22.9.1982, K1-2. *People's Daily*, 'Stabilise and perfect the system of contracted responsibilities with payment linked to output', 1.9.1981 tr FBIS/DR/PRC 24.1.1983, K2-9.
21   *People's Daily*, 'An investigation of, and views about, several present rural systems whereby responsibility is linked to output', 1.9.1981 tr FBIS/DR/PRC 9.9.1981, K7-15.
22   *People's Daily* 18.9.1982, op cit.
23   Zi Kunyi, 'A brief discussion of the improvement of the contract responsibility system of the commodity grain base of the Dongting Hu plain region', *Nongye Jingji Wenti (Problems of Agricultural Economics)* 1983 (10) pp 27-30, tr FBIS/CR/A 26.2.1984, pp 73-80.
24   Wang Xinglong, 'A humble opinion on the transfer of contracts for rural households at the present stage', *Red Flag*, 16.4.1984 tr JPRS/CR/RF No 8, pp 42-9.
25   Zi Kunyi, op cit.
26   Ibid.
27   Wang Xinglong, op cit.
28   Ibid.
29   Zi Kunyi, op cit.
30   Wang Xinglong, op cit.
31   Zi Kunyi, op cit. Lin Zili (b), 'The new situation in the Chinese economy and its basic direction', *Social Sciences in China*, 1983 (3) pp 112-46.
32   Zi Kunyi, op cit.
33   *Beijing Review*, 'Rural contract', 10.11.1980 23 (45) pp 5-6.
34   Diu Qingqi *et al*, op cit. An Gang, Song Cheng & Huang Yuejun, 'There is hope for the vigorous development of agriculture in China - commenting on the controversy over safeguarding of peasants interests', *People's Daily*, 9.7.1981 tr FBIS/DR/PRC 23.7.1981, K11-18.
35   Wu Xiang (a), op cit.
36   *People's Daily*, 'To do a good job in year-end distribution is a matter of importance', 18.12.1981 tr FBIS/DR/PRC 29.12.1981, K7-9. *Liaoning*

*Ribao* (*Liaoning Daily*), 'What has "happened"? - written to dispel the doubts of rural cadres', 22.2.1982 tr FBIS/DR/PRC 17.3.1982, S1. Yi Zhi, 'We should as strictly control the use of cultivable land as we do population growth', JPRS/CR/RF 16.10.1980 tr JPRS/CR/RF No 20, pp 64-71.

37  *People's Daily*, 'An important measure to improve the purchase and sales contract system', 10.2.1984b tr FBIS/DR/PRC 16.2.1984, K1-2.

38  R M Pfeffer, 'Contracts in China revisited, with a focus on agriculture, 1949-63', *China Quarterly*, 1963 (14) pp 106-29.

39  *People's Daily*, 'How to perfect the responsibility system in agriculture', 6.2.1982 tr FBIS/DR/PRC 18.2.1982, K12-16. *Xinhua Radio*, 'CCP issues minutes of 1981 rural work conference', 5.4.1982 tr FBIS/DR/PRC 7.4.1982, K1-13.

40  *Xinhua Radio*, 5.4.1982, op cit. Zhou Cheng (b), 'Discourse on fixed farm output quotas for each household', *Jingji Guanli* (*Economic Management*), 1981 (2) quoted by Guo Ming, op cit.

41  CCPCC administrative office, 'An investigation of, and views about, several present rural systems whereby responsibility is linked to output', *People's Daily*, 1.9.1981 tr FBIS/DR/PRC 9.9.1981, K2-15.

42  *People's Daily*, 'Policies must be consistently stable, problems must be solved in real earnest - on summing up and perfecting the agricultural production responsibility system', 3.4.1982 tr FBIS/DR/PRC 15.4.1982, K1-3.

43  *People's Daily*, 6.2.1982, op cit.

44  Yu Guoyao (a), 'How to approach the fixing of output quotas for each household', *Red Flag*, 16.10.1980 tr JPRS/CR/RF No 20, pp 19-26. *People's Daily*, 'Protecting collective property means protecting productive forces', 4.10.1981 tr SWB/DR/FE 14.10.1981 B (2) pp 1-2.

45  *People's Daily*, 'Several questions of cognition on perfecting the agricultural production responsibility systems', 27.4.1982 tr FBIS/DR/PRC 5.5.1982, K18-23.

46  Wu Xiang (a), op cit.

47  J Gray, 'Whatever happened to Dazhai?', *New Society*, 12.3.1981, pp 458-9.

48  *Ban Yue Tan* (*Semi-monthly talks*), 'Communes and production brigades must take charge of the things that ought to be taken charge of', 25.2.1982 tr FBIS/DR/PRC 11.3.1982, K11-13.

49  *Nongmin Ribao* (*Peasant's Daily*), 'Nongmin Ribao on role of rural cooperatives', 30.4.1985 tr FBIS/DR/PRC 10.5.1985, K10-11. Li Xudong, 'Perfectly unified management and "*Baogan daohu*" systems', *Hebei Ribao* (*Hebei Daily*), quoted by Guo Ming, op cit. Feng Jixin, 'Bring out the superiority of the system of contracted responsibilities on the household basis', *People's Daily*, 24.2.1983 tr *Chinese Economic Studies*, 1984 17 (3) pp 18-26.

50  Baoding prefecture CPCC, 'The establishment and development of specialised service companies for agricultural production - a major step in

the further restructuring of the agricultural economic system', *Nongye Jingji Wenti* 1983 (10) pp 9-14 tr FBIS/CR/A 26.2.1984, pp 61-71.

51 *People's Daily*, 'Restraining house-building in rural areas', 17.9.1981 tr SWB/DR/FE 2.10.1981 B (2) pp 7-8. Hsiao Chen-mei, 'The system of contracted farm production', *Issues and Studies*, 1983 19 (8) pp 10-12. Gi Mingchen, 'Peasants richer, build more houses', *China Daily*, 24.9.1983 in FBIS/DR/PRC 26.9.1983, K9-10.

52 *Hubei Radio*, 'Resolutely check unauthorised seizure and use of cultivated land', 28.4.1982 tr FBIS/DR/PRC 6.5.1982, P1-2.

53 *Xinhua Radio*, 'State council issues housing-construction rules', 5.3.1982 tr FBIS/DR/PRC 9.3.1982, K20-21. *Xinhua Radio*, 'Document regulates farmland housing construction', 5.11.1982 tr FBIS/DR/PRC 8.11.1982, K16-18.

54 He Kang, quoted by *Shijie Jingji Daobao*, 'Gradual reduction of farmland has become a hidden peril in China's countryside', 1.4.1985 tr FBIS/DR/PRC 12.4.1985, K20-21.

55 Li Jie, 'The defects in the workstyle of certain Henan cadres should be vigorously corrected', *People's Daily*, 8.6.1985 tr FBIS/DR/PRC 11.6.1985, K4-5.

56 Chang Wen & Xin Hai, 'How to do family planning work after output quotas were assigned to groups in agriculture - an investigation of the family planning work in Mianzhu county, Sichuan province', in *Zhongguo Renkou Kexue Lunji (Symposium of Chinese Population Science)* (Chinese Academic Publishers: 1981). Marie-Claire Bergère, 'On the historical origins of Chinese underdevelopment', *Theory and Society*, 1984 13 (3) pp 327-37.

57 Liu Zheng (a), 'Strive to bring population growth under control', *Red Flag*, 16.10.1981 tr JPRS/CR/RF No 20, pp 58-63. CCPCC Administrative Office, op cit. Yu Guoyao (a), op cit. Xu Xuehan, 'Resolutely implement the policy on rural population', *People's Daily*, 5.2.1982 tr FBIS/DR/PRC 16.2.1982, K11-16.

58 *Liaoning Radio*, untitled, 25.10.1981 tr SWB/FE/DR 30.10.1981 B (2) pp 12-13.

59 *Ban Yue Tan*, 25.2.1982, op cit. *Sichuan Ribao*, 20.12.1981, op cit.

60 Chang Wen *et al*, op cit.

61 *People's Daily*, 'Rely on two kinds of initiative in arrangements for surplus labour', 8.11.1981, p 2. *Inner Mongolia Radio*, 'Inner Mongolia's Zhou Hui on use of surplus labour', 20.5.1982 tr FBIS/DR/PRC 26.5.1982, R1.

62 Crook, op cit.

63 Du Runsheng (c), 'The agricultural responsibility system and the reform of the rural economic system', *Red Flag*, 1.10.1981 tr JPRS/CR/RF No 19, pp 24-39.

64 Sun Xiangjian & Pei Changhong, 'A probe into the question of our country's present internal agricultural accumulation', *Red Flag*, 1.5.1983 tr JPRS/CR/RF No 9, pp 37-44.

65 Ibid.

66 *Xinhua Radio*, 'Strive to achieve even greater development in agricultural production this year', 4.2.1982 quoting a *People's Daily*, 4.2.1982 editorial, tr FBIS/DR/PRC, K1-3. *People's Daily* 3.4.1982, op cit.

67 *People's Daily*, 'Rural policy research centre of the secretariat of the CCPCC gives explanations on land contracting in the central document', 3.7.1984 tr FBIS/DR/PRC 6.7.1984, K3-8.

68 *Xinhua Radio*, 'No more "Lord Ye's love of dragons"', 11.10.1984 tr FBIS/DR/PRC 17.10.1984, K15-17.

69 *Hunan Radio*, 'Discussion on rural policies', 22.2.1984 tr FBIS/DR/PRC 27.2.1984, P3-5.

70 *Shaanxi Ribao* (*Shaanxi Daily*), 'Seriously study and resolutely implement the CCPCC Document no 1 - questions and answers on rural work at present', 11.2.1984 tr FBIS/DR/PRC 22.2.1984, T10-15. *Ninxia Ribao*, 'Certain stipulations formulated by the regional CPCC and people's government on implementing Document no 1 of the CCPCC (24.3.1984)', 8.4.1984 tr FBIS/DR/PRC, T3-9.

71 Gray, op cit.

72 Wu Xiang (a), op cit.

73 Y Y Kueh (a), 'A weather index for analysing grain yield instability in China, 1912-1981', *China Quarterly*, 1984 (97) pp 68-83. Du Runsheng (b), op cit.

74 K R Walker (b), 'Chinese agriculture during the period of readjustment 1978-1983', *China Quarterly*, 1984 (100) pp 783-812.

75 *Xinhua*, 'Further report on farm purchase prices', 24.10.1979 in FBIS/DR/PRC 26.10.1979, L2-3.

76 *Xinhua*, 'CCPCC circular announces food price rise', 31.10.1979 in FBIS/DR/PRC 31.10.1979, L12-13.

77 W Klatt, 'The staff of life: living standards in China 1971-1981', *China Quarterly*, 1983 (93) pp 17-50.

78 *Beijing Radio*, 'Peasants must become well-to-do by developing production', 2.4.1982 tr FBIS/DR/PRC 6.4.1982, K6-7.

79 Zhao Ziyang, 'Loosen control over the prices of farm products to promote the readjustment of the production structure in rural areas', *Red Flag*, 1.2.1985 tr JPRS/CR/RF No 3, pp 14-20. *Xinhua Radio*, '1985 Document No 1 on rural economic reform', 24.3.1985 tr FBIS/DR/PRC 25.3.1985, K1-7. *Xinhua Radio*, 'Cheng Zhiping discusses price control for 1985', 12.4.1985 tr FBIS/DR/PRC 19.4.1985, K7-10.

80 *Red Flag*, 'Decision of the CCPCC on reform of the economic structure - adopted by the 3rd plenary session of the 12th CCPCC on 20.10.1984', 21.10.1984 tr JPRS/CR/RF No 20, pp 1-20.

81 Gu Lei & Xu Zhongying, 'Private plots ought to be in fact what they are in name', *People's Daily*, 24.4.1979 tr JPRS/CR/Political, Sociological and Military Affairs, 25.7.1979 No 4, pp 19-24.
82 *People's Daily*, 'We must not adhere to any new "uniform system"', 22.9.1981 tr FBIS/DR/PRC 29.9.1981, K15-16.
83 *Xinhua Radio*, 5.10.1979, op cit.
84 *Beijing Review*, 'Small plots for private use', 29.6.1981 24 (26) pp 3-4.
85 Ibid.
86 K R Walker (a), *Planning in Chinese agriculture: socialization and the private sector 1956-62*, (Frank Cass: London, 1965).
87 B Brugger, 'Rural policy', in *China since the Gang of four*, B Brugger ed, (Croom Helm: 1980), quoting *Beijing Review*, 17.10.1975.
88 Klatt, op cit.
89 *People's Daily* editorial, 'It is necessary to develop the diversified economy on a larger scale', 9.5.1982 tr FBIS/DR/PRC 13.5.1982, K2-4.
90 Dai Guoqiang, Liu Erning & Wan Wuyi, 'Shaanxi: Ankeng develops diversified economy', *Xinhua Radio*, 6.6.1982 tr FBIS/DR/PRC 9.6.1982, T2-3. *Beijing Review*, 'Restructuring the agricultural economy', 23.6.1980 23 (25) pp 4-5.
91 Yuan Ming, 'Important changes in rural economic structures', *People's Daily*, 22.2.1982 quoted by Leeming, op cit.
92 Wei Min, 'Wanzai county diversifies its economy', *Beijing Review*, 17.8.1981 24 (33) pp 25-7.
93 Ibid.
94 *Beijing Review*, Diversified rural economy', 4.5.1981 24 (18) pp 5-6.
95 Wei Min, op cit.
96 Zhang Yi, 'Actively develop the farm and sideline products processing industries in rural areas', *Red Flag*, 16.4.1984 tr JPRS/CR/RF No 8, pp 52-8.
97 J Sigurdson, *Rural industrialization in China*, (Harvard, 1977). C Riskin (a), 'Small industry and the Chinese model of development', *China Quarterly*, 1971 (46) pp 245-73. C Riskin (b), 'China's rural industries: self-reliant systems or independent kingdoms', *China Quarterly*, 1978 (73) pp 77-98. D Perkins, (Chairman, American rural industry delegation), *Rural small-scale industry in the People's Republic of China*, (California: 1977).
98 C R Wong, *Rural industrialization in China: Development of the 'five small industries'* (University microfilms international: 1983).
99 *Xinhua Radio*, 5.10.1979, op cit.
100 S H & J M Potter, *Socialism and the Chinese peasant: an anthropological perspective*, (Unpublished manuscript). Shi Qian, Cao Dichen, Yi Hongren, Shao Xiuyun & Li Chunxia, 'Investigative report. A few problems involved in the effort to speed up agricultural mechanisation as seen from the experience at Wuming', *Jingji Yanjiu*, 1978, (3) pp 37-42 tr *Chinese Economic Studies*, 1979 13 (1-2) pp 58-73.

101 *People's Daily*, 'Support and guide commune- and brigade-run enterprises in developing healthily', 23.2.1984 tr FBIS/DR/PRC 1.3.1984, K17-19. Luo Zicheng, 'Several questions about perfecting the output-related contract system in the rural areas', *Guangming Ribao*, 25.3.1984 tr FBIS/DR/PRC 12.4.1984, K10-15.

102 *Xinhua Radio*, 'Rural commune-, brigade-run enterprises develop', 14.8.1982 tr FBIS/DR/PRC, K6-7. *Xinhua*, 'Poor areas prosper in rural industrial boom', 12.4.1984 in FBIS/DR/PRC 12.4.1984, K16.

103 *Hebei Radio*, 'Guo Yang urges developing Hebei rural industries', 25.5.1984 tr FBIS/DR/PRC 8.6.1984, R1-2. *Guangzhou Daily*, 'Panyu county promptly studies the way out for the surplus labour force in the rural areas', 23.1.1983 tr FBIS/DR/PRC 17.2.1983, P1-2.

104 *Xinhua Radio*, 'Excerpts of commune, brigade enterprises report', 17.3.1984 tr FBIS/DR/PRC 23.3.1984, K7-17.

105 *China Statistical Abstract, 1990*, (Praeger: New York).

106 Zhang Yulin, Yang Chengxun & Guo Xiping, 'Contracting output quotas to households under unified management: the responsibility system in the Xiaotan people's commune', *Social Sciences in China*, 1983 (2) pp 121-45. Ma Zhongming & Liu Guanghui, 'There is no deviation in orientation and policy - a discussion by several prefectural party committee secretaries in Jiangxi on the current rural situation', *Xinhua Radio*, 13.5.1980 tr FBIS/DR/PRC 15.5.1980, L14-19. CCPCC Administrative Office, op cit.

# Chapter Three

# Commercial Production: Specialisation and the Commercial System

## Introduction

> The basic principles of farming are: choose the right time, break up the soil, see to its fertility, hoe early and harvest early. With the choice of appropriate time and favourable conditions of the soil, a harvest of 10 *shi* per *mou* (1200 *jin/mu*) is obtainable even from very poor land.[1]

Since the 1978 reforms it is possible to discern two broad development emphases which rural production units within the Chinese countryside might adopt in the long-term to break free of the traditional limitations of small-scale grain farming. Though discussed separately, these emphases should not be thought to represent alternative development paths. On the contrary, they may often complement each other, but they do represent two distinct political viewpoints.

Initially at least, post-1978 pronouncements continued to argue that further improvement in the incomes and livelihood of peasants engaged in farming production - especially grain farming - would largely come through a reduction in the amount of land, labour and capital used to satisfy grain contract demands. That is, increasing per-unit yields and multi-cropping levels would free resources for the production of more lucrative cash crops and diversified undertakings. These arguments represented little more than a continuation of the established Maoist standpoint. Indeed, as illustrated by the quote above from an agricultural text dating from the first century BC, this view offers little different from traditional agricultural treatises.

To increase per-unit yields and multi-cropping levels, rural production units were urged to implement a wide array of measures to enhance the condition of the agricultural resource base and raise agricultural productivity: improving water conservation, land reclamation and land preservation;[2] raising the levels of agricultural mechanisation;[3] utilising fine-seed strains and so forth.[4]

Yet, an extension of Table 1 from Chapter One indicates that while there is evidence of a commitment to a modernised agriculture since 1978, this support seems patchy.

**Table 1  Inputs to farming**

| | 1978 | 1979 | 1980 | 1981 | 1982 | 1983 | 1984 | 1985 |
|---|---|---|---|---|---|---|---|---|
| Tractors (excluding small tractors - 1000's) | 56 | 67 | 75 | 79 | 81 | 84 | 85 | 85 |
| Powered irrigation (mn hp) | 66 | 71 | 75 | 75 | 76 | 78 | 78 | 78 |
| Artificial fertilisers (*jin/mu* sown area) | 7.9 | 9.8 | 11.6 | 12.3 | 13.9 | 15.4 | 16.1 | 16.3 |
| Output of artificial fertilisers (mn tons) | 8.7 | 10.6 | 12.3 | 12.4 | 12.8 | 13.8 | 14.6 | 13.2 |
| Farm inputs sold at retail (100 mn *yuan*) | 294 | 324 | 346 | 347 | 388 | 423 | 477 | 501 |
| Pesticide sales (mn tons) | 1.5 | 1.5 | 1.5 | 1.5 | 1.6 | 1.2 | 0.8 | 0.7 |
| Tractor and agricultural machinery sales (mn hp) | 21.4 | 21.2 | 14.7 | 11.3 | 12.3 | 14.8 | 14.3 | 14.6 |

Some figures deduced. Compiled from materials in *Chinese Statistical Yearbook* 1981; 1982; 1983; 1984; 1986.

Several points arise out of Table 1. First, the increases in the levels of inputs to farming since 1978 are significant. However, it would seem that those increases were possibly beginning to level off after 1981. Certainly, the amount of large-scale agricultural machinery (large tractors and combine harvesters for example) used in Chinese farming does not increase to any great extent through the end of the 1980s. Most of the increased inputs to farming are in small-scale machinery, which is to be expected because of the emergence of the household as the basic production unit, as well as the use of artificial fertilisers.

Second, the commitment to modernised farming demonstrated in Table 1 echoes that illustrated in Chapter One, and it must be reemphasised strongly that there is nothing new about the arguments encapsulated within the first development emphasis proposed for rural production units. They are very Maoist in tone.

Finally, it should be seen that it is the whole range of post-1978 rural economic policies - a combination of increased advanced agricultural techniques with better incentives for rural producers - which has combined to create an atmosphere to facilitate large-scale increases in rural output. Indeed, it is only now that in many areas the significant Maoist investment in farming outputs, especially that between 1965 and 1976, is for the first time bearing fruit. Only since 1978 have peasants had the money and the incentive to utilise properly the advanced agricultural inputs available to them. This is an important and little-cited factor in explaining the extent of agricultural development since 1978.

In practice, of course, there continue to be numerous problems in the implementation of many of the measures mentioned above. These problems may not be as severe as they were in the 1960s and 1970s, but they are,

47

nonetheless, reminiscent of those encountered by the Maoists in the implementation of the same policy measures. Some units, for example, have adequate means of production at their disposal yet management remains weak and resources are squandered.[5] Alternatively, other units find themselves unable to acquire the necessary means of production.[6]

Furthermore, not only are supplies of the means of production insufficient, they are often high in price, low in quality and inferior in efficiency. Again, the level of technical skills currently available within rural China is inadequate, both in quantity and quality, a legacy of the Cultural Revolution when education in China virtually ceased.[7] Indeed, in 1983 only 117,000 scientific and technical personnel were acknowledged as part (0.034%) of the rural labour force.[8]

Most crucially, the high cost of these modern inputs of agriculture has resulted in more expensive agricultural production costs at the same time that prices for agricultural produce remain relatively low. The state was, and still is concerned that those areas which use modern agricultural inputs extensively to reap high outputs are also facing prohibitive production costs. In some areas these costs are such that it becomes more profitable to produce less. At present, and for the foreseeable future, the state needs the countryside to maximise output. Thus it is encouraging localities to subsidise agricultural production from the profits of rural industry in order that farmers can both maximise output and earn good incomes.[9] This is a theme which is examined more closely in the regional chapters below.

Clearly then, modernising Chinese agriculture remains an important task. It is a task which will present the state with its difficulties, in particular the need to offset increased production costs as a result of utilising modern techniques, by adequately rewarding increased output. This is especially true since the introduction of *baogan daohu*, where the household is increasingly responsible for investment in such modern inputs. It has already been noted that the tendency in rural households has been to purchase consumer goods rather than reinvest in their agricultural resource base. Given the reluctance of many households to undertake this important investment, especially in those areas where higher outputs do not necessarily result in proportionately higher incomes, the state must seek lasting solutions to these problems to maintain and develop peasant enthusiasm for rural production. At some point, and this can already be seen in some areas, such contradictions will serve to sap rural vitality and limit growth.

The second development emphasis proposed for rural production units is the generation of income through trade and commercial production.[10] In particular, the state is encouraging specialised production forms in an effort to improve commodity production. State encouragement of specialisation and trade is a clear reversal of Maoist rural policy. Under the Maoists, rural production units were encouraged to be 'small but complete', that is, self-sufficient. This was especially true for foodstuffs but also applied to all aspects of rural life. In this way, trade - for Mao the 'root of capitalism' - could be effectively curtailed and the Maoist political ideal of socialisation in the Chinese countryside more readily accomplished.

The reality was not quite so clear cut. To be sure much rural trade disappeared, but pockets of trade were to be found even at the height of the Cultural Revolution. But, for many peasants, this all important goal of self-sufficiency was economic necessity as state commercial organs became increasingly inefficient. Thus, most peasants naturally found themselves concerned with the personal satisfaction of foodstuffs and the paucity of rural markets often meant monotonous diets.

Reversing the trend whereby political concerns dominated economic decision-making, the 1978 reforms have sought to stimulate rural activity and rural trade by encouraging peasants to develop commodity production, perhaps specialising in one or two production activities to which their resources and skills are well suited. The satisfaction of personal foodstuff needs can be achieved not only through their own production, but also from purchases at the marketplace financed by produce sales. This is certainly a new policy direction and requires considerable attention.

The emphasis upon trade and commercial production has come to the fore more recently at a time of bumper grain harvests. This is an important development. In 1984, grain output topped 810 billion *jin*, over 90 billion *jin* above the target figure in the Sixth Five Year plan. Although the state admitted that backward areas - where basic food and clothing requirements had yet to be met - still existed, the basic situation in the Chinese countryside was declared excellent. Grain surpluses were repeatedly reported - the fact that some areas were still without grain at a time of apparent surplus being a reflection of the inadequate distribution network.[11]

The importance of grain surpluses to the state are numerous: first, they serve to legitimise the policies of the current regime; secondly, they consolidate its power base and are an invaluable propaganda tool; and thirdly, they open the way for commodity production of more lucrative cash crops, giving peasants the opportunity to improve their incomes through commodity sales in the market place.

However, if grain is so expensive to produce, local surpluses (and falling market prices) are not so welcome to the grain farmers. There is little doubt that in some rural areas this tension is appearing. A number of other important and interrelated points need to be raised. The state is clearly nervous about the possibility of a wholesale reduction in grain output. On the one hand, the propaganda value of grain surpluses is undeniable, on the other hand it does not want to encourage peasants to react to reports of surpluses by across-the-board reductions in grain output and a return to a situation of grain shortages.

Consequently, grain production is still heavily emphasised.[12] Indeed, the record grain harvest of 1984 was matched only once (and then barely in 1989). In part this was due to poor weather conditions (and the increasing vulnerability of the agricultural resource base to the elements), but in part also due to peasant disinclination to grow grain.

The relationship between the status of grain production and the state's strategy for future rural economic development is significant. At the most basic level, simply maintaining current consumption levels requires stable increases in grain outputs to match population growth. Essentially, the commercialisation of agriculture is to be built upon a foundation of stable grain supplies. In other words, local producers should satisfy local grain requirements before developing commodity production.

Furthermore, there can be little doubt that the ability of rural production units to engage in commodity production and trade remains widely different. Ironically, it appears that it is in precisely those areas where grain production requires a relatively greater investment in land, labour and capital, that the state is unwilling to reduce its current grain demands.

It is noted below for example, that in the fertile regions of Southern Jiangsu and Southern Guangdong, poorly-rewarded grain production has fallen significantly since 1978 in favour of more lucrative cash crop production. Moreover, the state appears to be consolidating such a situation by stating that the economically developed coastal areas and the suburbs of large- and medium-sized cities may be exempt from, or granted reductions in contracted grain requirements.[13]

If the economically developed coastal and periurban areas produce less grain, the burden for grain production falls heavily upon the North China plain and the peripheral grain bases. Under such circumstances, it is difficult to see how the agricultural resource bases in such areas would support the necessary grain production and simultaneously facilitate extensive commodity production. Commitments of production inputs to grain farming would be so heavy as to preclude significant production of cash crops, limiting rural income and employment opportunities.

The state has encouraged specialisation as a possible way out for grain-burdened areas. However, as will be discussed at greater length below, it seems unlikely that specialisation - in particular specialisation in grain production - will alleviate the problems of such regions. Indeed, increasing specialisation in rural production seems likely to further polarisation in the Chinese countryside.

Those areas with a high proportion of specialised agricultural production can benefit from economies of specialisation as well as high commodity rates and increased rural trade. Peasants, of course, can profit both from these economies and the rural trade. Alternatively, those areas which are dominated by a landscape of small-scale grain farming, find that they have little opportunity to enter the commodity market, nor do they reap any economies of specialisation. Production costs remain high and they fail to benefit from rural trade.

Thus, for the North China plain and the peripheral grain bases, which at first sight appear to be those areas upon which the burdens of grain production must fall, it is the traditional line of increasing per-unit yields and multi-cropping levels which seems to be the only effective way of developing grain production sufficiently in order to be able to divert inputs into the production of other commodities. Given longstanding difficulties in capital accumulation in such areas (the bottom line for real improvements in the resource base and increased use of advanced agricultural techniques), this will prove hard. Neither will state investment help. The proportion of state investment committed to agriculture in the current phase is lower than at any time since liberation.

Table 2  State investment in capital construction by sector (%)

|  | Ind | Construction | Agric | Trans | Commerce | Other |
|---|---|---|---|---|---|---|
| 1953-57 | 42.5 | 3.7 | 7.1 | 15.3 | 3.6 | 27.3 |
| 1958-62 | 60.4 | 1.4 | 11.3 | 13.5 | 1.9 | 11.5 |
| 1963-65 | 49.9 | 2.1 | 17.6 | 12.7 | 2.5 | 15.2 |
| 1966-70 | 55.5 | 1.8 | 10.7 | 15.4 | 2.2 | 14.4 |
| 1971-75 | 55.4 | 1.6 | 9.8 | 18.0 | 2.9 | 12.3 |
| 1976-80 | 52.9 | 1.9 | 10.6 | 13.0 | 3.8 | 17.8 |
| 1981-85 | 45.4 | 1.8 | 5.0 | 13.3 | 5.9 | 28.6 |
| 1986-89 | 49.9 | 1.2 | 3.5 | 14.5 | 3.5 | 27.9 |

Some figures deduced.  Compiled from material in *Statistical Yearbook of China*, 1986, 1990.

The need for rural development to be self-financing is an argument which will be developed further in the regional chapters which follow.

However, first it remains necessary to outline in more detail state proposals for the development of commodity production and trade in the Chinese countryside.  Particular emphasis is given to those organisational forms which have been promoted in order to tackle the grain question.

## Specialised households

Within China the specialised household is emerging as a distinct production form in the countryside.  From the outset it must be said that a variety of expressions are used in the media for specialised households, in particular distinguishing between 'key' and 'specialised' household - the 'two' households. In Foshan prefecture, Guangdong for example, a key household represents an intermediate level of specialisation, superior to those households engaged in normal diversified undertakings but inferior to the level of specialisation normally associated with specialised households.[14]  For the purpose of this study the distinction is ignored.  The lack of clarity in the media over such a distinction, however, can be taken as a sign of the somewhat confused and haphazard nature of development in the rural economy at present.

In 1983, 9.4% of all rural households (16 million) were considered specialists.[15] This figure had risen to 13.6% (c 23.4 million) by mid-1984.[16] Its emergence came with the introduction of responsibility systems which gave the peasants decision-making power over production. Peasants were urged to use surplus resources to develop sideline production and engage in diversified undertakings. In particular, peasants with special skills and management ability began to distinguish themselves by moving beyond the normal diversity associated with household production to engage in several or even just one specialised line of production. As production was developed, earnings from these undertakings surpassed the earnings from contracted farming outputs and households began to make sideline occupation their economic mainstay. In this way, households became specialised in one or two pursuits. Alongside these households which gradually emerged as specialised households, in the initial round of contracting some peasant households were contracted to perform specific tasks and they too were known as specialised producers.[17]

Initially, payments to specialised households for fulfilment of tasks encompassed a variety of methods including work-points, awards, and the distribution of profits.[18] However, with the development of *baogan daohu*, specialised households became established as part of the contract system. They contract responsibility land in the normal way, fulfilling contracted output targets in their specialism alongside any other contractual demands (such as contributions to collective accumulation funds). They are free to dispose of surplus produce in the normal way.

The precise definition of specialised households varies from place to place. In Foshan prefecture, Guangdong, for example, to be considered a specialised producer, a household must: first, sell over 90% of the output of the specialised occupation as commodities (a figure of 70% for Guangdong is given elsewhere);[19] secondly, the household per capita income should be over 1000 *yuan*; and thirdly, the income from the specialised or principal occupation should account for the majority of the household total income.[20]

By contrast, qualifications for specialised households in Anhui differ somewhat. Those specialised households not involved in crop production must sell 80% of the specialised product as commodities with the output value of these commodities exceeding 65% of the total household value. For those households doing specialised jobs as well as crop cultivation, 50% of the output of the sideline occupation must be sold as commodities with the output value being 50% of the total household output value. However later reports indicate that the 50% values applied to all types of specialised household in Anhui.[21]

Variety is certainly the watchword for development in the countryside at this time. Specialised production in Nantong county, Jiangsu for example, exhibits five different modes of management.[22] First, self-management: that is, provision and management of labour and capital by the household, with control over production, marketing and supply and responsibility for their own profits and losses. Second, contracting, whereby the specialised household contracts with the collective to use collective land, facilities or equipment with output quotas determining remuneration. Third, linkage, which essentially is a form of 'putting-out' system, the specialised household contracting its labour while the collective (enterprise) provides capital, raw materials, and marketing services. Fourth, coordination, with groups of specialised households supporting one another in a combination of related services while retaining independent management. Finally, cooperation, the pooling of resources by a number of specialised households with joint production and distribution of profits commensurate with contribution of resources. In Nantong, 60% of the specialised households were organised as self-management households, with 10% as contract, 7% linkage, 15% coordination, and 8% cooperation.[23] This should not be surprising. Initially, specialised households can be expected to concentrate on household production and feel disinclined to integrate with others. More sophisticated relationships between households will only develop as circumstances warrant and the peasants feel comfortable doing so.

## Advantages of production by specialised households

Production by specialised households has the incentive and motivational advantages of *baogan daohu*. Additional advantages are also claimed. By building on local economic advantages for example, it is argued that specialised households can better utilise surplus labour, especially in the development of diversified undertakings previously suppressed by the Maoists.[24] Furthermore, growing pressure on land resources requires increasing amounts of rural employment be created in non-agricultural activities.

Since the 1978 policy relaxations, employment opportunities in handicrafts, industry, construction and commerce are once again available. In favoured areas such as Nantong county specialised producers have been particularly important in creating employment in handicrafts, services such as construction and transportation, and commerce.

Two important points need to be made here: first, specialised households predominantly utilise the experience and skill of individuals existing within the rural community.[25] In a sample of 150 specialised households in Nantong county, for example, it was estimated that 70% were based on traditional skills within that household (although this distinction was becoming more difficult to make with technical innovation in traditional undertakings).[26] Secondly, it is argued that the release of traditional skills into the economy combined with a greater individual freedom in production should allow a more rational development of local environments and resources.[27]

Allied to this more rational use of land resources, is the claim that specialised households better utilise advanced agricultural techniques.[28] It is argued that specialised households can reap the benefits from such techniques at the same time as keeping costs down relative to investment thereby increasing profit. The state believes such specialist producers are able to use small investments to gain quick returns with low levels of costs and high levels of efficiency.[29]

Collective units also stand to gain from the development of specialised households in that collective retention will increase, although this may be only in absolute terms and not relative to the increase in income being demonstrated by specialised households. Nevertheless this retention is important in determining the depth of local development.[30]

For the state, specialised households have two important benefits. First, they are active commodity producers and have helped considerably in increasing commodity production in the current phase.[31] With the current improvements in personal incomes, this increase in available market produce is crucial if the economy - especially the rural sector - is to maintain its current momentum. Secondly, it would appear from examples offered by the media, that specialisation often stimulates a welcome increase in grain production.[32] Without denying that specialisation in production may well lead to an increase in grain output, these examples also serve the state's desire to maintain an emphasis on grain production, and few detail exactly how such improved outputs are achieved.

## Problems of specialised households

It should not be thought that specialised households are without their problems. As with *baogan daohu*, specialised households face problems with local cadres tearing up agreed contracts; often this problem comes about when the production of a specialist producer far exceeds the allotted contract demands resulting in significant peasant incomes. Local cadres, many of whom were appointed under the Maoists, find this kind of wealth difficult to accept.[33]

Alternatively, the attraction of such potential income gains is pushing some producers with little in the way of production skills into specialised production with disastrous results. In Kaiping and Enping counties, Guangdong, for example, at least 200 specialised households were making losses through 'blind management, errors in technology, or overexpansion of production'.[34] Indeed, the losses can be quite significant. The same source gives the example of one specialised household which overexpanded and undertook responsibility for a large pig farm. As a result of technical incompetence and mismanagement, the household lost 60,000 *yuan* as well as over 600 pigs in just one year.[35]

Again, the development of specialised households, as with *baogan daohu*, will make collective influence over such matters as birth control and resource base management more difficult. The emergence of specialised commodity producers has made increased demand on the weak state commercial system.

While demand for agricultural goods seems at present to be almost inexhaustible, the peasant's ability to market agricultural produce as well as purchase producer goods remains poor. The inefficiency of the commercial system, despite the emergence of specialist traders, for example, could be a major stumbling block to the potential development of specialised households as well as the rural economy in general.[36] (A fuller discussion of the commercial system will follow below).

Additionally, specialised households have specific technical needs which have to be met. If specialised households are going to be effective then not only must producer goods be available, but pre-production and post-production services must also be catered for. In other words, division of labour must develop further. Without this development the extent of specialisation must remain low.[37]

The problem of inequality also becomes important. As already stated incomes from specialised production are relatively high. Within a locality this can easily create tension and conflict. Furthermore, it is inevitable that areas with well-endowed resource bases and access to markets and the means of production can exploit the advantages of specialised production more than less-developed regions. This is something Chinese planners are currently willing to accept but which may promote political difficulties if maintained.

Finally, there is the complex question of land transfer, a subject which merits detailed attention. For rural households to effectively specialise production and maximise production efficiency, land must be organised into manageable parcels. This in turn requires a system of land transfer. It should be reemphasised that in the initial contracting of responsibility land, land was commonly allocated on a pro rata basis ignoring the strengths and weaknesses of individual households. In order to overcome the situation whereby land is either poorly or under utilised, and to allow households to develop according to their abilities (ie specialise), the state has encouraged land transfers. Indeed, it emphasises land transfer as a 'necessary phenomenon' for agricultural specialisation.[38]

Land transfers to benefit specialised production can be done in two ways: through the collective, that is a peasant returns unused land to the collective which proceeds to reallocate it; or on an individual basis whereby the peasants merely register transfers with the collective.[39] The state would prefer all transfers to go through collective channels, in the hope of preventing the illegal rent payments found in some rural areas. However, this does not prevent corruption amongst officials who can 'favour' households in any subsequent distribution of transferred land.

There are many reasons why individual households might wish to reduce the amount of land they farm. Consider the example of Putuan commune, Hubei, a commune of 5756 households with 51,100 *mu* of cultivable land. In Putuan commune, between 1981 and 1983, 380 households (6.6%) transferred a total of 2155 *mu* of the commune's cultivable land (4.3%) through sub-contracts.[40]

Various reasons were given for these transfers, including the excessive burdens of agricultural tasks; a shortage of labour (both because of the demands of other activities and through out-migration from the countryside to nearby cities); a lack of funds and equipment; indebtedness; and the inaccessibility of assigned land.

Whatever reasons peasants have for wanting to transfer land, it is clear that the state feels it is right for them to do so in order that rural units - if they are able - can specialise production and develop in this way. Transferring land in order to promote specialisation can, however, cause problems not least because the land has been regarded by peasants as their 'lifeblood'.[41] In theory these transfers are voluntary. In Datong county, Shanxi, county authorities were faced with demands from commodity grain households to increase land allotments to them by 11,000 *mu*. (It is unclear how the county came to be handling this). The county authorities needed to utilise various sources to secure this land, including 5100 *mu* transferred from hardship, ordinary contract and specialised contract households.[42] Inevitably it must be asked if county authorities, anxious to consolidate landholdings to facilitate greater specialised production and thereby reap the potential benefits, may have sweetened the transfers with incentives, indulged in 'commandism', or possibly straight corruption. Certainly, in Nantong county, Jiangsu, the county authorities offered numerous incentives, such as welfare benefits, to peasants in order to persuade them to transfer their land to skilled farmers.[43]

Similarly, individual peasants may come under severe pressure from wealthier neighbours to relinquish responsibility lands. Indeed, it seems likely that a number of individual agreements could come to proliferate in the countryside, with wealthier peasants able to accumulate land and poorer peasants becoming little more than wage labour. Whatever the specific case, local officials - themselves known to take advantage of their position[44] - are certainly under pressure from a variety of sources when considering the redistribution of transferred land.

Furthermore, there is the question of payment of compensation to peasants who do transfer land, either voluntarily or at the expiry of a contract period when redistribution of land is possible due to changed household circumstances. If households have improved and made long-term investments in the land, making the same plot of land yield higher incomes (with the expectation that it would continue to do so), it is considered only right to compensate them for that investment. Indeed, such compensation payments are necessary to encourage peasants to improve their land resources.[45] Without compensation payments, it is easy to see that peasants would refuse to make significant investments in contracted land.

However, it is evident that this issue can be contentious. The arrangement of compensation payments is very unclear in state pronouncements. Language such as 'the specific measures of investment compensation should be determined through the negotiation of the cadres and the masses' obviously subsumes many areas of potential and actual conflict.[46] While some comment is made of fixing compensation according to factors such as the grade of land transferred and the amount of capital invested in the land - comment obviously aimed at allaying fears of arbitrary transfer of land with minimal (if any) compensation - no definite picture emerges. Inevitably it seems that compensation payments will vary in value and effectiveness from place to place. In this sense, while such payments should promote a stable rural atmosphere, in practice they could have the opposite effect.

In the rural suburbs of Ezhou city, Hubei, for example, two forms of compensation have been adopted. The first compensates for the additional expenditure those transferring will incur in purchasing their grain ration. The second grants compensation greater than that of satisfying the grain ration, but no detail is given.[47] Interestingly, the first method of compensation is preferred by the authorities in Ezhou. The second is deemed open to abuse from peasants demanding compensation for non-existent investment. It is not difficult to see why peasants in Ezhou would feel little reassured by these statements. Compensation payments are clearly poorly defined and difficult to obtain.

## Grain-producing specialised households

Thus many questions still remain as to the exact workings of land transfer and compensation payments. Nevertheless, locally, it would appear that solutions have been developed to allow specialisation to emerge as an important force in the rural economy. However, the impact of specialisation remains dependent upon adequate supplies of grain. Early specialist producers, as might be expected, were specialists in a wide range of agricultural undertakings, but rarely grain. The question as to how the state is able to reconcile the need for increased grain outputs with a policy goal of stimulating commodity production is an important one. One proposed solution is the development of grain specialists, in particular grain-producing specialised households.

Grain specialist households have emerged quite dramatically in the past decade. In 1981 only 'a few' households specialised in grain.[48] By late 1983, grain specialists accounted for 34.2% (c 5.5 million) of all specialised households.[49] This upsurge undoubtedly reflects the state's concern to maintain commodity grain supplies at a time when first, most specialised households were giving up grain production where possible to concentrate exclusively on their speciality; secondly, state contracted demands for grain remain below levels of consumer need, in particular from non-productive urban populations which have increased in the 1980s; and thirdly, it has become permissible for households to 'fulfil' contracted grain targets by payment of a cash equivalent.

The impact and potential of grain specialists is well illustrated by material from Yangxin county in the extreme southeast of Hubei.[50] Yangxin county implemented *baogan daohu* in 1981 and in 1982 specialisation began to emerge, including specialisation in grain production.

Although the data on grain specialists in Yangxin county are based on only 35 households, a number of the potential benefits claimed for specialised households can be quickly identified. First, the commodity rate of grain specialists is relatively high, 45% of total production compared to the county average of 20%. Secondly, against the backdrop of the traditional competition for land between grain and cash crops, the increase in per-unit grain yields obtained through specialisation (631.3 *jin/mu* for grain specialists compared to a county average of 485 *jin/mu*) is very welcome, enabling reductions (however small) in the land devoted to grain and an increase in more lucrative cash crop production. Thirdly, grain specialists use investment funds in a relatively effective manner, (grain production costs for specialists are 2.53 *yuan/100 jin* compared to a county average of 3.5 *yuan/100 jin*), facilitating the breaking of the prevailing rural cycle whereby insufficient investment funds promotes poor economic results which in turn yield insufficient investment funds. Finally, grain specialists can provide conditions in which other enterprises can develop through a reduction in the grain burden placed upon other peasants.

However, two questions need immediate answers. First, how can grain specialists accumulate sufficient consolidated landholdings to reap the economies of scale claimed for Yangxin county? Secondly, how are they to earn high incomes from grain production given low state grain contract prices? Briefly, the answer to the former is land transfer (as discussed above); and to the latter, incentives, of various kinds, to the grain specialists to make their incomes at least comparable with those of households engaged in other agricultural undertakings. The issue of incentives in particular is an interesting one and will be discussed at greater length in the regional chapters that follow.

## Specialised households: conclusions

Specialised households - including grain households - are without doubt an important production management form in the Chinese countryside. They are not without problems in organisation and they certainly present challenges to the state in terms of the inequality of incomes discernible between specialised and non-specialised households within local areas and also regionally. On the one hand there is a need for increased commodity production, on the other the risk of 'state-sponsored' emergence of class differentiation (and exploitation). Tension and conflict between individuals is already apparent.

Those difficulties notwithstanding, specialised households seem to be a permanent production form within the countryside. Indeed, in time it is hoped that they will become the 'building-blocks' for allegedly more sophisticated production forms at a variety of spatial levels.[51] Some of these more sophisticated production forms are more developed on the ground than others. It is to these more concrete production forms that discussion now turns.

## Commodity production bases: definitions; issues

Commodity production bases are areas within which production of one crop is dominant. Typically a group of counties, these bases are involved in a style of production where 'one crop is king' but a strong and varied diversified economy also exists. The key is that amount of production which is commodity production, production beyond local need and demand. It is from such areas that the state expects to be able to obtain significant amounts of foodstuffs to feed the non-agricultural population as well as supply key industries with raw materials such as cotton.[52]

It would be expected that these bases have a tradition of commodity production, with the local environment suited to a certain product and a history of production which would have facilitated the accumulation of production and managerial expertise. Secondly, the commodity rate of farm produce is already high. Thirdly, the potential for further expansion of specialised production must be high, either through increased per-unit yields or land reclamation to expand the sown area.

Fourthly, there must exist good internal and external communications and transport networks so that access to markets is convenient. Fifthly, where possible, production should be centralised to facilitate planning and the construction of any major capital construction projects which are deemed necessary. Finally, pre-existence of produce processing industry is also considered advantageous.[53]

The advantages and difficulties associated with commodity production bases are broadly similar to those already expressed above for specialised households and will not be further elaborated upon here. What are more important are the issues that arise out of the establishment of these bases: how to establish commodity grain bases and maintain peasant enthusiasm for grain production within those bases; the competition between areas for the production of known high-income crops; the importance of state perceptions of an area; and the question of regional differentiation.

## Commodity grain bases: Poyang lake commodity grain base

It is worth reemphasising that grain production remains central within Chinese agriculture, 'never slackening grain production and energetically developing a diversified economy' is the new slogan, not much different from those used by the Maoists.[54] Grain output in China is basically unstable because of the deteriorating condition of the agricultural resource base and low productivity.

Contracted and private sales of grain still only amount to about 15% of total grain production.[55]

Furthermore, market sales of grain are drawn from a small number of counties. Almost half of total grain sales is drawn from only 15% (or 344) of China's 2321 counties. The per-unit yields in these counties are almost one-third higher than the average for China, and per capita grain sales are almost twice as high.[56]

Given that such a large proportion of China's marketable grain comes from such a small number of counties, the state's desire to establish commodity grain bases in order to ensure stable grain supplies is understandable. The state must continue to rely on a small number of bases for its grain and thus it needs to ensure that these 'granaries' continue to supply the grain it needs. However, with relatively low grain prices, grain production for the market makes little sense. The state believes that grain commodity bases may be a way to reconcile state demands for stable grain supplies with peasant demands to earn incomes commensurate with those obtainable from the production of more lucrative cash crops.

Furthermore, only through ensuring the stable supply of grain can the state establish commodity bases which concentrate on other foodstuffs.[57] While it should not be thought that the state envisages large areas producing nothing but one crop without any grain production, it concedes that to expect self-sufficiency in grain foodstuffs from designated non-grain commodity bases would impede their development and limit the extent of rural trade.[58]

The Poyang lake area of Northern Jiangxi more than fits state criteria for a commodity base, in this case for grain. With plentiful water supplies, a suitable subtropical humid climate and ample sunlight, the Poyang lake area has been an important agricultural base since the Han dynasty, and supplies about 40% of all the grain sold to the state in Jiangxi.

Grain is the key crop in the area, not surprising given the concentration of major cities, including Nanning, and rural population in the area. Cotton, oil-bearing crops, animal husbandry and aquatic produce are also important as well as traditional specialities such as silk in Nanning county, sugar in Dongxiang county, and fruits in Qingjiang county.[59] Although the area is prone to flooding, grain production in the region is considered stable, with relatively high output levels and commodity rate. Furthermore, communications and transport networks are considered good and expansion of grain production is possible with the existence of 2.3 million *mu* of wasteland available to be converted to grain production.[60]

However, the problems associated with commodity grain bases in general and in the Poyang lake region in particular are numerous. Grain production costs for example, have risen steadily from 3.4 *yuan*/100 *jin* in the early 1950s, to 5 *yuan*/100 *jin* in the 1970s and 7.5 *yuan*/100 *jin* in the mid-1980s.[61]

At the same time as costs have risen, the price of grain relative to cash crops has fallen and incomes of grain farmers are relatively low. Furthermore, incomes are considered unstable. One particularly bleak picture of grain farming in China states that:

> Grain farmers have an unstable income. The grain production period is long, natural restrictions are great and droughts, floods, blights, pests and natural disasters are frequent, so income is unstable. Although those engaged in industry and sideline occupations also are influenced by market changes, in the final analysis they are a little safer than those engaged in agricultural occupations.[62]

Again, the burden placed upon the grain farmer is heavy. The costs charged to grain farmers for ploughing and irrigation for example are considered high, and at the same time non-productive expenses (administrative costs) are too numerous.[63] Furthermore, not only are procurement contract targets in the old-established commodity grain areas too high, but above-quota prices for grain are relatively low. Both have important disincentive effects.[64]

Commercial difficulties within commodity grain districts also create problems for grain producers even though it would be expected that the state has more incentive in such areas to ensure commercial efficiency.[65] Criticism of the official commercial system, its inability to handle the most basic purchasing and sales tasks required of it by grain farmers, has been by Chinese standards harsh.[66] However, critics stop short of attacking the CCPCC for its continuing failure adequately to reform a system which still moves the bulk of China's commodity grain. But such criticism needs to be made.

Together these difficulties make grain production a relatively unattractive proposition. Grain is recognised as the 'treasure of treasures' but grain farmers are becoming relatively impoverished and 'socially unpopular'.[67] If commodity grain bases are to develop, it would seem necessary that the bases must offer subsidies to grain producers in order to make their incomes more comparable with those of others both within, and beyond, the base area who are involved in the production of more lucrative economic crops. Indeed, without such subsidies it is difficult to see how commodity grain bases will develop except through 'commandism'.

Crucially, it would appear that for the most part it will be the local unit (county level and below) which will determine the extent and range of subsidies that are available and not the state.[68]

The material on the Poyang lake grain base is conspicuously silent on the issue of subsidies. Elsewhere however, local subsidies are openly discussed. Yuyao county, Zhejiang has encouraged commodity grain production through the introduction of eight forms of subsidy including a dispersal of non-productive expenses, subsidised chemical fertilisers and priority for many forms of agricultural goods and materials.[69]

That subsidies are for the most part locally financed is an important issue. It is conceded that some state aid is necessary in the workings of commodity grain bases. Yet it is also generally accepted that any such aid will be of only marginal importance.[70] For most local units, it is the hard cash accumulated from the profits of the commune- and brigade-run enterprises and the diversified economy which determine the ability of local units to generate such subsidies.[71]

It should be said that in the more marginal rural areas, where local economies cannot bear the cost of these subsidies, state aid is essential if any progress is to be made with commodity grain production. In Guangxi for example, provincial authorities have established commodity grain bases around several communes. More commonly grain bases are established within the framework of several counties. However, the nature of the physical landscape in Guangxi, with small and dispersed areas of plainland suited to farming, makes the commune a more suitable unit for commodity grain production.

In order to provide the financial basis - in terms of capital to subsidise production and improve the agricultural resource base - for such bases, the chosen units first develop industrial and diversified undertakings. In Guangxi this has involved a substantial amount of provincial short-term 'priority funding' to finance the necessary capital construction and production inputs. Such a capital allocation strategy may benefit those units fortunate enough to be designated as bases (most likely those units with already well-established economies), but only at the expense of the more needy marginal units.[72]

By contrast, it is obvious that those areas with agricultural resource bases capable of significant commodity grain production can easily support more lucrative cash crop production. Indeed, commentators have watched with some alarm the two traditional 'granaries' of Taihu basin (Jiangsu) and Zhujiang (Pearl river) delta (Guangdong), where between 1978 and 1981 grain production fell by 18.8% and 5.5% respectively.[73] Similarly, Walker comments upon the growing crop specialisation within the Chinese countryside and its impact upon provincial grain production as follows:

> the general point can be made, however, that the emerging trends in grain production ... are not to the entire satisfaction of the central government. This question will merit detailed research as time passes, but there is no doubt that the declining sown area of grain under the more market-orientated, decentralized planning system introduced, has been considerably greater than the government intended.[74]

From this, two issues become important. First, the state's perception of an area. If an area is perceived by the state as an important supplier of commodity grain then the potential production of cash crops is limited. Subsidies and incentives to produce grain will offset to some extent the impact of deleterious state grain prices, but it is open to debate how much they can be expected to fully equate incomes from grain production with those possible from cash crops. Secondly, and following on from this, competition between areas to promote their claims to produce commodity cash crops (which would involve cutting back on grain production) is intense. An example of such competition will be given below with material from Guangdong.

## Commodity sugar-cane production: competition between Zhanjiang and Zhujiang

Within Guangdong the prime areas of sugar-cane production are found south of 24 degrees latitude: the Zhujiang plain, Chaoshan, Zhanjiang and the tropical island of Hainan.[75] High winter temperatures remove the hazard of frost. Rainfall and soils are both well suited to sugar cane production.[76]

In comparison to sugar cane production in other provinces, the amount of land needed to produce one ton of refined sugar in Guangdong is low, 1.5 *mu*/ton for paddy fields, compared to 3 *mu*/ton in Jiangxi and 6 *mu*/ton in Hunan; and 3.4 *mu*/ton on dry-slope fields, compared to 8 *mu*/ton in the Yangzi river basin.[77] This reflects both the relative fertility of land in Guangdong, as well as the fact that extraction rates of sugar from cane are higher here than elsewhere.[78]

In addition, the abundance of navigable waterways makes the transport of bulky sugar cane both more convenient and relatively inexpensive.[79] The existing processing facilities are also underutilised with a spare capacity of about 30%, thus the expansion of sugar cane production would require little if any additional investment in processing facilities.[80]

However, in the current climate of growing local autonomy, many local authorities, attracted by high profits, have set up their own mills to compete with state mills. This results in the continued excess capacity of large state mills and the production of more inferior quality, high cost, sugar. This is an example of what the state sees as an increasingly common phenomenon of 'wasteful competition'.[81] However, it is also inevitable in the current economic climate where to 'get rich is glorious'. Local peasants want to develop highly-rewarded industrial undertakings and reap the levels of incomes which they read of in the press. Competition - wasteful or otherwise - is the result.

In addressing the question of competition between areas to produce sugar cane, the benefits of such production can be quickly given. Despite protests from some officials that the value to the producer of its sugar cane is still relatively low (1.69 *yuan* per ton of sugar cane which will purchase three *jin* of refined sugar while the state can actually extract 13 *jin* of sugar plus the value of the waste products), sugar cane production gives a higher return for labour than grain production.[82]

The collectives stand to gain principally from their ability to develop sideline industries around sugar cane production - even though they may compete with state and other collective facilities. These industries include sugar mills and an assortment of enterprises using the by-products of sugar cane refining to produce fibreboard, alcohol, paper and fodder.[83] The profits generated by these industries are important in rural economic development and they also employ surplus labour. The state benefits from increased taxation and also from increased supplies of refined sugar which reduce the necessity of expensive imports.

The most important advantage to the sugar cane producers is the reduction in the state demands for grain in return for increased demands for sugar cane, something the producers are willing to accept because the value of their production surplus to state demands will be that much more for producing sugar cane that that under grain production.

Under a series of exchange agreements the state will guarantee grain supplies to sugar cane producers.[84] These grain supplies are usually in the form of husked rice (thereby avoiding earlier problems in Fujian for example, when the state supplied locally unpopular sweet potatoes, under a similar agreement).[85] This advantage takes on even greater significance in terms of the local competition for sugar cane production when it is considered that a reduction in the grain production of one area must in all probability be met by an increase in the grain production of another nearby (given the commercial difficulties common throughout China, long-distance transfers of grain are unlikely). Indeed, in the material concerning competition for commodity status between Zhanjiang and Zhujiang, the emphasis becomes not so much one of stressing an ability to produce sugar cane but more a relative inability to produce grain.

The arguments concerning Zhujiang and Zhanjiang were made in 1981. These are the kinds of arguments which have been heard throughout China in recent years, with different localities arguing their case for official status as commodity bases. The competition between Zhanjiang and Zhujiang in 1981 was intense.[86] Chaoshan and Hainan island, being the more 'junior' production areas, could only expect to increase their sugar cane production through raising per-unit yields rather than by an expansion of the area sown with sugar cane. The rich alluvial soils of the Zhujiang plain represent much better growing conditions for sugar cane than those in Zhanjiang where the soils are sandy and thin. Furthermore, 90% of Zhanjiang's sugar cane production is on dry-slope land whilst the Zhujiang plain has a mixture of dry-slope and paddy fields. However, while the natural advantages of the Zhujiang plain make for more efficient sugar cane production than that of Zhanjiang, at the same time (not unnaturally) the same advantages make grain production more efficient.

Ultimately, it seems it is the relative land-cost of grain production in Zhanjiang which is the key argument. Zhujiang, it is said, should concentrate on commodity grain production (for which it has ideal conditions),[87] while Zhanjiang should be allowed to expand commodity sugar cane production.[88] This despite Zhujiang's obvious superiority in sugar cane production.

Other factors which influence such a conclusion include the relative abundance of barren land within Zhanjiang which can be reclaimed for sugar cane production and the relatively high level of centralised production. However, it is clearly grain which remains the key issue.

As a way round this intra-provincial competition, several commentators suggested that inter-provincial supplies of grain can increase with less efficient sugar cane producers in other provinces turning their land over to grain production in order to supply Guangdong sugar cane producers.[89] In this way both Zhujiang and Zhanjiang could grow commodity sugar cane. However, such a proposal would scarcely be welcomed in sugar cane regions where production is less efficient but the impact of sugar cane upon the local economy is no less valuable. It merely passes the problem of who grows grain to another region. Furthermore, some peasants remain fearful of over-dependence upon an outside source for supplies of staple grain foodstuffs.[90] Given China's internal commercial difficulties these fears are quite justified.

Finally, it is also suggested that grain might be imported into Guangdong from abroad using money generated from increased sugar production, in particular from international market sales of sugar.[91] This solution is likely to be unsatisfactory for a number of reasons. First, it reduces the amount of available sugar for the domestic market. Secondly, it utilises foreign currency which is more urgently needed to import, for example, foreign technology and equipment. Thirdly, the state places much weight on its claims of self-sufficiency in grain and such a switch to grain imports in Guangdong would reduce the propaganda value of these claims as well as perhaps encouraging dramatic shifts away from grain production elsewhere.

It is difficult to judge how the competition outlined above between Zhanjiang and Zhujiang was eventually resolved. Certainly Zhujiang remains an important commodity grain base but it also contains areas of sugar cane commodity production.[92] Presumably some level of compromise was reached although it is unclear what this compromise might have entailed and how satisfactorily it has worked.

## Commodity production bases: conclusions

Commodity production bases are emerging as another level of administrative organisation of production in the countryside. It would appear however, that such bases continue to serve bureaucratic functions more closely than economic ones. Ideally, profitable commodity production should become widespread in suitable areas, although the state would continue to insist upon substantial amounts of grain outputs - if not grain self-sufficiency. However, this is difficult to envisage on three counts. First, the complexity and essentially small-scale nature of production continues to prove an intolerable strain upon state commerce. Secondly, the emphasis upon natural advantages would seem to exacerbate widening income differences within the countryside, perhaps beyond tolerable limits. Thirdly, grain production in non-grain commodity bases will make too many demands upon production inputs, thereby limiting the extent of commodity production unless substantial amounts of commodity grain can be grown in, and transferred from commodity, grain areas. These areas, however, face their own problems. Thus, it remains to be seen if commodity production bases can develop as envisaged by Chinese planners.

# Agricultural-industrial-commercial complexes

The development of agricultural-industrial-commercial integrated complexes (A-I-C complexes) is another example of rural production specialisation designed to stimulate commodity production.[93] Furthermore, the material on this subject can be used to illustrate a number of problems and issues associated with the study of rural China: first, the Chinese often label something as if a concrete entity, yet in the field it proves to be somewhat confused and even contradictory. Secondly, the rapidity of change in the Chinese countryside can radically alter the definition and shape of a management form in a short period. Finally, it is important to establish, where possible, a broad historical as well as geographic framework for specific contemporary local materials in order to fully understand the significance of developments claimed within such materials.

Initially it appeared that the A-I-C complex was to be a distinct production management form. Its conception was to aid the development of small-scale rural processing industry. The A-I-C would utilise the agricultural and sideline products of the locality as the principal raw materials; the peasant households providing the local raw materials, the enterprises run by the communes or the production brigades providing the processing facilities and the collective marketing organisations handling sales and purchases.[94] In this way, it was argued, local units could break the traditional agricultural mould where farming was the only occupation. Ideally such organisations - as is claimed for most of the state's preferred organisational forms and policy goals - could be set up quickly at little cost and yield high returns.[95]

The gains from organising production in this way are essentially economies of specialisation and scale, together with those of vertical integration. Agricultural producers can be confident of selling their produce at a reasonable price which should encourage them to develop production, perhaps even become more specialised, and invest in the land. The processing enterprise gains not only a stable supply of raw materials but also, it is claimed, improved commodity circulation.

Again, such integration should ensure that local natural advantages are fully and effectively utilised.[96] The higher utilisation of raw materials in turn effectively increases their value.[97] Furthermore, by in situ processing of rural raw materials, utilisation of agricultural by-products, for example as fodder or manure, previously wasted by the processing industries of the cities and towns is made easier. Similarly, transport and storage costs can be cut.[98]

A-I-C complexes could also cut out some of the many 'links' in the commercial system.[99] This is particularly important with products which have to be processed quickly and sold fresh. A-I-C complexes on the outskirts of Tianjin for instance, after integration in February 1979, emphasised milk production and surpassed all previous production records. Improved production and processing together with better market connections provided guaranteed supplies to the city at guaranteed prices. After an absence of ten years shops were once again supplied with fresh milk, butter and condensed milk.[100]

Other claimed benefits include the utilisation of rural surplus labour;[101] the ability to accumulate capital construction funds;[102] and increases in output, profits, taxes and distributed income.[103]

Of course not all instances of integration are successful. A-I-C complexes must recognise the limits of their economic environment - investment capability, transport capacity, processing facilities and so forth. Some integrated units have over-extended themselves and blindly developed. Others find that integration brings about an increase in gross agricultural output value, but all too often costs rise at a greater rate and incomes do not improve. Yet others come into competition for resources and markets with state-owned facilities and presumably, although nothing is said, with other collective enterprises.[104]

Not all the difficulties are of the A-I-C complexes' own making. As with other units they are hampered by an official planning system they feel is still too rigid. The management structure seems to have too many bureaucratic links, a bureaucracy which delays availability of funds, equipment, and raw, processed and other materials.

## The example of Liuzhuang production brigade

One of the best examples given of an A-I-C complex is Liuzhuang brigade in Qiliying commune, Xinxiang county, Henan. In 1982 Liuzhuang, located on the North Henan plain, had a population of 1230 (207 households) and a total cultivable area of 1904 *mu* predominantly sown with grain and cotton, only about 5% (c 95 *mu*) used for fruit and vegetables. Development since liberation can be traced as follows.

**Table 3  Liuzhuang brigade. Economic performance. Various indicators**

|                          | 1949 | 1957 | 1968/9 | 1975   | 1978   | 1981 |
|--------------------------|------|------|--------|--------|--------|------|
| Grain yields (*jin/mu*)  | 100  | 430  | 1000   | c 1600 | c 1600 | 1700 |
| Cotton yields (*jin/mu*) | 20   | 100  | 176    | 150    | 150    | 175  |
| Total collective income (mn *yuan*) | 0.04 | n/a | 0.32 | 0.54 | 1.26 | 2.52 |
| Peasant income (*yuan*/capita) | 20 | 79 | 140 | n/a | n/a | 2050 |

Compiled from material in *Red Flag* 16.6.1982, see note 105.

The development of Liuzhuang can be divided into distinct phases. From 1949 to 1957 the brigade concentrated on providing the basic needs of food and clothing, what the peasants described as 'a stage to lay foundations for eliminating poverty and achieving prosperity'.[105]

Between 1957 and 1968, Liuzhuang concentrated on developing production through the establishment of stable high-yield land - principally by means of well and canal irrigation - and by increased mechanisation of farm production. From 1968 until 1978 Liuzhuang turned its attention to utilising the surplus labour created by increased mechanisation in farming. To this end, a number of local industrial enterprises were established including a flour mill and a cottonseed oil processing factory. Indeed, by 1975, 42% of the total collective income came from industrial and sideline production (compared to only 7.7% in 1969).

Since 1978, Liuzhuang has been established as an A-I-C complex, consolidating and further expanding industrial and sideline production to include 10 factories and workshops. At the same time, improvements in farming production have taken place, principally through the extension of advanced agricultural techniques as well as the adoption of specialised production forms. Significant increases in collective income, public accumulation funds and improved peasant livelihoods - in the form of per capita incomes, welfare facilities, savings, surplus grain, improved diet, new housing and increased purchases of consumer goods - have all been reported since the integration.[106]

There the Chinese media effectively leaves the argument: integration of economic function in Liuzhuang has prompted great prosperity. However, closer inspection of the material on Liuzhuang can give numerous insights into difficulties associated with Chinese media coverage of the countryside. It should not be thought for example that Liuzhuang is in any way a 'typical' production brigade - even in the sense of being a 'typical rich' unit. Qiliying commune, of which Liuzhuang as noted above is one brigade, was an important Maoist model of development through intensification on the North China plain and one of the first communes established in 1958.

It is interesting to note that Liuzhuang was able to become relatively prosperous under the Maoists when prosperity continued to elude other units similarly placed environmentally. Leeming offers three possible lines of explanation. First, that cotton production continued to bring in a cash income from the state. Secondly, that the burdens of grain production were more tolerable. Thirdly, that Liuzhuang may have possessed certain privileges which others did not. Certainly, Liuzhuang was able to develop local industrial enterprises relatively early, perhaps as a result of its privileged position.[107]

For Liuzhuang, the 1978 reforms gave the chance to openly and actively generate income, further developing its already strong economic base. Thus, only limited conclusions can be drawn from Liuzhuang about the potential for more widespread economic integration. It would be expected that, in the post-1978 economic environment, Liuzhuang would expand and prosper.

Indeed, it can be easily deduced from the materials that A-I-C complexes are more likely to be found in areas of comparable natural advantage. Only relatively well-developed units will be able to supply the necessary investment funds to develop processing industries, have the transport networks - roads and vehicles - needed to ensure access to markets and so forth. It is interesting to note that many of the examples of integrated units in the materials are drawn from the periurban fringe.[108]

This was also true for an A-I-C complex visited by the author in 1983: Huaxi brigade, Jiangyin county, Jiangsu. Huaxi also has other advantages. Located on the Southern Jiangsu plain, Huaxi has flat land ideal for mechanisation. Water supplies are abundant, facilitating irrigation and the creation of high stable-yield land - grain yields are as high as 2000 *jin/mu*. The brigade also has good transport links with the manufacturing city of Changzhou, itself a national model for light industry and planned births, about 15 kilometres away.

In other words, it is difficult to see how an A-I-C complex is anything more than a bureaucratic label for what are essentially wealthy communes and brigades which possess a variety of enterprises in addition to high levels of crop production. Although the literature would claim that they are more than this, on the ground they may be simple extensions to (or even an excuse to extend) already well-established rural enterprises and local economies, extensions motivated by other emerging organisational forms, a reemphasis on diversification and rural industry, and most importantly greater profits.

Given this critique is there any justification for distinguishing the A-I-C complex as an economic/social form in the Chinese countryside? Probably not. They appear to be little more than a label - even bureaucratic justification - for well-established and relatively prosperous units. However, they do act as a signpost for distinguishing areas of relative rural wealth in the Chinese materials.

It is also apparent that many economic combinations between specialised households are also now known as A-I-C integrated units.[109] In this respect and others the A-I-C complex has become a more generalised term for many kinds of rural development. Nevertheless, the experience of these integrated units, illustrates the kinds of advantages - economic, geographical and political - which are required for commercial success in rural China. Even with them, success is not guaranteed; without them, rural progress is very slow.

## Specialisation: summary

In the current phase there has been, and continues to be, a move towards specialisation of rural production, such specialisation being an important part of the development of commodity production and the rural economy in general. The success of these moves towards increased local - and regional - specialisation is greatly determined by the ability of local economies to move beyond the traditional limitations of small-scale grain farming.

It is also recognised that there are difficulties involved in specialisation. The major difficulties which have been identified include the extent of competition for resources and markets within rural China; the question of who grows the grain; the distinctions emerging (or more precisely being consolidated) between regions; and finally the inefficiency within the rural commercial system. The first three points have been discussed above, and will continue to be discussed. At this point what is needed is a more detailed assessment of rural commerce. Organisational reform in production systems has been bold and striking. But to assess the production potential of specialised production forms, *baogan daohu*, diversification and rural industry - that is, the policy of commercialisation - some understanding is required of the commercial organisation which is supposed to both market what is produced, and supply producers with important inputs.

## Commerce

Since the implementation of the system of contracted responsibilities with payment linked to output, the enthusiasm of the peasant has risen, household subsidiary pursuits and diversified operations have rapidly developed and there has been an upsurge of specialized households and households doing specialized jobs. On the other hand, in the circulation sector, old and antiquated systems and methods are still in use, while the circulation channels are few and the links are numerous. There are difficulties in both buying and selling and while in some places goods have to be stockpiled, in other places, goods are out of stock. Contradictions are thus being daily intensified. The time has indeed come for the reform of rural commerce.[110]

The changed economic conditions in the Chinese countryside since 1978 have prompted significant improvements in the performance of the rural sector. However, it is generally accepted that commercial conditions remain poor. If potential advances in the Chinese countryside are not to be limited, commercial change needs to be an important element in the Chinese reforms package.[111]

## Problems in rural commerce

Two broad groups of problems can be identified in rural commerce: first, the organisational problems; and secondly, the infrastructural problems. The official commercial system dominates in China. The actual amount of farm outputs purchased by the official commercial system in 1983 is estimated at between 87% and 90%.[112]

The dominance displayed by the official system in the rural sector is matched only by its unwieldy nature and the friction generated amongst its various parts: 'the channels of circulation are too few, the links are too many'.[113]

Commercial bureaucratic mismanagement has been attributed to a variety of causes. One factor is traditional (Confucian) hostility towards commerce, mirrored some thousands of years later by leftist attitudes among bureaucrats, attitudes which continue to disrupt the official system.[114] Some of the complaints about difficulties in finding food, clothing repair services, vegetable supply and transport services can be attributed to the dramatic fall in retail outlets under the Maoists from 1.01 million in 1957 to 280,000 in 1979.[115]

It must also be said that commercial departments and organisations are short of qualified management personnel.[116] After decades without market influences, bureaucrats must now be able to respond to market conditions. Not surprisingly this has created its own problems.[117] In addition, until recently such personnel had little incentive to carry out their work efficiently or with enthusiasm and rather more to stick to the rules and organise committees upon which to sit.

Rural commerce has become increasingly complex since the introduction of production responsibility systems and the emergence of varied production forms in the Chinese countryside. In the past dealings were with the communes and their subdivisions, but now dealings are often with families and individuals. It is claimed, inevitably, that this has complicated commercial work and made management tasks much more difficult.[118]

Furthermore, not only is the official system faced with an increased volume of products coming onto the market, increasingly cash settling of accounts is becoming common with payments occurring at the time of sale. The multiplicity of prices - according to the status of the product in the sale - is also said to be confusing.[119]

The commercial system is also beset by a growing problem of corruption.[120] This can range from petty corruption by local bureaucrats to 'official' corruption by state organs themselves. The latter is a reference to such practices by commercial departments as compulsorily purchasing scarce farm and sideline products at prices below those the peasants are entitled to receive or downgrading products and deliberately manipulating prices, forcing them down.[121]

Not surprisingly, the official commercial departments have tried to deflect criticism for their poor performance onto other state organisations. They argue that mismanagement in production departments gives rise to problems for which the official commercial system is wrongly blamed.

In 1982 for example, production departments expanded the acreage sown with tobacco to more than 13 million *mu*. Output exceeded 3 billion *jin*, far above actual demand. In 1983 the situation was reversed with the sown acreage of tobacco reduced so dramatically that tobacco imports had to be made. Tobacco producers blamed the commercial departments for the limited production of 1983; the commercial departments in turn blamed the blind production developments of production departments.[122]

Alongside the organisational problems are the infrastructural problems. There is no doubt that poor communication links and insufficient storage and preserving facilities have a detrimental effect on rural commerce.[123] This is especially pointed since the improvement in China's rural production, the increase in commodity production serving to illustrate the inadequacies in transport and storage.[124]

Roads are the cornerstone of the Chinese transport infrastructure. However, they are generally narrow, poor in quality and unevenly distributed.[125] Mountain areas in particular suffer from lack of access to potential markets. In 1984, over 200,000 production brigades (27.8%) were still not physically accessible by truck.[126]

In all, China has a total of a little over 1 million kilometres of road. This gives a figure of only 10 kilometres of road per 100 square kilometres and 9 kilometres per 10,000 head of population. Furthermore, it is acknowledged that 40% of China's roads do not meet the lowest standards stipulated by the state, as many as 25% being earthen roads and virtually impassable in periods of heavy rainfall.[127]

Similar problems are reported for rail transport. Interestingly, it is suggested that grain is especially unwelcome on the railway because the fees charged for transporting grains are relatively low. Grains also carry greater risk in terms of compensation payments for loss damage than other materials.[128]

To put it simply, Hu Yaobang commented at the 12th CCP National Congress that China's current transport and communications capacity can barely cope with the current increase in the volume of cargo and traffic.[129]

There are also difficulties with the means of transport. Total carrying capacity is too small, services are few in number and seldom prompt, and haulage fees are high.[130] In 1982 for example, of 2,037,600 rural transport vehicles, 1,831,200 were tractors; and just over half of China's total cargo capacity in the rural sector is in the form of tractors.[131] The use of tractors for haulage is both slow and costly. However, they are available to the peasants.

Finally, storage facilities are poor and inadequate. Materials for Chuxian prefecture, Anhui illustrate this problem. In 1983 the total storage capacity for grains and edible oils was 800 million *jin*. The state grain purchase alone in 1983 was 1.37 billion *jin*. In addition, many granaries were already about 80% full with grain from the previous year. As a result grain was stockpiled outdoors. In one county alone, 179 wheat dumps, 200 rice dumps and 19 rapeseed dumps were established, all illegally. Enormous losses of foodstuffs occurred from exposure to the elements and vermin.[132]

Similarly, in a well-publicised case, in the second quarter of 1983 Shanghai received shipments of 410 million *jin* of rice, of which 713,000 *jin* was inedible and more than 49 million *jin* had fermented and had to be reprocessed. This arose because of inadequate storage facilities in the producer areas and subsequent outdoor stockpiling of grain before shipment which gave rise to much of the rice having an excess moisture content; and also inadequate storage facilities in Shanghai itself with grain shipments rotting in railroad cars and ships.[133]

The state is also quick to point an accusing finger at the bureaucrats in the producer areas who seem more concerned with getting rid of their grain than ensuring its condition; what is called 'moving the burden' to the consumer is sharply criticised.[134] However, it is difficult not to have some sympathy for rural bureaucrats who, on the one hand are under pressure from rural producers to sell foodstuffs under less than perfect commercial conditions, and on the other hand contemplate increasing demands from urban areas for sufficient food supplies to feed growing urban populations.

The consequences of the commercial, organisational and infrastructural problems are certainly damaging to rural enthusiasm for production. Too many commentators report that throughout China astonishing quantities of fruit become rotten, fresh milk soured, fish and shrimps spoiled and grain mildewed because of commercial inefficiency.[135] All too often it appears that goods are procured or purchased but the distribution network is such that the goods spoil before they can be re-sold. This situation is frustrating both to rural producers and consumers everywhere, frustrations made worse by reports of stockpiles in some areas at the same time as shortages in others.[136]

Similarly, just as peasant sales are difficult, the increasingly large peasant demand for consumer goods is a further burden for the system.[137] Numerous reports reveal that the supply of consumer goods to rural areas is well short of demand. In Hunan for example, many durable and semi-durable consumer goods were in short supply including furniture, kitchen utensils, knives, scissors, pottery and clothing.[138]

Similarly, a report from Sanhe commune in Hebei notes that while rural purchasing power in 1979 and 1980 rose by 26% and 38% respectively over the previous year, the volume of commodities available in Sanhe commune rose by only 10% and 6% respectively. Goods such as sugar, cigarettes, wines, clothing, clocks, soap, furniture, bicycles and electrical appliances were all in short supply.[139]

More significantly for rural producers are reported difficulties in purchasing production inputs. Fertilisers, pesticides, diesel oil and other means of production are increasingly in short supply.[140] Failure to rectify this situation will seriously harm the initiative of peasants in developing both the production of grain and other agricultural products.[141]

Unless the supply of producer goods to the countryside improves, the 'black market' for such goods which has already developed will only become more widespread.[142] This shortfall in the supply of modern agricultural inputs is naturally related to the wider issue of China's industrial production and commentators are quick to point out the problems which continue to beset industrial production of tractors and chemicals for instance. Nevertheless, the same commentators do not use these wider concerns about China's industrial performance to excuse commercial mismanagement and the paucity of commercial infrastructure.

Crucially, commercial inadequacy - both of organisational and physical infrastructure - can only serve to prevent the widespread commercialisation of the rural sector. The development of such rural production management forms as specialised households - including grain specialists - and commodity production bases for example, depends heavily on an efficient commercial system.[143] Without such a system development would at best be limited, at worst impossible. At the most basic level for example the commercial system must at least be able to guarantee stable supplies of grain to those specialised producers not engaged in farming. It is this kind of basic inadequacy which has prompted the state to offer some reforms in the rural commercial system.

## The reform of rural commerce

The most widely reported aspect of Chinese commercial reform in the western media is the growing number of individuals engaging in rural commerce. Certainly, individual traders were a rare sight in the Chinese countryside until recent years.[144] It is claimed that the emergence of these individual traders has not only served to improve the flow of consumer and producer goods into the urban and rural markets, but also to utilise surplus labour and stimulate rural incomes.[145]

The contribution of these individual households to rural commercial circulation in certain areas is undoubtedly considerable. In Pujiang county, Zhejiang for example, one-third of all agricultural produce is carried by individuals. Similarly, in Haian county, Jiangsu, 50% of all of the produce of specialised households is carried by individuals.[146]

However, while there is little doubt that the current regime views individual commerce with a good deal more sympathy than the Maoists - who had none at all - the scope of individual commerce is generally extremely limited.[147]

The state accepts that individual traders can fill the gaps left uncatered for by the official system. Indeed, it accepts that they offer greater flexibility than that exhibited by official organs and will be more efficient at the local level. But, the state sees individual commerce as supplementary to state-run commerce and cooperative commerce. Individual commerce is of 'limited strength and cannot be of much help'.[148]

The truth of the matter is that the state is determined to limit the role of individual traders. It fears that their proliferation could undermine the state plan, result in arbitrary price rises, increased fraud, and the promotion of black markets. (Though, of course, the same conditions are being witnessed through the inefficiency of the official system.)

There have been reports detailing complaints from consumers about precisely these kinds of problems with individual traders - although much of this may be due to resentment at the high incomes being earned by these traders rather than the existence of any sharp practice. In Jiangsu for example, the price of mullet at the quayside is 0.5 *yuan/jin*. At surrounding commune markets this rises to 0.7 to 0.8 *yuan/jin*. In the local county town each *jin* fetches one *yuan*, while in the larger cities the price is 1.8 *yuan/jin*. The individual trader bringing fish from the quayside and making the trip to the city can make 200 *yuan* net profit per trip.[149]

Interestingly, the same source, while noting urban consumer complaints about high prices and profits, does not decry the individual traders but in fact urges the state and collective commerce to develop to meet urban demand and effectively compete with individual traders. Thus, for some time to come, given continuing high levels of consumer demand, such individual traders will clearly have a role in commerce, a role which may be far greater than that intended by the state.

The state is unwilling to be flexible towards the development of individual commercial activities for important political reasons. Furthermore, there are logistical reasons for curtailing such activities, not least, for example, limited rural supplies of diesel oil. If the state allows too much growth in individual transport, a profitable undertaking despite the use of inefficient tractors, this can only exacerbate the shortfall in supplies of diesel oil and have a detrimental impact on agricultural production.

The state has a more tolerant attitude, however, towards collective commerce. During the 1950s and continuing through the mid 1970s collective commerce - Supply and Marketing Cooperatives (SMC) - was in effect part of the official state system with little, if any, autonomy. In 1982, following the 'Summary of the National Conference on rural work' document, reforms of the SMCs were initiated in selected places. The content of these reforms essentially aims to increase peasant shareholding, renew the cooperative nature of these organisations, and restore the good traditions of the SMCs of the 1950s, that is, restore some measure of local autonomy to these organisations. By 1983 the document 'Some questions on current rural economic policies' affirmed that the reforms of the SMC should be implemented nationwide, with considerable emphasis being placed on the SMC organisation based in the county town.[150] The new status of the SMC (as well as the growing but still minor role of individual traders) is well illustrated in the following table detailing the source of retail sales by organisation.

**Table 4  Source of retail sales**

| | State | Collective (SMC) | Individual | Peasant sales to non-agrarian pop |
|---|---|---|---|---|
| 1952 | 34.6 | - | 61.2 | 4.3 |
| 1957 | 73.9 | 19.5 | 3.2 | 3.3 |
| 1965 | 83.3 | 12.9 | 1.9 | 1.9 |
| 1978 | 90.5 | 7.4 | 0.1 | 1.9 |
| 1979 | 88.3 | 8.9 | 0.2 | 2.6 |
| 1980 | 84.0 | 12.0 | 0.7 | 3.2 |
| 1981 | 80.1 | 14.5 | 1.6 | 3.8 |
| 1982 | 76.6 | 16.1 | 2.9 | 4.3 |
| 1983 | 72.2 | 16.7 | 6.5 | 4.7 |
| 1984 | 45.7 | 39.7 | 9.6 | 8.6 |
| 1985 | 40.5 | 37.3 | 15.4 | 6.8 |
| 1986 | 39.4 | 36.4 | 16.3 | 7.6 |
| 1987 | 38.6 | 35.7 | 17.4 | 7.9 |
| 1988 | 39.5 | 34.4 | 17.8 | 8.0 |
| 1989 | 39.1 | 33.2 | 18.6 | 8.6 |

Compiled from materials in *Statistical Yearbook of China*, 1986. *China Statistical Abstract, 1990*.

The key statistic here is the change in 1984 of the role of the SMC. Not only has the state reaffirmed the role of the SMCs it has also begun to relax its monopoly over the control of first and second category agricultural and sideline products, a necessary step if the SMCs are to have a role other than that of picking up the 'leftovers' from the official state system.

The SMCs can also interact with the emerging rural production forms as well as individuals engaged in rural commerce in what are described as 'joint operations', though undoubtedly throughout China, such organisations have a wide variety of names.[151]

'Joint operations' aim to link production and circulation, thereby enhancing the economic interests of the peasants. Examples of joint operations include: first, joint operation in purchasing and marketing whereby the SMCs sign contracts with production units (of all kinds) and undertake responsibility for the purchasing and marketing of products. Such contracts stipulate the quantity and quality of produce to be delivered. Secondly, joint operation of local commodity bases whereby the SMCs provide funds, technology and materials, and production units provide labour and land. Finally, as discussed earlier, an A-I-C one-chain system with the SMCs undertaking the commercial functions.[152]

It is claimed that the role of the SMC in such joint operations can provide a fixed market outlet and price stability for producers thereby giving them confidence and security to invest in production. This is especially true for specialised producers who need to be assured of produce sales in order to purchase appropriate agricultural inputs as well as basic foodstuffs.

However, the state's motivations for developing SMCs are more concerned with its own interests. Firstly, the successful development of SMCs will, it hopes, limit the role of individual traders. Secondly, the state feels that SMCs can more effectively combine peasant interests with the needs of the state plan, that is, forming a 'link between planned regulations and regulation by market mechanism'.[153] It is evident that it is the state plan which continues to be of paramount concern, and this concern translates itself into a continued emphasis upon the official state commercial system.[154]

Indeed, while much has been made of SMC administrative reform (in particular to emphasise its own identity as distinct from the official system), real limitations on SMC functioning must be said to continue. State monopolies, though reduced, still apply to key agricultural products such as pigs, poultry, herbal medicine, cotton, tobacco, and wine. Although this situation is liable to change, it may be a change back to more state control rather than to more liberalisation. Furthermore, the SMC may still suffer from its close links with the state commercial system, both in terms of the bureaucracy which is simply renamed, and also peasant attitudes based on longstanding difficulties in commerce.

Transport and storage difficulties also beset cooperative commerce as much as they do the official system. While many Chinese commentators are confident in tone about the ability of the SMC to stimulate rural commercial circulation, the material remains confused, bureaucratic in nature, and there is continued difficulty in determining the autonomous nature of the SMC.

Similar confusion is true of the proposed reforms within the official state system. The State Council's 'Regulations for trial implementation' of 1983, for example, advises the commercial system to 'open all avenues of circulation and change the practice of rigid control, monopoly and single channel of circulation'.[155] Yet those same regulations continue to emphasise the monopoly to be retained by the state over key agricultural products, in addition to close control over prices.[156]

Koziara *et al* commenting specifically on the distribution system for producer goods note recent reforms which include a reduction in the state monopoly over producer goods, new distribution approaches, better facilities, improved services and an effort to reduce stockpiling. However, despite conceding that improvements are being made, they state that three key areas of concern remain: the difficulty of coordinating supply and demand in an inadequate state planning system; the problem of further loosening state monopolies in distribution; and the inadequate distribution network (warehousing, retail outlets and so forth). They argue that the prospects for solving these problems are poor given the continued piecemeal approach to them, the continuing transport bottlenecks, the low rate of worker incentives, and the continued dominance of political concerns over economic practices.[157]

Some improvement in rural commerce can only be made with huge amounts of capital investment in roads, railways, warehouses, and refrigerated storage facilities. The state has improved its contribution to investment in commercial facilities, but this investment remains inadequate to clear all the stumbling-blocks in the way of real commercial improvement.

However, real improvements could be made to the commercial system with little investment. The relaxation of rigid state controls within the commercial system would certainly improve rural circulation but only by sacrificing considerable political principle. The current regime has shown it is willing to make such sacrifices in the realm of rural production, but as yet it is unclear if it wants, or is strong enough to make, parallel sacrifices in the commercial sphere.

## Conclusions

There is a clear need for reform in commercial circulation, a need which is recognised by the state. Yet recent proposals purporting to open the way to better commercial circulation appear too weak to change the current situation significantly. Flexibility, offered through more individual commerce, price reform, and cooperative commerce, is in reality severely limited. The necessity - in the state's eyes - for a state monopoly on the most important agricultural products makes rigidity and bureaucratic inefficiency almost inevitable. To these must be added continuing opportunities for corruption at all levels.

It must be doubted if basic contradictions will disappear quickly - if at all. The state's desire to maintain stable supplies of basic agricultural products continues to stimulate relative efficiency in the procurement of goods from the countryside, in stark contrast to its languid attempts to deliver goods to the ever-growing rural market. Such inefficiency, alongside the comparatively low agricultural product prices paid by the state in contrast to those paid for industrial goods, will continue to encourage peasants to operate outside the state system, even in those goods where the state monopoly applies, as far as it is physically possible.

All this places reservations against the state's continued ability to develop the rural economy along the lines it wishes, that is limiting the potential impact of much of the material discussed in the earlier sections of this chapter. Furthermore, it indicates the complexity and depth of problems which Chinese rural planners face, from woefully inadequate infrastructure to deeply-entrenched bureaucrats.

# Notes to Chapter Three

1 Fan Shengzhi, *Fan Shengzhi shu - An agriculturalist book of China written by Fan Shengzhi in the 1st century BC*, tr Shi Shenghan, (Science Press: Beijing, 1982).

2 *People's Daily*, editorial, 'Farmland water conservation construction must be guided by prevailing circumstances', 5.1.1982 tr FBIS/DR/PRC 18.1.1982, K8-9. *People's Daily*, 'China's irrigated farmland area ranks first in the world', 16.8.1984 tr FBIS/DR/PRC 23.8.1984, K13-14. *Henan Radio*, 'Henan rural construction', 4.2.1982 tr FBIS/DR/PRC 10.2.1982, P1. *Shijie Jingji Daobao*, 'The heavenly land faces a soil crisis', 19.4.1982 tr FBIS/DR/PRC 11.5.1982, Q1-2.

3 *People's Daily* editorial, 'Correct policy for accelerating agricultural mechanisation', 6.2.1979 as quoted by *Xinhua Radio*, 6.2.1979 tr FBIS/DR/PRC 9.2.1979, E17-20. *Xinhua Radio*, 5.10.1979, op cit. Shandong province planning committee, 'The fundamental way out for agriculture lies in mechanisation', *Jingji Yanjiu*, 1978 (2) pp 53-8, tr *Chinese Economic Studies*, 1979 13 (1-2) pp 40-57.

4 *Xinhua Radio*, 'People's Republic of China to breed, popularise fine crop seeds', 20.1.1982 tr FBIS/DR/PRC 22.1.1982, K6. Zheng Youyun, 'The tremendous successes attained in the reforms of the rural economic structure', *Red Flag*, 21.10.1984 tr JPRS/CR/RF No 20, pp 77-80.

5 Zhou Cheng (a), 'A trial exposition on the question of "increasing production and income" in the rural people's communes', *Jingji Yanjiu*, 1978 (6) pp 23-6, tr *Chinese Economic Studies*, 1979 13 (1-2) pp 74-85.

6 *People's Daily*, 'Pay close attention to increasing production of small farming machines', 30.1.1982 tr FBIS/DR/PRC 3.2.1982, K20-21. Huang Daoxia, Zhu Peiwei & Chen Peishen, 'A brief talk on technological transformation in Chinese agriculture', *People's Daily*, 1.2.1984 tr FBIS/DR/PRC, K25-29. *People's Daily*, 6.2.1979, op cit.

7 Zhan Wu & Liu Wenpu (b), 'The 3rd plenary session of the 11th CCPCC creates the new path for agricultural development in our country', *Red Flag*, 1.9.1982 tr JPRS/CR/RF No 17, pp 29-38.

8 *Chinese Statistical Yearbook 1984*, (Beijing, 1984).

9 *Xinhua Radio*, 17.3.1984, op cit.

10 *Shaanxi Ribao*, 11.2.1984, op cit.

11 Yuan Mu, 'An initial analysis of the present economic situation', *Liaowang*, No 32 12.8.1985 tr FBIS/DR/PRC 29.8.1985, K1-6.

12 *Xinhua*, 'Ministry warns against relaxing grain production', 14.3.1985 in FBIS/DR/PRC 19.3.1985, K12-13. *People's Daily*, 'In no way should the grip of grain production be relaxed', 19.3.1985 tr FBIS/DR/PRC, K9-10. *Jingji Ribao (Economic Daily)*, 'Do not forget grain production', 16.3.1985 tr FBIS/DR/PRC 19.3.1985, K14-15.

13  *Xinhua Radio*, 'Excerpts of Wan Li December speech on rural work', 28.2.1985 tr FBIS/DR/PRC 4.3.1985, K1-10.

14  Wu Xiang, Liu Qing & Gu Haiyan, 'The system of contracted responsibilities on the household basis and the rural economy in Foshan prefecture', *Red Flag*, 1.5.1983 tr JPRS/CR/RF No 9, pp 11-27.

15  Lie Bang, 'Specialised households are a boon to the rural economy', *Xinhua*, 26.9.1983 tr FBIS/DR/PRC 28.9.1983, K2-4.

16  Yu Guoyao (b), 'A brief discussion on specialised households', *Red Flag*, 16.4.1984 tr JPRS/CR/RF No 8, pp 32-41.

17  *People's Daily*, 1.9.1981, op cit. See also Wang Lanxi & Li Tong, 'Notes on a trip to Hainan island', *Red Flag*, 16.5.1983 tr JPRS/CR/RF No 10, pp 74-80.

18  Li Yong, 'Breeding by specialised households - a good way to develop animal husbandry', *Red Flag*, 1.10.1983 tr JPRS/CR/RF No 19, pp 41-6.

19  Ma Enchang, 'Characteristics and trends of development of rural specialised households', *Yangcheng Ribao*, tr FBIS/CR/A 18.4.1983, pp 102-6.

20  Wu Xiang *et al*, op cit.

21  *Anhui Radio*, 'Anhui regulations on specialised households', 3.6.1983 tr FBIS/DR/PRC, 8.6.1983, O1. *Anhui Radio*, 'Anhui issues regulations on specialised households', 22.4.1984 tr FBIS/DR/PRC 26.4.1984, D1-2.

22  Song Linfei (a), 'The employment of the surplus labour force in the countryside - a survey of Nantong county, Jiangsu province', *Social Sciences in China*, 1983 (2) pp 105-25.

23  Song Linfei (a), op cit.

24  Jing Ping (a), 'This is where the great hope of our country's rural areas lies', *Red Flag*, 1.12.1982 tr JPRS/CR/RF No 23, pp 23-8. Wang Youfeng, 'South-East Shanxi agricultural region enthusiastically supports the need to develop the "two households"', *Jingji Guanli* (*Economic Management*), 1983 (7) pp 39-51.

25  Li Yong, op cit. Jing Ping (a), op cit. Wang Lanxi *et al*, op cit.

26  Song Linfei (a), op cit.

27  Guangdong CPCC policy study office, Kaiping county CPCC and Enping county CPCC, 'The vigour of the specialised households lies in their great beneficial results - investigation report on the specialised households in Kaiping and Enping counties', *Red Flag*, 1.11.1984 tr JPRS/CR/RF No 21, pp 45-52.

28  Ibid.

29  Wu Xiang *et al*, op cit.

30  Li Yong, op cit. Wu Xiang *et al*, op cit. Zhan Wu *et al* (b), op cit.

31  Guangdong CPCC, op cit.

32  Zhan Wu *et al* (a), 'On the responsibility system of contracting by specialisation', *Jingji Yanjiu*, 1981 (4), pp 55-9, 73.

33  *Jingji Ribao*, 'Loudly appeal to the public for specialised households', 20.3.1984 tr FBIS/DR/PRC 26.3.1984, K9-10.
34  Guangdong CPCC, op cit.
35  Ibid.
36  *People's Daily*, 'Developing specialised households is a major policy', 23.1.1984 tr FBIS/DR/PRC 2.2.1984, K1-2.
37  Guangdong CPCC, op cit. Yuyang prefecture CPCC research office, 'Several questions concerning grain specialised households', *Nongye Jingji Wenti*, 1984 (1) pp 14-17.
38  Lu Wen, 'New trends in the development of cooperative economy in the Chinese countryside', *Jingji Yanjiu*, 20.11.1983 tr FBIS/CR/A 6.2.1984, pp 15-21. Song Linfei (a), op cit.
39  *People's Daily*, 7.3.1984, op cit.
40  Wang Xinglong, op cit.
41  Guangdong CPCC, op cit.
42  Datong county party committee and people's government, 'Increasing the number of households specialising in commodity grain production to convert an agro-economy into a commodity economy', *Nongye Jingji Wenti*, 1984 (10) pp 50-2.
43  Song Linfei (a), op cit.
44  Shi Qingmin, Xie Chengjin & Li Darong, 'Pi county earnestly deals with violations in housebuilding regulations by party members and cadres', *Xinhua Radio*, 2.4.1983, p 2.
45  *People's Daily*, 3.7.1984, op cit.
46  Ibid.
47  Wang Xinglong, op cit.
48  *People's Daily*, 21.3.1980, quoted by F A Leeming, unpublished manuscript on Heilongjiang.
49  *Xinhua Radio*, 'Rural centre says specialised households mounting', 24.9.1983 tr FBIS/DR/PRC 26.9.1983, K10-11.
50  Fang Jianzhong, Yan Yiping, Chai Liming & Liu Ming, 'Present status and future development of specialist grain households in the rural economy', *Nongye Jingji Wenti*, 1983 (8) pp 48-51, 47.
51  *People's Daily*, 'Further develop the new phase of agriculture which has already opened up', 23.11.1982 tr FBIS/DR/PRC 4.1.1983, K2-20. *People's Daily*, 'Make continued efforts in developing a new situation in rural areas', 4.2.1984 tr FBIS/DR/PRC 6.2.1984, K3-5. Song Linfei (b), 'The present state and future prospects of specialised households in rural China', *Social Sciences in China*, 1984 (4) pp 107-30. Zhan Wu *et al* (c), op cit. *Guangzhou Daily* 23.1.1983, op cit. *Fujian Radio*, 'Praises specialised households', 17.2.1984 tr FBIS/DR/PRC 21.7.1984, O3-4. Chen Fudong, 'Investigations into five specialised villages', *Red Flag*, 16.6.1984 tr JPRS/CR/RF No 12, pp 34-41.

52  Chen Jun & Cai Renqun, 'A probe into the question of an equitable distribution of agricultural commodity bases', *Nongye Buju Yu Quhua* (*Agricultural Distribution and Zoning*), 1982 (March) pp 180-3, tr FBIS/CR/A 1.2.1983, pp 6-11.

53  Ibid.

54  Ningbo agricultural committee, 'Implementing microeconomic adjustments, safeguarding the interest of the grain farmers', *Nongye Jingji Wenti*, 1983 (12) pp 122-7, tr FBIS/CR/A 1.5.1984, pp 76-88.

55  Jing Ping (b), 'It is necessary to stabilise the acreage grown with grain', *Red Flag*, 1.3.1983 tr JPRS/CR/RF No 5, pp 53-5.

56  Nong Yan, op.cit.

57  Chen Jun *et al*, op cit.

58  Ibid.

59  Liu Junde, 'Problems of a commodity grain base - the case of Jiangxi province', *Jingji Dili* (*Economic Geography*), 1981 (1) pp 28-33.

60  Lu Xinxian, 'The question of specialisation and comprehensive development of agricultural production in Jiangxi province', *Jingji Dili*, 1982 (2) pp 95-100.

61  Nong Yan, p 9.

62  Ningbo agricultural committee, op cit.

63  Ibid.

64  Nong Yan, 'Protect the production of old high-output commodity grain districts', *Nongye Jishu Jingji* (*Economics for Agricultural Production Technology*), 1983 (10) pp 15-16, tr FBIS/CR/A 20.3.1984, pp 8-10.

65  Ding Shengjun, 'The reform of the system of buying and selling of commodity grain', *Jingji Yanjiu*, 1984 (8) pp 26-8, 25.

66  Ningbo agricultural committee, op cit.

67  Ibid.

68  Ibid.

69  Ibid.

70  *People's Daily*, 'Build commodity grain bases through self-reliance', 30.1.1983 tr FBIS/DR/PRC 3.2.1983, K3-4. Ministry of agriculture survey team, 'Self-reliance in establishment of commodity grain bases', *Nongcun Gongzuo Tongxun* (*Rural Work Newsletter*), 1982 (10) pp 43-4, tr FBIS/CR/A 16.2.1983, pp 31-4.

71  Ningbo agricultural committee, op cit. Liu Junde, op cit. Ministry of Agriculture, op cit.

72  Ministry of Agriculture, op cit.

73  Nong Yan, op cit.

74  Walker (b), op cit.

75  Zhen Tianxiang *et al*, 'Develop Guangdong's Zhanjiang area's potential as a sugar-cane production base', *Jingji Dili*, 1981 (1) pp 34-7, 76.

76 Ibid. Wu Youwen, 'Exploration of the building of a Pearl River delta commodity grain base', *Nongye Buju Yu Quhua*, 1982 (April) tr FBIS/CR/A 28.2.1983, pp 19-27. Chen Jun *et al*, op cit.

77 Zhen Tianxiang *et al*, op cit, Zhao Hua, op cit, Liang Zhao *et al*, op cit.

78 Liang Zhao, Liu Xiaotie & Li Pumi, 'An investigation into developing the strong points of sugar-cane production in Guangdong', *Red Flag*, 16.1.1981 tr JPRS/CR/RF No 2, pp 36-41.

79 Zhao Hua, 'Make the Zhujiang river delta into a production base for sugar-cane', *People's Daily*, 4.5.1980, p 3.

80 Liang Zhao *et al*, op cit.

81 Wu Xiang *et al*, op cit.

82 Doumen county propaganda committee, 'Two questions concerning individual, collective and state benefits in sugar-cane areas', *Jingji Yanjiu*, 1979 (6) pp 79-80.

83 Zhao Hua, op cit. Doumen County, op cit.

84 Liang Zhao *et al*, op cit.

85 Xi Huijia, 'Sugar production in Xianyu county, Fujian province', *People's Daily*, 18.10.1979, p 2.

86 Zhen Tianxiang *et al*, op cit.

87 Wu Youwen, op cit.

88 Zhen Tianxiang *et al*, op cit.

89 Liang Zhao *et al*, op cit. Zhen Tianxiang *et al*, op cit.

90 Zhao Hua, op cit.

91 Liang Zhao *et al*, op cit.

92 Chen Jun *et al*, op cit.

93 Zhang Gensheng, 'How does our province run the agriculture-industry-commerce integrated enterprise on trial?', *Jingji Guanli*, 1982 (1) pp 22-5.

94 Wu Xiang (b), 'Develop rural cooperative commerce', *Red Flag*, 16.1.1983 tr JPRS/CR/RF No 2, pp 39-47. Zhang Genshang, op cit.

95 *People's Daily*, 'A new way of rejuvenating agriculture', 20.8.1981 tr FBIS/DR/PRC 26.8.1982, K6-9. Wu Xiang (b), op cit. Bai Rubing, 'Readjust the agricultural sector, improve economic results', *Red Flag*, 1.4.1982 tr JPRS/CR/RF No 7, pp 25-34.

96 *Heilongjiang Radio*, 'Li Lian speaks at Heilongjiang rural work meeting', 19.1.1984 tr FBIS/DR/PRC 20.1.1984, S1-3.

97 Bai Rubing, op cit.

98 *People's Daily*, 20.8.1981, op cit.

99 Yichun county committee, 'Speeding up the building of commodity production centres by the joint management of agriculture, industry and commerce', *Nongye Jingji Wenti*, 1984 (3) pp 39-40, 48.

100 Wang Songpei, op cit.

101 Ren Zili, 'State farms to integrate farm, industry, commerce', *Xinhua*, 1.3.1983 tr FBIS/DR/PRC 2.3.1983, K20-21.

102 Zhan Wu, 'Take the road of agricultural modernisation the Chinese way', *Jingji Guanli*, 1979 (9) pp 11-17, 58, tr *Chinese Economic Studies*, 1981 (14) pp 48-89.

103 Ren Zili, op cit. *Xinhua*, 'On agriculture, industry, commerce link', 8.1.1982 in FBIS/DR/PRC 8.1.1982, K2. Wang Songpei, op cit. *Beijing Radio*, 'The broadening road of integrated farming, industry and commercial operations for state-farm land reclamation departments', 24.9.1983 tr FBIS/DR/PRC 26.9.1983, K11-12.

104 Wang Songpei, op cit.

105 *Red Flag*, 'Investigation in Liuzhuang', 16.6.1982 tr JPRS/CR/RF No 12, pp 33-43.

106 Ibid.

107 Leeming, op cit.

108 Wang Songpei, op cit. *People's Daily*, 'City suburbs can become prosperous faster', 7.10.1982 tr FBIS/DR/PRC 14.10.1982, K11-13.

109 Kong Qingyuan, 'A talk on the joint Agricultural-Industrial-Commercial enterprises', *People's Daily*, 1.6.1984 tr FBIS/CR/A 27.6.1984, pp 25-8.

110 Wu Xiang (b), op cit.

111 Lin Zili (c), 'More on the distinctively Chinese path of developing socialist agriculture', *Social Sciences in China*, 1984 (1) pp 79-123. *People's Daily*, 'Make great efforts to promote circulation - on an urgent problem in developing rural commodity production', 28.2.1984 tr FBIS/DR/PRC 6.3.1984, K15-1.

112 *China Daily*, 'Peasants may sell surplus agriculture nationwide', 5.2.1983 in FBIS/DR/PRC 5.2.1983, K16. Duan Yingbi, 'Some situations in and opinions on farm product procurement', *Nongye Jishu Jingji*, 1983 (7) pp 25-8, tr FBIS/CR/A 26.1.1984, pp 8-14.

113 Xue Muqiao (b), op cit.

114 *Xinhua Radio*, 'Obstacles to rural commodity production cited', 30.3.1984 tr FBIS/DR/PRC 3.4.1984, K10-14.

115 *China Daily* 5.2.1983, op cit. *People's Daily*, 'Renmin Ribao discusses commodity circulation', 8.7.1981 tr FBIS/DR/PRC 28.7.1981, K8-10.

116 *People's Daily*, 'Smooth commodity circulation needed in rural areas', 6.8.1981 tr FBIS/DR/PRC 9.8.1981, K6-7. Zai Fang, Gu Xiulin, Zheng Yanan & Hua Sheng, 'Investigation of difficulties in selling grains reported', *Nongye Jingji Wenti*, 1983 (8) pp 52-4, tr FBIS/CR/A 4.4.1984, pp 43-8.

117 Gao Dichen, 'State-run commerce should take an active part in regulation by market mechanism', *People's Daily*, 12.4.1985 tr FBIS/DR/PRC 19.4.1985, K4-7.

118 *Red Flag*, 'Study comrade Chen Yun's works published during the period after the founding of the country', 1.5.1983 tr JPRS/CR/RF No 9, pp 70-9.

119 Zai Fang *et al*, op cit.

120  Gong Xiaolan & Zhang Hang, 'Develop county trade fairs and individual, industrial and commercial households, promote rural commodity production - central task for industrial and commercial management departments in implementing Document No 1 of the central authorities', *Jingji Ribao*, 15.2.1984 tr FBIS/DR/PRC 27.2.1984, K18-19.

121  *Xinhua Radio*, 'Renmin Ribao on farm produce procurement', 28.11.1981 tr FBIS/DR/PRC 1.12.1981, K25-27.

122  Zhao Huazhou *et al*, op cit.

123  *People's Daily*, 6.8.1981, op cit.

124  *Xinhua Radio*, 'No more "Lord Ye's love of dragons"', 11.10.1984 tr FBIS/DR/PRC 17.10.1984, K15-17.

125  Deng Yiming, 'Making great efforts to develop rural road transport', *Nongye Jingji Wenti*, 1984 (9) pp 59-60.

126  *People's Daily*, 6.8.1981, op cit. Deng Yiming, op cit.

127  Xian Lizhi, 'Vigorously develop highway construction and road transport', *Red Flag*, 1.12.1983 tr JPRS/CR/RF No 23, pp 46-52.

128  Zai Fang *et al*, op cit.

129  Reported in Jin Luzhong & Zhang Bingfu, 'On readjustment of the transport and communications set-up', *Red Flag*, 16.9.1984 tr JPRS/CR/RF No 18, pp 62-9.

130  Mi Henian, 'Transform the transport management system, promote the development of commodity production', *Jingji Guanli*, 1985 (6) pp 11-13.

131  Deng Yiming, op cit.

132  Zai Fang *et al*, op cit.

133  Pan Gang, 'The CCPCC discipline inspection commission and the Ministry of Commerce are handling the incident of mouldy rice being sent to Shanghai by several provinces', *People's Daily*, 14.2.1984 tr FBIS/DR/PRC 22.2.1984, K1.

134  *People's Daily*, 'Serious consequence of incorrect ideas in management', 14.2.1984 tr FBIS/DR/PRC 22.2.1984, K2. Pan Gang, op cit.

135  Wan Li (b), 'Wan Li speech on rural work progress, problems', *People's Daily*, 8.1.1984 tr FBIS/DR/PRC 28.1.1984, K1-9. See also Yang Chengzun, 'Several characteristics of rural commodity production in our country', *People's Daily*, 13.2.1984 tr FBIS/DR/PRC 2.3.1984, K15-16.

136  *People's Daily*, 28.2.1984, op cit. Tian Jiyun, 'Further develop commodity production and increase commodity circulation', *Red Flag*, 16.3.1984 tr JPRS/CR/RF No 6, pp 8-20. Wan Li (b), op cit.

137  Jing Ping (a), op cit.

138  Hunan province No 2 light industry supply corporation, 'What items does the rural market need at present?', *Jingji Guanli*, 1982 (7) p 14.

139  Han Jinduo, 'Pay attention to the problem of supplying manufactured goods to the countryside', *Red Flag*, 16.10.1981 tr JPRS/CR/RF No 20, pp 75-6.

140  *People's Daily*, 28.2.1984, op cit.

141 Hunan province, op cit.
142 Xue Xin, Xu Daohe, Sun Ming & Sun Jing, 'Some problems in the rural market for industrial goods', *Jingji Yanjiu*, 1984 (3) pp 34-40, tr FBIS/CR/A 8.6.1984, pp 3-15.
143 Wu Xiang (b), op cit. Lin Zili (a), op cit.
144 Tian Jiyun, op cit. Wang Fang, 'Thinking should be suited to the developing situation of rural commodity production', *Red Flag*, 16.4.1984 tr JPRS/CR/RF No 8, pp 26-31. Gong Xiaolan *et al*, op cit.
145 *Zhongguo Nongmin Bao*, Untitled, 4.12.1983 tr FBIS/CR/A 14.5.1984, pp 26-7.
146 *Zhongguo Nongmin Bao* 4.12.1983, op cit. Pujiang county, op cit.
147 Lin Zili (c), op cit. Xue Xin *et al*, op cit. Wu Xiang (b), op cit. *Xinhua Radio*, 'Policy explained', 30.1.1983 tr FBIS/DR/PRC 4.10.1984, K17-18.
148 Wu Xiang (b), op cit.
149 Wang Hao, 'Why are differences in city and countryside prices so large', *Xinhua Ribao*, 26.5.1983, p 2.
150 Lin Zili (c), op cit.
151 Wu Xiang (b), op cit. Diao Xinshen, 'Reform of the wholesale market and the sphere of circulation of agricultural and sideline products', *Red Flag*, 1.9.1984 tr JPRS/CR/RF No 17, pp 45-52.
152 Wu Xiang (b), op cit
153 *People's Daily*, 'Grasp firmly the structural reform of supply and marketing cooperatives', 10.6.1984 tr FBIS/DR/PRC 19.6.1984, K14-16.
154 *People's Daily*, 'Enliven commodity circulation in the countryside', 28.1.1983 tr FBIS/DR/PRC 2.2.1983, K16-18.
155 *Xinhua Radio*, 'State council rural commodity circulation rules', 26.2.1983 tr FBIS/DR/PRC 10.3.1983, K13-16.
156 *Xinhua Radio*, 'Circular issued on agricultural, sideline goods', 5.8.1981 tr FBIS/DR/PRC 6.8.1981, K22-24. *Xinhua Radio*, 'Regulations on price of farm, sideline products', 6.6.1981 tr FBIS/DR/PRC 12.8.1981, K3-6. Ge Quanlun & Zhu Weiwen, 'Some questions concerning the negotiated purchase and sale of agricultural and subsidiary products', *Red Flag*, 16.2.1983 tr JPRS/CR/RF No 4, pp 66-71.
157 E C Koziara & Chiou-shuang Yan, 'The distribution system for producer goods in China', *China Quarterly*, 1983 (96) pp 689-702.

# Chapter Four

# The Rural Economy on the Urban Fringe: Nanjing Municipality

The materials collected for this chapter represent a sample of the variety of production experiences drawn from the Nanjing area, this sample being used to suggest some conclusions about rural production since the 1978 reforms in a periurban environment.[1] Of particular importance are the advantages which the rural production units within Nanjing gain from physical proximity to a major city, as well as the unique problems which they face.

## Nanjing: the setting

One common location of relative prosperity in the current phase of development is on the urban fringe. The extent and depth of development will vary from city to city, but belts of significant rural wealth are to be found on the outskirts of most Chinese cities.

Throughout history, Nanjing has been one of China's most important cities. First settled in 472 BC, Nanjing has at various times been China's capital. The old city, situated on a plain in south-west Jiangsu province, Eastern China, Nanjing is surrounded by a terrain of low hills and rivers, most notably the Yangzi. Nanjing is now an important administrative centre as the provincial capital of Jiangsu with a number of important educational and cultural institutions also located in the city.

The urban core is surrounded by suburban city districts of mixed land use - Dachang, Qixia, Yuhuatai and Pukou. Industrial concerns, including petroleum, metallurgy and electrical goods industries, are important alongside land sown with vegetables. Beyond the suburban districts are the five city-administered rural counties - Jiangpu, Jiangning, Liuhe, Lishui and Gaochun - with the bulk of the municipality's cultivable land resources. (See Figure 4.) Food production dominates the resource base, although processing industries are becoming increasingly important. The periphery also contains a diversity of mineral wealth including deposits of iron, gypsum, lead, zinc and manganese as well as limestone and sandstone. Agriculture and rural industry are both well developed.

Nanjing saw a rapid growth in its population in the 1920s and 1930s as a result of once again becoming China's capital. From a population of only 300,000 in the early 1920s, by the end of the 1930s Nanjing was a city of over one million. Nanjing suffered badly during the Japanese occupation but grew significantly in the 1950s, a period of rural-urban migration. Population growth stalled in the late 1960s and early 1970s (the period of the Cultural Revolution) through a policy of rustification, in which significant numbers of city dwellers were forcibly moved to the countryside. However, by the end of the 1970s, with the return of those sent to the countryside during the rustification movement, the city population continued to grow to over two million inhabitants.

Growing pressure upon available space and infrastructure throughout Nanjing poses important challenges for Nanjing planners in terms of rural development. Some problems are common to all rural planners: raising capital for agricultural investment; improving commercial organisations and infrastructure; and developing income and employment opportunities. However, for the peasants of Nanjing, these problems are not as striking as elsewhere because of proximity to urban markets and the relative wealth of their resource base. Cash crop production, agricultural sideline undertakings and rural industry are flourishing.

This is an environment rich in income opportunities. Furthermore, the development of rural production in Nanjing appears to have been energetically and flexibly promoted within the limits allowed by the state reforms.[2] This has not been the case everywhere.[3]

But the periurban environment also faces distinct development problems. There is a clear need to deflect further growth from an already overcrowded urban core. Of particular concern is how to manage industrial growth effectively. Increasingly, large industrial enterprises are found in the rural counties offering employment opportunities but also pollution problems.

This industrial growth is also accompanied by a growing 'urbanisation' of the urban fringe, with the emergence of significant urban settlements from what were once small rural villages and townships. The effective development of these settlements - which presents its own opportunities and difficulties - is a unique concern of the periurban environment.

There is also the challenge of feeding the city. Chinese municipalities are, as much as possible, to be self-sufficient in foodstuffs. This places the grain question very much in focus and has interesting implications for spatial distributions of relative wealth within the limits of the municipality.


## Industrial growth and satellite towns

The expansion of industrial activity within the city centre has long been a problem for Nanjing planners. In the 1930s Nanjing had little in the way of an industrial base, its size and stature reflecting its role as capital city with all the administrative and bureaucratic organs which accompany such a position.[4] Industrial growth in Nanjing after liberation was rapid. By the mid 1980s, there were almost 3000 industrial enterprises in the municipality, employing almost 600,000 workers, a far cry from the 10,000 employed at Liberation. In 1949, only 28% of Nanjing's gross output value was derived from industry; by 1977, this figure was 93%.[5]

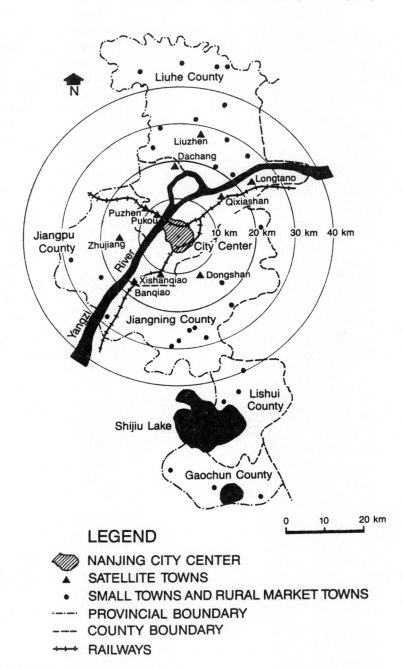

**Figure 4 Nanjing municipality**

The first expansion of industry was predominantly within the urban core. By the late 1950s, expansion of industrial activity was so extensive that shortages of housing, public utilities and other support services were becoming increasingly evident. In the 1960s, enterprises began to locate in the suburban districts to accommodate further industrial growth. Small townships such as Dachang, Banqiao and Xishanqiao developed into significant industrial zones.[6] (See Figure 5.) However, development was somewhat mismanaged, with industrial development often conducted at the expense of the most productive farmland surrounding the urban core, a major source of vegetables for urban consumption.

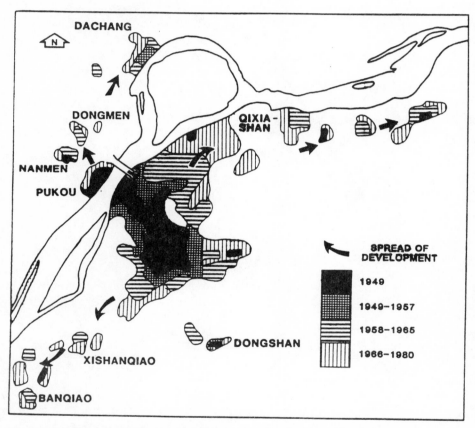

**Figure 5 The spread of industry in Nanjing municipality, 1949-80**

By the 1970s, industrial space in the urban core was all but saturated. Further growth, even if physically possible, would only exacerbate urban overcrowding, and pollution and waste disposal problems. Thus, Nanjing planners continued the established trend of developing the industrial zone in the suburbs. By this time, the diversity of industrial concerns in the city centre and suburbs was considerable, including mining, metallurgy, telecommunications, machine-building, petrochemicals, trucks and chemical fibres.

Currently, the suburbs themselves are becoming overcrowded. Industrial growth is expanding through the suburbs into the city-administered rural counties. In an effort to control this expansion effectively, planners have tried to channel growth into designated satellite towns, such as the rural townships of Liuzhen, Zhujiang and Dongshan.[7] The suburban townships of Dachang, Longtan, Banqiao and Xishanqiao, *de facto* satellite towns for a number of years, were included in this group.

The concept of satellite towns was first put forward by Chinese planners in the early 1950s. Ideally, such towns would range in size from 50,000 to 200,000 people. While access to the nearby city was considered important, it was perceived that satellite towns would be independent urban entities and the location of a significant number of urban-based employment opportunities, and adequate urban facilities.

The main objective of satellite towns was to relieve the pressures on China's overcrowded cities: industrial enterprises realised that expansion was limited by a lack of space; traffic congestion was growing; housing shortages were marked - a situation made worse by the significant in-migration to Chinese cities in the 1950s; and the levels of pollution - industrial and domestic - were rising, exacerbated by growing overcrowding.

However, the experience of satellite towns in Nanjing reveals a sharp divergence between planning theory and practical achievement. First, satellite town development has failed to match industrial growth with the construction of adequate urban infrastructure. Living conditions are poor, while living costs are high. Transport and communication links - even to the city centre - are weak. Education and sanitary standards are low.

Furthermore, much-needed capital investment funds are largely unavailable. While Kirkby reports that since 1982 some improvements in this situation are being made in the suburban satellite towns, the situation in the rural satellites remains bleak.[8]

Satellite towns also suffer from poor management. All too often land-use planning is weak, resulting in the siting of incompatible uses (for example, chemical plants located next to hospitals and schools). The weakness of planning measures is also well illustrated by reports both of misuse and waste of valuable cultivable land around satellite towns.[9]

Currently the illegal use of land for housing construction around the rural satellites is of particular concern. In 1984, all but 3.4% of residential building space under construction by the state and collective units was located in the city centre and suburbs.[10] For the most part, individuals in the rural satellites are responsible for housing construction. In many cases this has resulted in housing being built on land designated for other purposes. Between 1976 and 1981 for example, 15,000 *mu* of cultivable land was lost in the municipality to housing construction as well as brickworks, factories and commercial enterprises.[11] One can only speculate that this figure has been substantially increased since the reforms have taken hold more completely in the countryside and incomes improved.

In the suburban satellites, the issue now is not so much illegal use of land, but an absolute lack of land. The rate of construction is increasing, with 10-storey residential buildings becoming more common. Population densities are rising, putting a severe strain on the already over-burdened infrastructure.

Clearly, in both the suburban and rural satellite towns, much capital investment in infrastructure is needed. Too much of what little capital investment does take place serves only to create further pressure on the already weak existing infrastructure. This is a difficult situation with no easy solutions.

A further concern is that the industrial base which has been developed in the satellite towns, ostensibly providing the foundation for autonomous urban development, is weak. A distinction must be drawn here between the industry of suburban satellites, and that of the more recently-established rural satellites. The industrial base of the suburbs appears to be solid. Over 90% of Nanjing's Gross Industrial Output Value is derived from the urban core and suburbs. While numerically the rural industrial base is large, and its share of gross industrial output value is rising, in practice too much of it consists of small-scale undertakings using obsolete equipment with inferior technical levels.

Lack of capital is another distinguishing factor here, as is poor planning. Supply of certain key raw materials is limited, and the planning system remains unable to meet the increasing demands for these materials from the wide range of enterprises which require them, leading to frustration and economic hardship.[12] The industrial base of Zhujiang for example, faces competition from more efficient, well-established factories for both markets and raw materials. In the current economic climate, in which industrial wage levels are linked to productivity and performance in the marketplace, there is little room for sentiment amongst competing factories. In this environment, fledgling industrial enterprises in the rural satellites will continue to find competition intense and growth difficult.[13]

In Nanjing, the burden of deflecting future growth away from the urban core lies principally with the rural satellite towns. The suburban satellite towns have, in many respects, done as much as they are able to do in reducing pressure on the urban centre. Their future role in this regard is limited. Given this fact, the relatively severe difficulties currently experienced by rural satellite towns must be of critical concern to planners.

At this time, the rural satellite towns have only a weak industrial basis from which to develop a wide range of urban-based employment. Their urban infrastructure is even less developed. Currently, their population growth owes more to peasants moving in from the countryside than any movement out from the city centre. Furthermore, unless living conditions improve markedly, it is unlikely that any such movement from the city centre will occur without a great deal of pressure from the authorities. While these towns may be promoting some localised wealth in the countryside around them, these benefits do little to ease the burden of overcrowding in the urban core.

For the moment, improvements remain unlikely. Investment capital is limited, and much of what is available continues to be used to patch up longstanding problems within the urban and suburban districts. It is difficult to see a way out of this situation. Significant inputs of capital and strict controls over current growth in the city centre, suburbs, and rural counties are needed. Neither seem to be forthcoming.

## Rural growth: feeding the city

It has long been a planning goal that Chinese cities should, as much as possible, be self-sufficient in providing food. To attain this goal, cities have included neighbouring rural counties within their municipal boundaries. Self-sufficiency as a planning goal is politically important, in that it gives a city a significant element of independence from the state planning system. It is also a reflection of economic reality, because it is important that cities avoid long distance inter-provincial trade and transfers of foodstuffs. Such movements inevitably involve high transport costs, excessive spoilage and waste, and place a heavy burden upon an already fragile transport and commercial system.

In pursuit of self-sufficiency, Nanjing planners have established two distinct production zones within the municipality. The first is a zone of 340,500 *mu* of cultivable land in the suburban districts, and is a zone with grain production but also 70,500 *mu* of vegetable land, as well as significant fruit production and animal husbandry. The second, the rural counties, with almost three million *mu* of cultivable land, is a zone dominated by grain production. Almost 94% of the grain produced in Nanjing comes from the rural counties. However, the rural areas are also diversifying rapidly. While, in 1981, the suburban districts produced over 80% of the city's vegetable output, by the mid-1980s the rural counties were producing almost 50%.[14]

The establishment of a periurban vegetable production zone has numerous advantages. Vegetable producers have easy access to urban markets for sales to consumers as well as to vegetable processing plants. This proximity minimises both spoilage and wastage losses incurred during shipment, as well as transport costs. There is also a plentiful water supply and the availability of night soil collected daily from the urban core. Pig breeding is strongly associated with vegetable production, and in Nanjing, periurban pig production is an important part of the city's meat supplies.

In Nanjing, this zone of vegetable production was formally established in 1959. Production is highly specialised and intensive, with heavy inputs of both labour and fertiliser. Production is also mechanised to a significant degree.[15] This zone has produced and continues to produce substantial quantities of vegetables for the city. The only exception to this was during the early 1970s when with much of China, Nanjing's vegetable base was cut to allow increased grain production. In the current phase, for vegetable producers, the high unit value of vegetable production combined with easy access to city markets, makes for comparative prosperity.[16]

Beyond this zone, significant amounts of vegetables are produced in the rural counties; however, grain is still the dominant crop, with vegetable production occupying a subsidiary role.

Even for a city the size of Nanjing, with its fertile agricultural resource base, achieving a goal of self-sufficiency is not easy. As noted above for instance, there is still continuing pressure on periurban cultivable land for use in building projects. Of greater significance are difficulties in grain production, a problem which is especially severe around major cities such as Nanjing with their large non-productive populations.

The 1978 reforms have undoubtedly stimulated grain production within the municipality. In Nanjing as elsewhere, the household has emerged as the basic production unit. After some early difficulties, commentators have praised *baogan daohu* for its ability to stimulate peasant enthusiasm for agricultural production, including grain.[17] In addition, increases in sideline outputs such as pigs have been seen both to increase peasant incomes and to provide fertiliser for the grain fields - fertiliser supplies from the city in the form of night soil, also being available in large quantities.

Yet, pressure remains for further increases in grain output. Grain production remains unpopular with the peasants, and production beyond personal need and the allotted grain targets is discouraged by the low official price for grain.

However, the bare fulfilment of production targets alone does not satisfy urban grain demands. Thus, Nanjing planners are left with the problem of how to increase grain output even further. Raising grain output targets would not be readily tolerated in the rural counties. As elsewhere in China the extent to which peasants can prosper is determined by their ability to generate wealth - through agrarian or other occupations - once allotted grain targets have been met. Given that current target levels represent significant inputs of land, labour and capital, raising these targets would have an immediate impact upon peasant income levels, making it more difficult to engage in anything but grain farming, and severely impinging upon their enthusiasm for agricultural production.

The alternatives to higher grain targets are limited. In recent years, Nanjing has attempted to bolster its grain production by incorporating additional rural counties within the municipality. In 1974 Liuhe county was incorporated, followed in 1983, by Lishui and Gaochun counties. The effect of these latter additions upon agricultural output was marked. However, this impact was a one-time addition to production and cannot be seen in itself as an answer to Nanjing's future increasing demands for agricultural produce.

Future sources of extra grain will be sought from increases in the per-unit yields of existing grain fields. There are two elements to this increase. The first element is the improvement of yields of farmers who produce the bare minimum of grain allowed by targets. This would facilitate increases in outputs without necessarily increasing inputs of land, although this would involve increases in labour and capital inputs. Secondly, the yields of farmers who specialise almost exclusively in grain production must be increased.

To implement the first element outlined above, agricultural production within the Nanjing countryside is demonstrating a growing sophistication. A growing number of peasant households are moving away from agricultural production itself to provide a variety of skilled agricultural production services to other peasants. A case in point is provided by material from Jiangning county.[18]

Following the introduction of the household contract system into Dongshan township, the basic production units were changed from 198 production teams to about 5,000 agricultural households. While this change was welcomed by the peasants, the declining influence of the collective caused numerous problems in grain production.

First, an investigation into 500 households revealed that only one-fourteenth of the land used in paddy-rice rotation was kept for rice-seedling beds, an insufficient proportion to meet cultivable needs. Secondly, there were problems in the adoption of new and improved seed-strains. Many households lacked the technical knowledge to use such seed-strains effectively. Thirdly, a similar lack of technical knowledge was also found in such areas as disease protection, pest control and fertiliser application. Finally, there was the problem of ensuring supply and distribution of 'planned' materials and goods such as fertiliser, diesel oil and pesticides.

In response to these problems, 769 specialised households began contracting out for these specific service tasks. In this way, skills in such diverse areas as seedling cultivation, seed-strain development, disease and pest control, and fertiliser application were made available to a wider range of peasants. However, steady increases in per-unit yields will require that planners ensure that supplies of chemical fertiliser, pesticides and other key farming inputs are available so that the peasants can take advantage of the skills being offered to them. There have been reports that these supplies are both insufficient and irregular.[19]

Initial reports of grain specialists in Nanjing indicated that some considerable success was being achieved by specialisation. Commodity rates of 50% and above were being reported, with upwards of 10,000 *jin* being sold to the state by some households.[20] It must be expected that the key to this development is the amount of subsidy offered to these grain specialists. While there is no clear evidence from the Nanjing materials to substantiate this claim, such incentives are found elsewhere in Southern Jiangsu. This point is important. Despite initial successes by grain specialists in raising per-unit yields

95

and total output, subsidies are crucial to the future development of grain production, a development which is necessary to satisfy the city's future grain demands.

To be sure, failure to increase grain output will leave planners with hard choices about future developments in Nanjing. Increases in the non-productive population without concomitant increases in grain production will be difficult to sustain. Furthermore, it is already clear that there are significant tensions within the rural counties as a result of the current direction of rural development within the municipality.

There are tensions, for instance, caused by the relative concentration of vegetable production - a source of high producer incomes - in the suburban districts. Since the addition of Lishui and Gaochun counties in 1983, the rural counties have a much bigger share of the vegetable market, but it is unlikely that this increase has done much more than temporarily ease the tension.

Similarly, tensions are found within the rural counties. It is clear in the materials from the rural counties of Nanjing, that the expansion of sideline undertakings and rural industrial undertakings is bringing wealth to the countryside. The best illustration of this kind of prosperity is given for an individual household in Jiefang production brigade, Xingdian commune, Jiangpu county. The household, headed by Du Jiaying, comprises 7 people, of whom 5 are considered labourers. In 1981, the household farmed 14.7 *mu* of responsibility land as well as 40 *mu* of reservoir for fish-breeding. In 1982, household production figures and income were striking. The household sold over 20,000 *jin* of grain to the state (almost two-thirds of total production). The household also engaged in the production of various cash crops - peanuts and rapeseed - as well as raising fish, poultry and pigs. Incomes were high, with a household gross income of 14,600 *yuan*, and a net income of 11,000 *yuan*.[21]

This household is, of course, exceptional - production costs in particular seem especially low. However, this kind of development is demonstrated by other households - mostly specialists - in the rural counties.[22] More importantly, larger spatial groups, from households up to communes, are also reporting significant progress.[23]

However, progress is uneven with some producers clearly prospering ahead of others. One commune, Xingdian in Jiangpu county for example, found that in the initial round of contracting, peasants were reluctant to sign contracts to develop water resources. The peasants were wary about the stipulations of the contracts, not least the amount of money and fish to be given to the collective in return for use of the fish-ponds. Thus, in Xingdian commune, those peasants that did sign contracts became responsible for significant amounts of water resources. However, as it became clear that much prosperity could be gained from developing the breeding of fish, the number of people who wanted to develop fish-breeding increased. This increase was in excess of the contracts available, the number being limited to avoid over-fishing.[24] The problem then became how best to distribute contracts, something which is at the very least a problem, possibly not free from corruption, and certainly not free from some degree of arbitrariness. The problem becomes more serious as demands upon a finite resource base become more severe, and also as contract periods lengthen to 30 years or more.

More crucially, the further removed geographically peasants are from urban markets, the more difficult it becomes to take advantage of the current freedoms within the rural production system. Commercial and transport links to the city centre from the periphery - only a distance of perhaps 50 to 60 kilometres - are extremely weak. This is especially true to the north and west of the city beyond the Yangzi, and in the extreme south of the new city-administered counties of Lishui and Gaochun.

The Yangzi and the river network within the municipality offer transport links, although such links are not fully utilised, and of course are very much confined to the river margins. Indeed the Yangzi still represents a major barrier for peasants to the north and the west of the city. While the road and rail bridge has greatly eased the burden of crossing the Yangzi, communications between Zhujiang, the county seat of Jiangpu, and the city, for example, are still difficult. The major road is narrow and poor in quality, and beyond the major highways conditions deteriorate still further. Up to 30% of production teams (villages) in Jiangpu have no ready access to a public highway.[25] This seems to be true for much of the Nanjing periphery.[26]

The development of versatile transport facilities remains an important determinant of the extent of development, especially in the more peripheral, inaccessible parts of the municipality. However, such physical inaccessibility can only be due to a lack of adequate construction capital for investment in roads, waterways and bridges and not the inhospitability of the local terrain.

Little quantitative data - such as transport costs and the availability of services - exists on the adequacy or otherwise of the commercial system in Nanjing municipality. Most authors indicate that the situation is improving. Some of this improvement is due to investments by city and provincial authorities. Ferry services between Nanjing and Jiangpu county have been improved, for example, with many previously labour-powered ferries mechanised. Ferry services are now more common, having risen to eight from three or four crossings per day; they carry more passengers, now 50 from 10 per crossing; and are less influenced by floodwaters and high winds.[27]

Other improvements are prompted by the interventions of bodies outside the official state commercial system, for example through household specialisation in transport.[28] But there are still problems to overcome. These problems will inevitably prevent the rural economy of Nanjing municipality developing to its full potential despite the progress which has been made in recent years since the 1978 reforms. The more peripheral areas still experience quite severe commercial difficulties and here, improvements have yet to be made. This point was argued quite strongly in material outlining the improved commercial situation in the southern half of Liuhe county, at the same time illustrating the problems which continue to beset the more distant - albeit only 30-50 kilometres from the city - northern half of Liuhe county.

On the periphery, income and employment opportunities are increasingly limited to the arable. Commodity production is likewise limited, which in turn restricts the potential of the peripheral authorities to subsidise grain specialists. Thus, the extent to which other peasants are able to diversify beyond grain and local development in general is curtailed. This situation contrasts quite sharply with the prosperity illustrated by rural communities proximate to the city and suburbs.

Furthermore, producers closer to the city markets are more likely to be able to market their own produce, avoiding the overburdened official commercial organs. As one commentator writes: 'the rural economy has developed quickly, but commodity circulation has remained an outstanding problem'.[29]

There is little doubt that within Nanjing commercial activity beyond the official system has developed quite sharply to take full advantage of the commercial opportunities which are available. The number of individuals specialising in commercial activities is growing.[30] Such specialists are predominantly involved with the marketing of agricultural sideline products - fruit, aquatic produce and poultry for example. Similarly, it is hoped that supply and marketing cooperatives located in villages and small market towns throughout the municipality, can offer peasants a means of access to the city markets.[31]

But there is still caution about being over-zealous in promoting commercial activity beyond the official system. Where alternative commercial organisations have come into play, they have certainly helped local economic development. But they are by no means standard throughout the municipality. Undoubtedly, proximity to markets is still a big advantage.

Finally, it must be said, that even in the current phase of relative rural prosperity, agricultural production remains an unattractive proposition for many. As noted above, recent growth in rural satellites owes more to an influx of peasants from the countryside than a movement of urban dwellers from the city centre and suburbs. While living conditions in the rural satellites may not appeal to existing city dwellers, they are attractive to peasants in the surrounding countryside seeking more urban-based employment. Because agricultural work has traditionally been seen as less rewarding, and certainly more demanding than urban-based employment, it is difficult to maintain peasant enthusiasm for agricultural production, especially in the peripheries where rural wealth remains largely elusive. Thus, while planners are eager to develop rural satellites to relieve pressure on the city centre and suburbs, the same development has caused a movement away from agricultural production in the suburbs. While this may not necessarily be a bad thing for agriculture as it relieves some of the demand for rural resources, it does place the rural satellites in a position of being a magnet for rural in-migrants. This is something they simply cannot afford.

## Conclusions

Theoretical prescriptions for the development of the urban fringe of Nanjing have been quite readily made, but the reality of the economic environment in which these prescriptions have been implemented has produced only partial success. In Nanjing, the suburban satellite towns did much to relieve early pressure on the city centre, but they tended to be developed without the necessary investment in urban infrastructure, a deficiency which is only now being rectified. Given the limited capital available to them, planners will find it difficult to develop rural satellite towns effectively and prevent them from falling into the same trap.

Furthermore, while the current economic environment in China has certainly proved successful in generating growth (albeit perhaps only in the short run), policies of increasing competitiveness pose problems for planners and their development goals. Industrial growth in the rural satellites is subject to fierce competition, hindering planning aims to build a strong industrial base within each. Similarly, the opening up of urban markets to rural producers, combined with the low price of grain, has resulted in grain acreage being reduced in favour of more remunerative cash crops making self-sufficiency more difficult to achieve.

While the relative wealth of the Nanjing urban fringe reduces the importance of the distinction between those areas within it which have developed significantly ahead of others, this distinction is apparent. The key factor in making this distinction, even on the urban fringe, is grain production; that is to say, intervention by the state planning machinery.

Also important is the inadequacy and inefficiency of the official commercial system. The state's inability or unwillingness to invest in the basic commercial infrastructure of the more peripheral areas, combined with the inability of those peripheral production units to accumulate investment funds for such capital construction (because of the need to fulfil poorly-remunerated grain contracts), dictate that this weak commercial situation is likely to continue. In this way, the potential scale and spread of specialisation and development which might be possible in Nanjing municipality will be limited.

The development of the rural economy on the urban fringe in the current phase as illustrated in Nanjing municipality is considerable, in spite of some limitations which still hinder development. The periurban fringe of Nanjing is a rich rural environment - high-output-rich. However, the problems encountered in such a favoured environment must cast considerable doubt upon the potential for development in less favoured urban fringes, and even more so in exclusively rural environments.

# Notes to Chapter Four

1   A version of this chapter appears as Powell, 'Development on the Urban Fringe: Recent Chinese Experience', *Carolina Planning*, Spring 1988.
2   Sang Wangbang & Zhou Zhengrong, 'Nanjing's suburban counties emerge as breeders of popular milk cows', *Xinhua Ribao*, 16.3.1983, p 1.
3   Yu Huanchun, 'A prosperous enterprise meets new hardships - what Daqiu village in Tianjin municipality's Jinghai county has encountered on the road to prosperity', *People's Daily*, 10.6.1984 tr FBIS/DR/PRC 18.6.1984, K12-16.
4   G B Cressey, *China's Geographic Foundations*, (McGraw-Hill, 1934).
5   Shan Shumu, Wang Weiping, Wang Tinghua & Bian Zhu, *Jiangsu: Dili (Jiangsu: a geography)*, (Jiangsu, 1980).
6   Yao Shimou & Zhang Fubao, 'The development of Nanjing after liberation and its further rational development', *Jingji Dili*, 1982 (4) pp 306-10.
7   Li Shinwu, 'The distribution of cities and towns in the Nanjing area', *Jingji Dili*, 1982 (3) pp 228-32.
8   R J R Kirkby, *Urbanization in China: Town and Country in a Developing Economy 1949-2000 AD*, (Columbia, 1985).
9   Zhang Fubao, 'Preliminary research into the development of small towns in Jiangpu county', *Jingji Dili*, 1982 (2) pp 139-46.
10  *China Statistical Yearbook 1986*, op cit.
11  Liu Zhongchun, 'Put a stop to the evil practice of irregular occupation of vegetable land', *People's Daily*, 6.3.1982.
12  Zhang Fubao, op cit.
13  Ibid.
14  Li Shinwu, op cit.
15  Shan Shumu *et al*, op cit.
16  Wu Yiyang, 'Nanjing vegetable supply bases offer guarantees', *Xinhua Ribao*, 28.3.1983, p 1.
17  *Xinhua Radio*, 'Jiangsu party circular on peasant's burden', 2.7.1983 tr FBIS/DR/PRC 8.7.1983, O3-4. *Nanjing Radio*, 'Jiangsu's Nanjing city to lessen peasant's burden', 4.7.1983 tr FBIS/DR/PRC 8.7.1983, O4-5. Liu Ning, 'Nanjing's 84 specialised and key households are elected as agricultural models or advanced production units', *Xinhua Ribao*, Liu Jiaren, '10,000 character households appear in Nanjing's suburban counties', *Xinhua Ribao*, 1.1.1983, p 1.
18  Liu Daochun & Sheng Peide (c), 'Dongshan countryside's agricultural service company's seven points for households', *Xinhua Ribao*, 21.5.1983, p 1.
19  Liu Daochun, Jiang Yanghe & Ruan Yide (b), 'Enthusiastically support the peasants who are entering into circulation', *Xinhua Ribao*, 10.2.1983, p 1.
20  Liu Jiaren, op cit.
21  Liu Jiaren, op cit.

22  Liu Daochun & Sheng Peide (a), 'Undertake work on hillslopes - transforming burdens to riches', *Xinhua Ribao*, 24.1.1983, p 2.

23  Gao Tongzhi, 'Huashan production brigade plant over 500 *mu*, of tea plants', *Xinhua Ribao*, 20.3.1983, p 1. Zhou Zhengrong, 'Peasants from Nanjing voluntarily organise mink-breeding meeting', *Xinhua Ribao*, 4.2.1983, p 2. She Yong & Zhang Zhenshe (picture section), 'Poultry-breeding factory', *Xinhua Ribao*, 4.2.1983, p 2.

24  Xu Zhonghai, 'The hard-working style of a female model worker', *Xinhua Ribao*, 4.2.1983, p 2.

25  Zhang Fubao, op cit.

26  Shen Xing & Liu Youde, 'Shuangzhe commune supports peasants engaged in commercial transport', *Xinhua Ribao*, 17.2.1983, p 2.

27  Hu Xueyi, 'Nanjing and neighbouring counties' river ferries take on a new appearance', *Xinhua Ribao*, 2.4.1983, p 2.

28  Shen Xing, *et al*, op cit.

29  Liu Daochun, *et al* (b), op cit.

30  Ibid. Zou Yongxiang & Wang Yongcong, '700 households in Liuhe county engage in trade', *Xinhua Ribao*, 18.5.1983, p 2.

31  Li Shinwu, op cit.

# Chapter Five

# Development in Taihu Agricultural District

## Introduction

Taihu agricultural district in Southern Jiangsu is an area of comparative well-being in contemporary China. The aim of this chapter is to trace the development of the rural economy of Taihu in recent years, outlining the important policy decisions and advantages of the area which have worked to the benefit of the rural economy. In particular, the impact of Taihu's strong rural industrial base will be examined.

Taihu agricultural district is in itself not an administrative unit and inevitably the material used refers to a particular part of Taihu - be it prefecture, county, commune and so forth - rather than the district as a whole. While geographical differences are inevitable within Taihu, sufficient physical similarity exists at that level to justify viewing Taihu as a single geographical area and reaching conclusions about it.

## Taihu: the setting

Though Jiangsu is one of China's smallest provinces, marked regional differences in agricultural production and outputs exist. There are three different climatic zones contained within Jiangsu: from north to south these are first, a warm temperate zone of deciduous and broadleaf forest with brown earths; secondly, a northern sub-tropical zone of deciduous and broadleaf mixed forests with yellow-brown earths; and finally, a middle sub-tropical zone of evergreen and broadleaf forests with yellow earths.[1] The quantity of heat retained in the soil, and the water content of the soils in these zones, fluctuate and have a deep influence on the cropping systems.

Jiangsu has a varied topography and furthermore, because of their different proximity to the sea, the climates of eastern and western Jiangsu are somewhat different. These numerous factors have an important effect on farmland capital construction, soil improvement and the schedule of crops.

Since the early 1960s, on the basis of the natural conditions of the province, Jiangsu has been divided into six agricultural regions (see Figure 7). The general characteristics of these agricultural regions are as follows.

**Figure 6  The agricultural regions of Jiangsu province**

**Table 1 The six agricultural regions of Jiangsu**

| Agricultural district | Area (sq km) | Rural population (mns) | Cultivable land (mn *mu*) | Agricultural land availability (*mu* / capita) | Multi-cropping indices |
|---|---|---|---|---|---|
| Xuhuai | 34500 | 15 | 25+ | 1.7 | 160-180 |
| Lixiahe | 16700 | 7.7 | 11 | 1.43 | 180-210 |
| Yanhai | 10900 | 5.3 | 7.6 | 1.4 | 180-210 |
| Yanjiang | 10700 | 8 | 8 | 1 | 220-240 |
| Zhenyang | 14500 | 5.35 | 7.75 | 1.44 | 220-240 |
| Taihu | 14800 | 8.2 | 10.25 | 1.25 | 265 |

Compiled from materials in Shan Shumu *et al*, op cit.

The six agricultural districts can be divided into two groups. The first group consists of Xuhuai, Lixiahe and Yanhai (coastal) agricultural districts in the north of Jiangsu. Traditionally backward, these areas have seen much improvement in their agricultural resource base since 1949 following extensive agricultural capital construction.

By 1978 Xuhuai was Jiangsu's fourth largest commodity grain base and had a broadly-based economy, although its full potential still has to be realised (a fuller discussion of Xuhuai follows in Chapter Six). In 1978 Lixia was Jiangsu's second largest commodity grain base and was also developing into a pig-breeding base as well as exploiting its abundant aquatic resource potential. While dual problems of waterlogging and salinity keep grain yields low in Yanhai, cotton production has developed to such a degree that Yanhai is now Jiangsu's largest cotton base. In addition, Yanhai's fishing industry, centred on Beikan, Huanggang, Jianggang, and Huangshang, is strongly developed and the potential of its livestock resources is also growing.

The physical and economic characteristics of these three districts are synonymous with those of the North China plain, districts which have traditionally suffered from the high-output-poor trap. Yet, since 1949, they have made exceptional progress by the standards of the North China plain to a position today of comparative well-being.

In contrast, the second group of Yanjiang, Zhenyang and Taihu agricultural districts in the south of Jiangsu are markedly prosperous agricultural areas. While Zhenyang owes much of its prosperity to agricultural capital construction since liberation, all three districts now enjoy diversified economies and high commodity circulation rates.

Yanjiang grows cash crops - especially cotton, peanuts, jute, peppermint and spearmint - with much success. In addition its livestock economy is well developed. Zhenyang is considered to be a general foodstuffs commodity base, annually supplying the state with 1200 to 1400 million *jin* of foodstuffs.[2] In

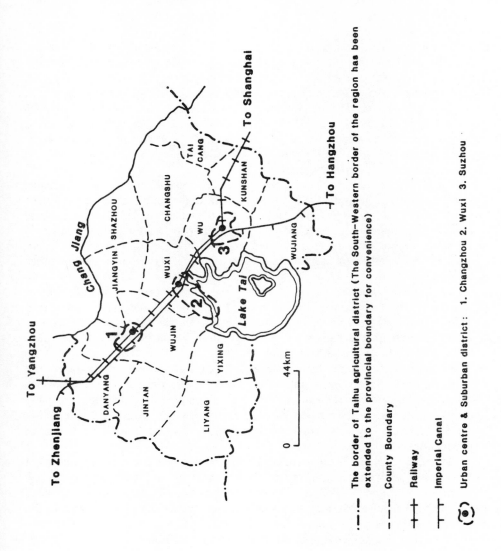

**Figure 7  Taihu agricultural district. Jiangsu province: the counties and major urban areas**

addition, the district has a (largely undeveloped) potential for livestock-breeding, as well as 37% of Jiangsu's forestry reserves - although Maoist over-emphasis upon grain had a serious negative impact upon the economic forests within Zhenyang.

Taihu, however, remains the most prosperous agricultural district of Jiangsu. It is the province's largest commodity grain base, annually supplying the state with 3000 to 3300 million *jin* (1.6 million tons) of grain - a commodity rate of approximately 35%. This represents about half of Jiangsu's commodity grain. Average per-unit yields of grain easily exceed 1000 *jin/mu* with yields of 1600 *jin/mu*, 2000 *jin/mu* and even 2400 *jin/mu* common.[3] At the same time, Taihu is an important base area for silkworm production, oil-bearing crops and fruit. Sideline production and commune- and brigade-run industrial enterprises have also developed to a marked degree.

In comparison to much of China, each of Jiangsu's agricultural districts would seem to be abundantly endowed with natural resources. However, there is little doubt that a distinction can be drawn between the southern agricultural districts of Jiangsu and those of the north. Furthermore, the superiority of Taihu's resource base seems quite evident. The multi-cropping index in Taihu (that is, the number of harvests per year) is much higher than that of other districts, in particular those of the north. A further key distinction between Taihu - and to a lesser extent Yanjiang - is the importance of non-farming sources of rural income. This chapter intends to use materials drawn from Taihu to indicate how, in recent years, that district has developed its resource base and built on the particular advantages that Taihu possesses which other areas may not have in such abundance, if at all.

In addition, material from the mid-1970s will be used to explore the influence of the Maoist grain policy on Taihu. Taihu suffered under the policies which sought to maximise grain production. Beginning in 1970, triple-cropping of grain was widely introduced into the region. While diversified production remained important, its potential was much reduced in favour of grain production.

Taihu, then, is one of the richest agricultural districts in China. It consists of 13 counties, as well as the three major urban areas of Changzhou, Wuxi and Suzhou (see Figure 7). Of the 13 counties, eight - Jiangyin, Shazhou, Wuxi, Changshu, Taicang, Wu, Kunshan and Wujiang - form Suzhou prefecture in the east of Taihu, whilst the other five - Yixing, Wujin, Liyang, Jintan and Danyang - make up part of Zhenjiang prefecture to the west of Taihu.

# Grain production in the 1970s

The heart of the grain emphasis in Taihu lay in the change from double-cropping to triple-cropping, a move which involved 70% of all grain fields.[4] A 'two-three system' of cropping was introduced. That is to say, where there had

106

formerly been a winter-crop and a summer-crop, there was now a winter-crop (barley, naked-barley or wheat), an early-maturing spring rice-crop after the harvesting of the winter-crop, and a late rice-crop.[5]

Results under triple-cropping were far removed from those anticipated. In Songjiang county for example, (in nearby Shanghai municipality but with similar agricultural conditions to those in Taihu) grain statistics for 1966 when the county double-cropped and 1976 when it triple-cropped using the two-three system compared badly. Grain yields were down from 1500-1700 *jin/mu* to 1400 *jin/mu*. The amount of labour used in grain farming increased as did farm costs. Not surprisingly, the value of the work day fell from one *yuan* to 0.84 *yuan*. Grain output, however, increased.[6]

Similar observations were made in Wuxi county.[7] Although yields were slightly higher under triple-cropping (1000 *jin/mu* in 1976 in comparison to 983 *jin/mu* in 1966 when there was double-cropping), after subtracting 60 *jin/mu* for extra seed requirements and also an amount to compensate for the lower processing rate of the rice grown under triple-cropping, the 1976 figure is effectively lower than that of 1966.

What difficulties were experienced with triple-cropping? Initially, the growing season itself is very limited. Taihu has a frost-free period of 200 to 230 days and a cumulative temperature value of 4600 to 5000 degrees C. This gives rise to tight planting schedules. Slightly adverse weather conditions can therefore have disastrous results. Tight planting schedules leave spring seedlings susceptible to frosts. The summer harvest may be forced early by high summer temperatures, and of course the size of the second summer crop is conditional in part upon the autumn weather.[8]

The tight planting schedules favour the extension of barley at the expense of wheat for the winter crop. However, in comparison to wheat, barley has a lower food value as well as a lower processing rate.[9]

Similarly, the intensity of the planting schedule leads to a rise in the use of Xian rice (with its shorter maturation period) at the expense of Geng rice. In Suzhou prefecture for example, whereas Xian rice constituted only 9.1% of the 1966 double-crop harvest, in 1976, with triple-cropping, it made up 45.6% of the harvest. Xian rice is inferior in quality to Geng rice and also has a lower processing rate. As a result of the change, there were shortages in supplies to urban centres of the preferred Geng rice.[10]

The tight planting schedule also increases the demand on labour. The two-three system of triple-cropping significantly increased the amount of work the peasants had to do.[11] Indeed, there were instances when harvesting and planting schedules could not be met because of labour shortages. As a result, in some areas yields fell sharply.[12] In addition, the long hours, especially in paddy fields, were claimed to be the cause of increasing sickness amongst the peasants. Peasants also complained that the amount of work necessary in grain production left little time for sideline occupations (although Taihu remained better off than most in this respect[13]).

Not only did demands upon labour rise, at the same time, increasing production costs often meant lower incomes. In 1976, production costs in Taihu were as much as 40% of gross agricultural revenue.[14]

There were also problems with fertilisers. More often than not there were shortages. Even in Suzhou prefecture where local supplies were available, it was only of one variety of chemical fertiliser. The soil in the prefecture lacks phosphorus and potassium and such trace elements as copper and molybdenum. Agricultural chemicals with low toxicity, high effectiveness and low residual toxicity were still in short supply.[15] Furthermore, the increased use of pesticides with the introduction of triple-cropping resulted in the building up of a higher resistance in the various pest populations to the chemicals used.

Finally, there was a decline in soil fertility. Increased flooding of the land under triple-cropping reduced the organic matter content of the soil and the constant ploughing and tilling lowered the soil quality. Commentators concluded that: first, the plough layer was becoming shallower and the soil in it rigid and more difficult to cultivate; secondly, the layer beneath the plough layer was becoming thicker with a deeper hard pan developing; and thirdly, the nutrient balance was lost.[16]

However, not all the Chinese media materials expressed like opinions. Some accused others of 'not seeking truth from facts', that is of making false claims about production costs and income figures.[17] One commentator reported figures for Suzhou prefecture which ran counter to those given by others opposed to triple-cropping. It was claimed for example, the in the years 1971 to 1979, using the two-three system, total grain production in Suzhou prefecture was 54,860 million *jin* (an annual average output of 6850 million *jin* - 3.425 million tons) whereas grain production during the years 1963 to 1970, when only one summer crop was harvested, was only 42,900 million *jin* (an annual average output of 5360 million *jin* - 2.68 million tons).[18]

While some supporters of triple-cropping conceded that increased yields had been achieved only at the expense of high production costs which had lowered income, the fault for that, they argued, lay not with the system itself but with inefficient management and the continued existence of the 'price scissors' (the high cost of inputs to grain production relative to grain prices).[19]

It seems most likely that triple-cropping under the two-three system did prompt increased outputs of grain, but only at the expense of high production costs and lower incomes. Consider the following material for Suzhou prefecture.

**Table 2 Suzhou prefecture. Grain production figures (100 mn *jin* unless stated)**

| | Winter crop: | | | Paddy: | | | Total |
|---|---|---|---|---|---|---|---|
| | Wheat | Barley | Sub-total | Xian | Geng | Sub-total | grain output |
| 1966 (double-crop) | 649 | 228 | 877 | 476 | 4732 | 5208 | 6084 |
| 1978 (triple-crop) | 1144 | 577 | 1721 | 2688 | 3472 | 6160 | 7880 |
| Inc 1978 over 1966 | 494 | 349 | 844 | 2212 | -1260 | 952 | 1796 |
| Net increase after processing | | | | | | | 1126 |
| | | | | | | | (sub-total) |
| Adjustments to 1978: | | | | | | | |
| 1 Extra seed | | | -34 | | | -251 | -285 |
| 2 Processing losses* | | | -59 | | | -176 | -235 |
| 3 Extra food requirements | | | | | | | -140 |
| Total 1978 adjustment | | | | | | | -660 |
| Actual increase 1978 over 1966 | | | | | | | 466 |

| | 1966 Double-cropping | 1978 Triple-cropping |
|---|---|---|
| Labour cost per *mu* (units of labour day) | 74.42 | 108.68 |
| Material expenses (*yuan/mu*) | 64.27 | 82.85 |
| Gross farm income | | 181 |
| Gross farm expenditure | | 191 |
| Net farm income | | -10 |

(all mns of *yuan* above the 1966 figure)

*100 *jin* of Xian rice is equivalent to 92 *jin* of Geng rice; 100 *jin* of barley is equivalent to 83 *jin* of wheat.
Compiled from materials in Zhang Liufang, 'We must adjust and reform the cropping system when the gains cannot offset the losses', *Guangming Ribao*, 13.12.1979, p 2.

Ultimately, whether triple-cropping in Taihu was judged a success or failure by individual commentators depends on their political standpoints. Those who see increased output as the measure of success will claim that triple-cropping under the two-three system is successful.[20] As one commentator argued: 'in the final analysis does the two-three system increase output or not? This is the major criterion for weighing the success of this cropping system'.[21]

Against this standpoint of increased grain production regardless of the impact upon income, are those who argued that incomes must not be sacrificed for the sake of marginal increases in grain production. These arguments were buttressed by claims that the state demands on Taihu for grain were really too high.[22]

Agricultural Reform in China

Eventually the mounting criticism of triple-cropping in Taihu, coming at a time both of adverse weather conditions which were reducing outputs and also political instability in the aftermath of Mao's death, culminated in a significant retreat from triple-cropping between 1976 and 1981. Within Suzhou prefecture for example, all aspects of grain production showed a decline in the period.

**Table 3  Suzhou prefecture. Aspects of grain production**

|  | 1976 | 1981 | Dec from 1976 to 1981 |
|---|---|---|---|
| Total sown area of grain crops (mn *mu*) | 13.38 | 11.78 | 1.6 |
| Double-cropping: net area (mn *mu*) | 4 | 2.04 | 1.96 |
| Triple-cropping: net area (mn *mu*) | 7.39 | 5.42 | 1.97 |
| Grain yields (*jin/mu*) | 1287 | 1019 | 268 |
| Gross grain output (bn *jin*) | 7.4 | 5.7 | 1.7 |
| Grain sales to the state (bn *jin*) | 1.951 | 0.7 | 1.3 |

Compiled from materials in Sun Ming *et al*, see note 24.

Furthermore, the figures for 1976 compared to earlier years show declining per-unit yields (from 1353 *jin/mu* in 1974), and a lower amount of grain (2.53 billion *jin* in 1975) sold to the state.[23]

Lower grain output in Suzhou has been attributed to inefficient management and production techniques. But the truth is that lower grain outputs in Suzhou prefecture and Taihu - as well as other fertile areas - have followed directly from the liberalisation of the rural economy since 1978. The reforms of the current phase did not so much change the rural economy of Taihu as essentially restore its ability to develop in a direction which it has always shown potential for: a strong rural industrial base, diversified agriculture and a strong degree of commercial vitality. In other words, the traditional strengths of the Taihu economy have been reemphasised.

This freer rein allowed to the area has made for a growing, vital rural economy - all too often depicted in the Chinese and western media as symptomatic of the national rural scene, but in fact representing the most prosperous rural picture. But, despite the prosperity exhibited by Taihu, there are still numerous questions which require investigation: what is the status of grain production? Can grain production be subsidised sufficiently to make it an attractive agricultural proposition? What kinds of strains are being created by the current direction of rural growth?

110

# The reestablishment of the Taihu economy: rural industry

In view of the weak financial position of the country, it will not be possible for a certain period to stimulate grain production by means of such measures as greatly raising the price for state grain purchases, or to lower the basic figure for grain purchases, or to expand the scope of excess-quota purchases. Hence, we should approve and actively encourage the use of profits from industry and sideline production to subsidise grain production.[24]

Rural industry has always been considered an important part of the rural economy in Taihu in particular and Jiangsu in general.[25] Within Jiangsu, the rural industry of five counties stands out: Wuxi, Jiangyin, Shazhou, Changshu and Wujin. All are in Taihu. Of the five, Wuxi is the most prominent.

Wuxi has a long history of rural industrialisation. More recently, emphasis has been placed on the development of agricultural machinery repair and spare parts factories and grain and silage processing enterprises. This follows the policy that industry should 'support' agriculture. Resource and labour allocations were structured accordingly. The county benefits from rural industry in a number of ways: first, it employs rural surplus labour;[26] secondly, it supplies - in situ - much-needed goods and services to the rural economy; thirdly, it provides for up to 90% of the county's investment funds for basic capital construction and agricultural mechanisation;[27] fourthly, it can provide a stable demand for agricultural raw materials, encouraging peasants to invest in production; and finally, funds from rural industry can also finance subsidies to farmers (especially grain farmers) in order to maintain an 'income standard' between farming and industrial occupations.[28]

Wuxi is exceptional. The successful development of rural industry requires the availability of local resources - both raw materials and capital; good transport links and commercial channels to large, local markets; and a sophisticated rural production system. All these are evident in Wuxi. Furthermore, Wuxi county benefits by being under the administrative control of Wuxi city, linking the rural enterprises with the better developed, large-scale city industry (though, conversely, the farmers may be now more obligated to sell grain to the city).[29] A 'putting-out' relationship is developing between the rural and urban industries, firmly establishing the place of rural undertakings. These conditions are not common in China, although the state clearly hopes that they will become much more widespread.

The kind of local development that is possible from a foundation of rural industry is well illustrated by Qianzhou commune in Wuxi county.

Qianzhou commune is one of the 35 communes in Wuxi county. It has a population of 36,000 occupying an area of 35 square kilometres. The commune has greatly prospered from the longstanding development of its industry in two key ways: first, as a source of income; and second, as a source of capital for investment in agricultural production.

Qianzhou has 80 commune- and brigade-run industrial enterprises including farm machinery plants, a small shipyard, brick and tile yards and grain and fodder processing workshops. Most of the profits from these enterprises contributed to collective accumulation funds. Thus, agriculture in Qianzhou benefited not only from the provision of goods and services but also from construction of water conservation projects financed by accumulation funds. Between 1970 and 1978 for example, Qianzhou commune built a 19 kilometre dyke across low-lying land, dug numerous river courses and underground drainage canals and set up 5 pumping stations. As a result of these and other improvements grain yields almost doubled.

Income subsidies are also important. In 1978, 54-65% of total peasant income was derived from distribution of industrial profits.[30] Qianzhou continues to develop its industrial capacity. It has established close links with city-based industries. For example, through the integration of dyeing and weaving operations between itself and a silkcloth printing and dyeing mill in Wuxi city, it has been able to increase output of high-quality silk. At the same time, it is argued that Qianzhou's managerial capabilities and access to market information, technical advice and price management have all been improved. In addition, the commune has better access to local and national markets. Essentially, both sides in these rural-urban arrangements can benefit from working together rather than being competitors, at least with each other.[31]

Growth of local industrial enterprises is being promoted with some vigour by local planners. Rural industries have followed the lead of agriculture and adopted a variety of production responsibility systems designed to build on the enthusiasm with which such systems were received on the arable. Such systems included: responsibility for quotas, based upon the fulfilment of output quotas, most common in enterprises with a comparatively large scope of production, where output value and profits are high; responsibility for profits, based upon the need to fulfil certain profit expectations, most common in small-scale industry where profits are low; responsibility for profits and losses on the part of the workers, most common in small concerns, handicraft industries and certain service trades; individual contract responsibility systems, in which an individual assumes responsibility for the completion of certain tasks, most commonly found in industries where numbers of workers are very small.[32]

However, while the balance of opinion expressed in the media on the rise of rural industry has been favourable (not surprisingly given the advantages to the state, plus demonstrated improvements in rural incomes and livelihood), there are still numerous problems to be faced. For example, the fall in Suzhou prefecture's grain production in recent years has been greeted with some alarm.[33] Given that almost 75% of Taihu's commodity grain output is derived from Suzhou prefecture, this concern is understandable.[34] Many local units have become attracted to industrial and sideline production because of their larger output value and greater profitability. Competition between investment in grain production and increasing income through investment in rural industry is being found in many rural units. Not surpisingly, grain is losing out.

Industrial enterprises have also been subject to blindness in development. There is much duplication of production and direct competition with state-owned industry despite moves towards integration as demonstrated in Qianzhou. As a result, productive capacity is not fully utilised. In addition, these commune- and brigade-run industries must be self-sufficient in raw material supplies. State plans will not - and cannot - provide the raw materials for such enterprises. Furthermore, many of the products produced are not included in state planning and the costs and risks of marketing must be borne by the enterprises themselves.

Authorities in Changshu county proposed to avoid excessive competition among its 2000 commune- and brigade-run industrial enterprises by supplying market information and analysis to reduce the commercial risks of each enterprise.[35]

Emphasis in Changshu has been put upon the development of traditional industries - textiles, embroidery, leather and hide manufacture and so forth - where local knowledge and skill can be utilised to the full. In this way, it is argued, Changshu county has been able to develop its industry avoiding excessive competition and market risks and reaping the benefits of increased incomes and an improved agricultural resource base.

In order that its rural enterprises complement rather than supplant larger-scale county-level industry or nearby state enterprises, the Changshu authorities have adopted wide-ranging control over rural industrial development. Yet, it is not clear that this intervention benefits rural industries. It may well help some, but at the same time offer protection to larger - and less efficient - factories.

Finally, it should also be noted that the impact of rural industrial development may not be as widespread as the state anticipates, even in areas like Taihu. Frequently, the accumulation funds generated from the profits of industrial enterprises are inappropriately used.[36] All too often the richer units develop their own cultural facilities rather than expanding the productive ability in poorer units.

In Shazhou county for example, accumulation funds were spent on such things as a basketball court, a stereoscope cultural gallery and a theatre. Yet, within Shazhou there are communes and teams with weak collective economies. But accumulation funds are quite rigidly controlled by units below the county-level, such units - not surprisingly given the fluctuations in rural policy since 1949 - preferring to improve their own lot rather than encouraging their weaker neighbours.[37]

This is a problem which will become more pressing as economic growth slows down and weaker units find local competition becoming more intense. For now, however, even these weaker units can enjoy a measure of prosperity, although less marked than that enjoyed by others.

## The diversified economy

Taihu is more than just an area with a strong industrial base. The diversified economy is also well-developed. Oil-bearing crops in Taihu for example, make up half of Jiangsu's total output. The same is true for silk. In addition, a third of Jiangsu's freshwater fishing industry and a quarter of the province's pigs are to be found in Taihu. Tea is also an important crop and 90% of the commodity production of oranges is developed within the district.[38] Other crops include cotton, hemp, tobacco and fruit.

This rich crop diversity, long important, has been fully exploited since 1978. The 1978 reforms themselves encouraged diversification and in Taihu, with the reversion to double-cropping in grain, cash crop production blossomed. Sophisticated production forms have emerged to effectively develop this rich resource base. Peasants in Taicang county for example, have established 'service companies' to supply peasants with market information, high-yield seeds, breeding techniques and even investment funds.[39] Similarly, agricultural research institutes have become more involved in rural production, encouraging peasants to utilise certain crop types to suit local conditions and how best to pursue local production.[40] Not surprisingly, in this rich environment, specialisation in agricultural production has become commonplace.[41]

Clearly, Taihu is beginning to exploit its rich agriculture resource fully. However, there are still some difficulties to be overcome. In some instances extension of the area sown with cash crops has occurred to the detriment of the resource base. For example, the enclosing of tideland to expand cash crop cultivation has led to a reduction in the water and fishing areas and an increase in silting. Similarly, peasants have begun to use water plants as fertiliser with the result that water quality has been lowered so much in some places that fish-breeding grounds were destroyed - ironically lowering fish yields at a time when more people are working in the fishing industry.[42]

More immediate is the threat which increased cash crop production poses for grain. In Suzhou prefecture alone, between 1976 and 1981, the sown area of cash crops increased by 440,000 *mu* at the same time as that of grain decreased by 1.6 million *mu*. Taihu, long a source of substantial amounts of commodity grain for the state, is moving away from poorly-rewarded grain production to more remunerative cash crop production. What has been the response of the Taihu authorities to this situation?[43]

## Grain production in Taihu

Initially it was believed that the introduction of production responsibility systems would provide sufficient flexibility for peasants to develop cash crop production as well as increase grain output.[44] Early reports indicated that this was the case, but grain outputs and sales to the state have never attained the levels reached in the mid-1970s. While part of this decline can be attributed to the slow readjustment of agriculture from triple-cropping to double-cropping - seed varieties suitable for the former only gradually being replaced in the revised cropping schedule, for instance[45] - the biggest cause of lower grain outputs and state sales has been the attraction of better rewarded rural occupations and activities, and the relative freedom for peasants to pursue them.

To combat this decline in grain performance, the Taihu authorities have encouraged the growth of grain-producing specialists. In some instances, a small number of grain specialists are fulfilling a significant percentage of the state grain targets. In Bacheng commune, Kunshan county, for example, authorities contracted out 15 *mu* of land to each of 403 grain specialists, the average contract being to produce over 16,000 *jin* of commodity grain.[46] This meant that only 8.2% of the total number of households in Bacheng commune contracted out 22% of the land in that commune and were responsible for 25% of the commodity grain which the commune had to produce. The commune assisted such grain specialists through subsidised fertiliser supplies, investment resources and scientific advice.

Such grain specialists, it is argued, should be able to reap economies of scale from the larger parcels of responsibility land which are allocated to them, although in Bacheng commune the economies do not appear to be that great. Of much greater significance, because specialising in grain production is less profitable than specialising in another crop or diversified undertaking, are the local subsidies which are available to grain specialists so that their incomes match those of other specialists.

An example of local subsidy to aid grain specialists is given in material from Yixing county on the west shore of Lake Tai.[47] In Yixing, at the end of the year, an amount is set aside from the profits of commune- and brigade-run industry, the profits of sideline occupations (often from specialised households) and other sources, and this amount is distributed amongst commune members who have contracted to engage in grain farming (the amount distributed based on the amount of marketable grain turned over to the state). In other words, industry and sideline production supports grain production through the provision of a local subsidy to grain producers.

Certainly this system seems to work in Yixing county. After its introduction in 1982, the summer grain harvest surpassed the previous record harvest by 14.4%, output per *mu* of early rice reaching 743 *jin*, 16.6% above the previous high. In all, 10% of the peasant households in Yixing contract 25% of the county's farmland and produce 40% of total grain output.[48]

# Conclusions

Freed to develop beyond the constraints imposed upon its rural economy by the excesses of grain farming in the triple-cropping system, Taihu is exhibiting 'all-round' development in its rural economy: a sound agricultural resource base; a wide range of diversified undertakings; many varied industrial enterprises; and a degree of commercial vitality. In comparison to much of China, incomes are high. Furthermore, the broadly based nature of the rural economy acts as an insurance against natural disasters. Although the impact of adverse weather conditions is still felt, such blows are now softened.

Some problems still remain. While Taihu remains self-sufficient in grain in terms of its rural population, it sells less to the state than the latter would like, especially when considering the large urban populations in the Taihu area, not to mention Shanghai. Of course the state does receive other agricultural produce in its stead, both in terms of produce which has supplanted grain, and also from more profitable utilisation of grain in pig-breeding or brewing for instance. However, this does increase the burden on other areas for grain foodstuffs required by the cities in the Southern Jiangsu area.

Industrial bottlenecks are still found and competition for materials and markets between rural industrial enterprises is getting more intense. Increasing integration between rural enterprises and those of the city will alleviate some of this competition, but not for ever. Commerce, relatively well-developed to begin with, is improving - often because of the intervention of bodies outside the official system. But there are still some problems with transport and storage.[49] These problems will become more severe as the rural economy develops.

Nevertheless, the structure of the rural economy exhibited by Taihu indicates that much potential exists for the gathering of accumulation funds from rural industry and sideline production for the strengthening of the agricultural resource base, subsidising agricultural incomes, and developing commercial infrastructure as needs arise.[50] Taihu then, is not only more likely to accumulate funds for investment in agricultural capital construction and hence further expand production ability, but is also able to subsidise local grain production in the face of low official grain prices, thereby ensuring as much as possible, continued high yields, high incomes and further specialisation in production - both in grain and lucrative commodity undertakings.

Yet, simply to offer up the development of Taihu as an example to others to follow, belies the fact that Taihu does possess numerous advantages which, if not unique to the area, certainly distinguish it from much of the Chinese countryside.

First, Taihu has a good natural resource base and has always been considered one of the richest areas of China. This underlying wealth helps Taihu to begin to solve some of its problems through a self-help policy - a policy necessary in the light of the state's inability to provide the resources for agricultural and other capital construction, or even to pay fair prices for commodities.[51] The ability of the production units of Taihu to accumulate investment funds because of the inherent strength of its resource base, especially in the current economic climate, is a crucial advantage in the further promotion of all aspects of the rural economy, not least by improving upon the weaknesses which still exist.

A second advantage which Taihu possesses is the proximity of major urban centres - Changzhou, Wuxi, Suzhou and Shanghai. Indeed, it must be said that the production of Taihu district bears many of the hallmarks of 'periurban' production, and it must draw considerable advantage from the various urban centres. The influence of the major urban centres upon Taihu's rural economy seems likely to increase in the future as recent administrative changes designate counties in Taihu as city-administered counties. (Though again, it may also invoke some strains on rural producers who may be expected to produce more grain for the city.)

A third advantage for Taihu is the density of small town urban development, that is to say the density of county towns and rural market towns, some of which may also be administrative headquarters. Taihu has the highest density of small towns in China.[52] Such small towns are important not only because much commune-run and all county-level industry is to be found in them, but also because they necessarily have adequate existing communications networks. Thus, it is argued that such small towns can further develop commercial functions and become key links in the commercial system which is able to serve the rural production units.[53]

The advantages outlined above become self-reinforcing. As Taihu's rural economy becomes richer, it can in turn improve itself. Indeed, Taihu has been able to take full advantage of the new management structures and changed state attitudes in agriculture in the current phase, compounding the benefits already bestowed upon it.

Furthermore, as noted in Yixing county, Taihu seems to want to fulfil its obligations to the state with the minimum disruption necessary to a goal of seeking the maximum gain possible from the fullest utilisation of its wide resource base. In Taihu, county and other authorities are using the management structures, and agricultural and industrial policy of the current phase to limit the state's role in their affairs as much as possible. This is shown for example, in the fact that decision-making authority involving large local accumulation funds remains very much at the county-level and below. Similarly, the flexibility inherent in *baogan daohu* gives Taihu's peasants greater control over its productive ability, ostensibly for a considerable period of time given the current prevalence of long-term agricultural contracts. This in turn should enable them to develop production to their own advantage.

This development is not spectacular in the context of East Asia outside China, but the apparent willingness of the state to allow production units to develop as they have done in Taihu is quite striking by Chinese standards. However, this may well be development the state ultimately feels it cannot tolerate. For the moment, the increases in tax revenue generated by rural industry, the higher outputs of cash crops, and the welcome offered by the peasants to the reforms are considered by the state to be sufficient compensation for the slacker grip it has over rural production.

Finally, the ability of the existing resource base to fulfil grain targets, produce surplus commodities and sustain diversified undertakings and industrial enterprises continues not only to be the way forward for Taihu, but is also the road to further polarisation of wealth in the Chinese countryside. The benefits and advantages which Taihu possesses, and has effectively utilised, have stimulated development in its rural economy, readily springing the high-output-poor trap. Those areas with a less advantageous resource base cannot expect similar development, and the prosperity which accompanies it, to be so readily forthcoming.

# Notes to Chapter Five

1    She Zhixiang, 'New characteristics developed in Jiangsu province's agricultural regions and new problems in agricultural distribution', *Dili Xuebao (Acta Geographica Sinica)*, 1979 34 (2) pp 104-15.

2    Shan Shumu *et al*, op cit.

3    Ibid.

4    Ibid.

5    Mu Jiajun & Ji Jincheng, 'Three times three equals nine is not as good as two times five equals ten', *People's Daily*, 13.1.1979 tr *Chinese Economic Studies*, 1981-82 (15) pp 37-44.

6    Mu Jiajun *et al*, op cit.

7    Zhou Zhengdu, 'A view of the 2-3 cropping system in Suzhou prefecture', *Guangming Daily*, 17.3.1979 tr *Chinese Economic Studies*, 1981-82 (15) pp 72-6.

8    Xiong Yi, 'Viewpoints and suggestions on the Southern Jiangsu cropping system', *People's Daily*, 13.1.1979 tr *Chinese Economic Studies*, 1981-82 (15) pp 45-7.

9    Zhou Zhengdu, op cit. Xiong Yi, op cit.

10   Yang Zuichen & Zheng Lizhi, 'Looking at the 2-3 system from the point of view of a survey of agricultural production costs and of the records of food grain distribution', *Guangming Daily*, tr *Chinese Economic Studies*, 1981-82 (15) pp 107-12.

11   Mu Jiajun *et al*, op cit.

12   Wujin county agricultural bureau, 'Looking at the 2-3 system from the production practice in our county', *Guangming Daily*, 31.3.1979 tr *Chinese Economic Studies*, 1981-82 (15) pp 77-81.

13   Wang Yongnian, 'The 2-3 system made peasants lose out', *Guangming Daily*, tr *Chinese Economic Studies*, 1981-82 (15) pp 99-101.

14   She Zhixiang, op cit.

15   *Red Flag*, 'Agricultural surveys in Jiangsu', 19.5.1980 tr JPRS/CR/RF No 10, pp 26-39.

16   Xiong Yi, op cit.

17   Huang Pinfu, 'Further discussions on viewpoints and suggestions on the southern Jiangsu cropping system', *People's Daily*, 15.3.1979 tr *Chinese Economic Studies*, 1981-82 (15) pp 64-71. Li Erhuang, 'Can't Suzhou prefecture's 2-3 system increase yield?', *Guangming Daily*, 20.6.1979 tr *Chinese Economic Studies*, 1981-82 (15) pp 93-8. Liu Sanhao & Wang Zaide, 'Decisions should be taken on the mainstream reforms in the cropping systems', *People's Daily*, 9.4.1979 tr *Chinese Economic Studies*, 1981-82 (15) pp 82-9.

18   Huang Pinfu, op cit.

19   Li Erhuang, op cit. Huang Pinfu, op cit.

20 Lu Shijian, 'In reforming the cropping system we must seek truth from facts', *Guangming Daily*, 11.9.1979 tr *Chinese Economic Studies*, 1981-82 (15) pp 105-6.

21 Li Erhuang, op cit.

22 Zhang Zhizheng, 'Farm production a matter of balance', *China Daily*, 23.5.1983, p 4.

23 *People's Daily*, 'Follow the path of "In agriculture learn from Dazhai" and advance in great strides', 17.9.1975, p 2.

24 Sun Ming, Zhu Gang, Kang Jian, Mei Xingbao, Bu Xinmen, Mu Fuxiang, Zhou Baosheng & Jie Hung, 'New questions which have cropped up in grain production in Suzhou prefecture', *Red Flag*, 1.8.1982 tr JPRS/CR/RF No 11, pp 50-7.

25 *Xinhua*, 'East China province develops local industry for agriculture', 12.2.1971 in SCMP 1971 (08) pp 66-7.

26 Shen Shisheng & Li Zhichang, 'Nansha commune organises over 3000 surplus labourers', *Xinhua Ribao*, 18.5.1983, p 2.

27 Hua Huiyi, Zhao Ming & Yuan Yanghe, 'This road must be followed - an investigation into the integrated development of agriculture, sideline production and industry in Wuxi county, Jiangsu province', *People's Daily*, 3.11.1978, p 2.

28 *Xinhua*, 'Wuxi county betters peasants' livelihood', 11.8.1978 in FBIS/DR/PRC 15.8.1978, E22-24.

29 Guo Zujin (a), 'Wuxi city management committee adopts measures to help commune- and brigade-run industrial enterprises', *Xinhua Ribao*, 13.5.1983, p 1. Guo Zujin (b), 'Industrial production in Wuxi's three city-administered counties has striking results', *Xinhua Ribao*, 13.5.1983, p 1. Bi Ruizhen, Jan Yongxi & Guo Zujin, 'Wuxi county becomes aware of the benefits of the new system of city administered counties', *Xinhua Ribao*, 7.4.1983, p 1.

30 Zhan Wu, op cit.

31 Bi Ruizhen *et al*, op cit.

32 Pan Shui & Zou Rongkun, 'Suzhou city suburban counties commune- and brigade-run enterprises practise all-round responsibility systems', *Xinhua Ribao*, 2.4.1983, p 2.

33 Sun Ming *et al*, op cit.

34 Shan Shumu *et al*, op cit. Sun Ming *et al*, op cit.

35 Wu Jiaming, Huang Canjiang & Zhu Lianghe, 'Chuangshu county gross industrial and agricultural output value increases by 95% in 4 years', *Xinhua Ribao*, 9.1.1983, p 1.

36 Hua Huiyi *et al*, op cit.

37 *Red Flag*, 'An important position in building rural spiritual civilisation - investigation of the rural market cultural centres set up in Shazhou county, Jiangsu province', 16.11.1983 tr JPRS/CR/RF No 22, pp 52-8.

38 She Zhixiang, op cit.

39  Chen Sheng, Shen Gengyuan & Ni Qianjian, 'Taicang county's diversified economy vigorously develops', *Xinhua Ribao*, 6.4.1983, p 2.

40  Shi Kaixi (a), 'An aquatic farming village emerges in East Taihu', *Xinhua Ribao*, 15.6.1983, p 2.  Shi Kaixi (b), 'Concerning the results of a unit investigating into techniques', *Xinhua Ribao*, 15.6.1983, p 2.

41  She Zhixiang, op cit.

42  Ibid.

43  Zhao Ming, 'Jiangsu province's commune- and brigade-run industrial enterprises output value in 36 counties and cities in 1982 exceeds 100 million *yuan*', *Xinhua Ribao*, 1.4.1983, p 1.

44  Kunshan county committee administrative office, 'Kunshan county commune members average per capita income reaches 400 *yuan*, in 1982', *Xinhua Ribao*, 25.1.1983, p 2.

45  Sun Ming *et al*, op cit.

46  Zhang Shucheng & Zhang Zhenghai, 'Bachang commune party committee stresses aiding grain contracting households', *Xinhua Ribao*, 9.6.1983, p 1.

47  Lin Zili (b), op cit.

48  Zhou Qiren & Du Ying, 'Specialised households: a preliminary study', *Social Sciences in China*, 1984 (3) pp 50-72.

49  Gu Hong, Yuan Siyi & Li Zhicheng, 'Taicang county communes establish service factories for the diversified economy', *Xinhua Ribao*, 18.2.1983, p 1.

50  Wang Liang (b), 'Wujiang county implements locally-run assistance plans', *Xinhua Ribao*, 9.5.1983, p 2.  Wang Liang (c), 'Dongshan commune's self-investment to construct a mountain road', *Xinhua Ribao*, 9.5.1983, p 2.

51  Ye Yuchang, 'Wuxi county sponsors a paddy-rice factory to train a rice-seedling cultivation team', *Xinhua Ribao*, 29.3.1983, p 1.  Lu Nianzu, 'Jiangyin county peasant education enterprises vigorously develop', *Xinhua Ribao*, 13.4.1983, p 4.

52  Zheng Zonghan, 'On small towns', *Social Sciences in China*, 1983 (4) pp 164-90.

53  Wu Xiang (b), op cit.

# Chapter Six

# Xuhuai: Rural Development in an Intermediate Area

## Introduction

Xuhuai agricultural district lies in the extreme south of the North China plain. Its physical and economic characteristics are synonymous with those of the North China plain and traditionally it has suffered from the high-output-poor trap (that is, relatively high agricultural output, usually of grain, but with a low agricultural output value) as well as containing significant pockets of poor, low-output units. It is considered by the state to be an intermediate area in terms of its development, especially in comparison to its more prosperous rural neighbours to the south.[1] This contrast is quite striking.

Even so, since 1949 Xuhuai has made exceptional progress by the standards of the North China plain to a position of comparative well-being. The main concern of this chapter is to examine how Xuhuai has been able to make such progress, and to assess how possible it might be for Xuhuai to leave the ranks of intermediate areas to join those regions which are considered well-developed.

## Xuhuai: the setting

Xuhuai agricultural district is the most northern agricultural district in Jiangsu (see figure 6). It broadly encompasses the warm temperate zone of deciduous and broadleaf forest with brown earths identified in Chapter Five.[2] Xuhuai is the largest and most important of Jiangsu's agricultural districts in a number of respects: gross area, rural population and cultivable land. In each of the above categories Xuhuai has about one-third of Jiangsu's total resources.

The physical characteristics of Xuhuai however, while considered favourable in comparison to much of China, are certainly inferior to other agricultural districts of Jiangsu, especially those of Yanjiang, Zhenyang and Taihu. Mean temperatures for example, differ by as much as 4.5 degrees C across the province. Accumulated temperature values show similar variation. The frost-free period in Xuhuai is between 185 and 200 days. This compares to 230 to 240 days in the south of the province.[3] Such differences in frost-free periods have a significant impact upon cropping systems.

Rainfall becomes more abundant in the south of the province. Finally, the soils of Southern Jiangsu are considered to be more fertile than those of the north, the organic content of the yellow-brown and yellow earths of Central and Southern Jiangsu reach 3.7%. In contrast the organic content of the yellow earths which predominate in Xuhuai reaches only 1%.[4] Variations in production conditions are apparent in details of the multi-cropping indices of

122

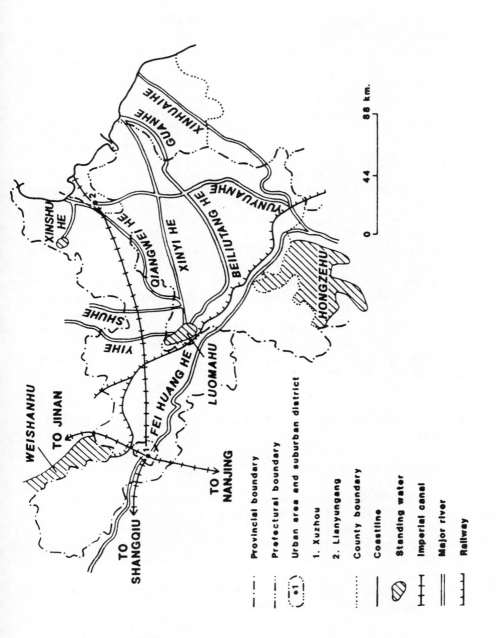

**Figure 8  Xuhuai agricultural district: major rivers; railways; and still water**

Jiangsu's various agricultural districts given above, and underline that the northern districts, in particular Xuhuai, are areas of inferior agricultural productivity compared with those of Southern Jiangsu.

Xuhuai does possess abundant water resources (see Figure 8) but the low-lying nature of the land - mostly below 50 metres above sea level - makes it liable to both flooding and waterlogging. Clearly, these variations in production conditions will do much to limit Xuhuai's economic potential in comparison to its more prosperous southern neighbours.

The distinction between Xuhuai and areas of Southern Jiangsu is reinforced from observations concerning the economic structure of the rural economies of the various districts. In particular, Xuhuai receives a relatively small contribution from sideline production to the gross agricultural output value in comparison to that of other districts. Capital accumulation from such sideline production remains markedly easier than from farming, and sideline production in Yanjiang and Taihu for example, is of crucial importance in any explanation of their relative wealth.

In human terms Xuhuai, like all of Jiangsu's agricultural districts, is not an administrative unit. Within Xuhuai are the two large urban areas (and their suburban districts) of Xuzhou and Lianyungang. Aside from these two urban centres, the district includes counties from Xuzhou, Huaiyin and Yancheng prefectures. In all there are 19 counties within Xuhuai: eight of Xuzhou prefecture - Suining, Feng, Pei, Pi, Xinyi, Donghai, Ganyu and Tongshan; nine from Huaiyin prefecture - Shuyang, Guanyun, Guannan, Huaiyin, Lianshui, Siyang, Sihong, Suqian and Huaian; and two from Yancheng prefecture - Xiangshui and Binhai (see Figure 9).

## Grain production - Xuhuai's emergence as a commodity grain producer

### Past improvements in grain production

> Take the Xuhuai agricultural area as an example. All throughout history, drought, flood and waterlogging, saline soil, low yield and many disasters were regarded as its special characteristics. The surface area of low yield soil occupied above 45% of all cultivable land, the level of fertiliser application was low, and cultivation was extensive.[5]
>
> A big rain brings a big disaster, a small rain a small disaster, and a scarcity of rain no less serious a disaster.[6]

Until the early-1970s, Xuhuai's characteristics - as outlined in the quotes above - allowed at best a cropping system of three crops in two years with priority given to corn, Chinese sorghum, sweet potato, soya bean and wheat crops. Grain

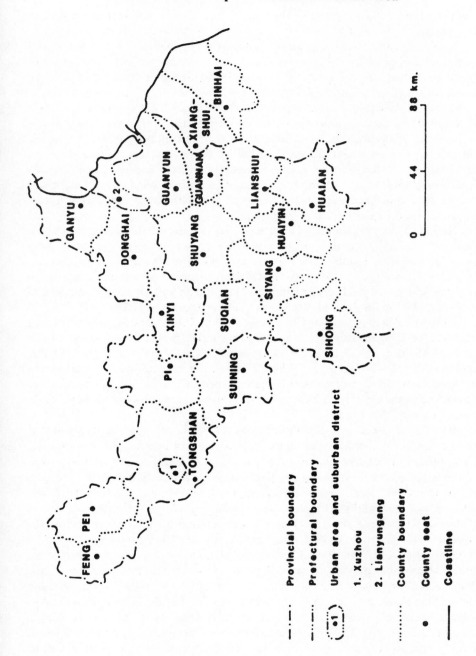

**Figure 9  Xuhuai agricultural district: counties and county seats**

yields remained low - typically 200 *jin/mu* - and the area had to rely upon state relief grain.

More recently however, grain production in Xuhuai has experienced profound changes. In 1972 for example, it was reported that the peasants had been organised to improve their agricultural resource base through the construction of farmland and water conservation projects. In this way, high-yield and stable-yield farmland had been established.[7] This improvement was a result of the mass mobilisation of labour, portrayed by the Maoist press as the solution to China's agricultural difficulties: the rural masses transforming the physical landscape under the exhortation of Chairman Mao. Alongside the mobilisation of labour, the Chinese media reported important changes in agricultural production and methods. Irrigation and drainage improvement was emphasised; mechanisation of agricultural production was encouraged; and improved seed strains were being developed.[8]

Numerous local examples of improvements in grain production as a result of changed production conditions and methods were to be found, including Dafei brigade, Lianshui county;[9] Suqian county;[10] Guanyun county;[11] and Dinglou brigade, Pi county.[12] Progress in Dinglou brigade for example, appeared striking, with grain yields rising from less than 100 *jin/mu* before Liberation and only 187.5 *jin/mu* in the mid-1960s, to 1500 *jin/mu* in the mid-1970s.[13]

At a wider spatial level, while change in the 1970s is not as striking as that claimed for Dinglou brigade, it appears that much progress was made. Total grain production in Xuhuai in 1969 for example, was 6.2 billion *jin*. By 1979, this had reached 12.9 billion *jin*.[14] While it should not be doubted that part of the increase came from an extension of grain crops in that period, a considerable part of the gain appears to have taken the form of a most welcome increase in per-unit yields.[15]

By 1973, it is claimed that Xuhuai was self-sufficient in grain.[16] Since that time it has developed into a commodity grain base of considerable importance. In addition to these improvements in per-unit yield and total output, there were also marked alterations in crop composition and in production stability.

In the 1970s alone, some 5 million *mu* of previously dry-field land was brought under irrigation. Much of this derived from large-scale capital projects to harness the Huai river.[17] This not only caused an upsurge in paddy-rice production - so much so that rice became the most important grain crop in Xuhuai - but also made possible the popularisation of double-cropping in an area which had previously struggled to grow three crops in two years. Furthermore, agricultural capital construction, of which irrigation work was the main component, helped improve production stability. By 1979 up to a third of Xuhuai's cultivable land (c 8.3 million *mu*) was stable high-yield land.[18] Another source puts this figure at a half (12.5 million *mu*) of Xuhuai's cultivable land.[19] The discrepancy here might be attributed to a problem of definition as to what exactly stable high-yield land is; alternatively it may involve the question of what is planned as stable high-yield land and what is actually completed.

The contribution of the state to large-scale agricultural capital construction projects within Xuhuai has been considerable. Between 1950 and 1979 state investment of more than 1.68 billion *yuan* was given to Xuhuai for irrigation projects alone, of which at least 1.2 billion *yuan* was spent on harnessing the Huai river.[20]

This 1.68 billion *yuan* represented 46.4% of total state investment (3.62 billion *yuan*) in irrigation throughout the province, Xuhuai receiving state investment in irrigation of 67.2 *yuan/mu* in comparison with an average of 42.5 *yuan/mu* for the remainder of Jiangsu.

In addition, collective investment in irrigation and other forms of agricultural capital construction, the purchase of agricultural machinery and other facilities was perhaps equal to that made by the state. This was especially true for those units more distant from the major Huai river projects, where collective investment in irrigation and other capital construction projects was much more dependent on collective reserves. Whatever its source, this investment was rewarded by improved grain yields, higher output and greater production stability.

Improvement in grain production was not achieved without problems, in particular those associated with double-cropping - paralleling those difficulties experienced following the popularisation of triple-cropping in Taihu. However, these difficulties were apparently either resolved or of only minor importance.

By the end of the 1970s, grain production was sufficiently developed for Xuhuai planners to contemplate widespread development and diversification in the production of industrial crops, forest produce, animal products, fish and sideline goods.[21] The problem of inadequate basic food and clothing supplies was largely solved. Large-scale agricultural capital construction - often state-financed - was seen to have wrought an impressive change in the living conditions of Xuhuai's peasants.

Yet, insofar as state investment was very much tied to improvements in grain production (either explicitly or implicitly), Xuhuai for the most part had moved only from the low-output-poor to the high-output-poor trap. Demands by grain production on resources of land, labour and capital remained prohibitively high and discouraged the wider development which Xuhuai planners hoped for.

## Grain production in the current phase

Having briefly outlined the stage of development reached by Xuhuai at the start of the current phase, the question remains how Xuhuai might further develop its grain production so as to reduce still more the excessive demands upon land, labour and capital made by grain production. Such a reduction would free resources to exploit Xuhuai's wider economic potential. Four points need to be considered: first, the need for further improvement in the quality of land resources to facilitate increases in per-unit yields; secondly, a need to increase mechanisation in grain production to reduce both seasonal labour shortages and the risks associated with tight planting schedules; thirdly, the desirability of appropriate measures to maintain enthusiasm for grain production - especially in commodity grain areas - given low state prices for contract grain production; and finally, the need to raise the scientific level of grain production.

Straight away, it must be said that these points are little removed from those development policies espoused during the 1970s and before that in the 1960s.[22] Xuhuai remains an increasingly important source of commodity grain for the state and although much improvement has been noted in Xuhuai's natural resource base since liberation there is still much work to be done. Basic improvements remain imperative. The average per unit grain yield of 850 *jin/mu* for Xuzhou prefecture in 1982 if taken as a proxy for Xuhuai is still below the provincial average. A provincial figure of 596 *jin/mu*/crop gives a provincial average grain yield of over 1000 *jin/mu*. Furthermore, the per-unit yield of 5 million *mu* of grain fields in Xuzhou prefecture for example, remains only 400 *jin/mu*.[23]

An illustration at a local level of the improvements in grain output and income that can be made by significant capital investment in the resource base is found in materials for the number nine production team, Chenlaozhuang brigade, Gupi commune, Suining county.[24] This team has 51 households and 234 people with a total of 537 *mu* of cultivable land (2.29 *mu* of cultivable land per head). Until recently, the team was backward with fields flooded and waterlogged nine years out of ten. However, between 1978 and 1980, peasants in the team constructed irrigation ditches to completely protect the cultivable land from flooding and waterlogging and created 350 *mu* of paddy fields. Enthusiasm for production was also stimulated by the introduction of *baogan daohu* and grain production and incomes showed remarkable improvement. Between 1977 and 1982 grain output in this brigade increased almost 400%, principally through an increase in per-unit grain yields from a little over 300 *jin/mu* to almost 1200 *jin/mu*. Grain sales to the state rose dramatically. The commodity rate for grain rose from a little under 5% to almost 50%. Incomes showed a similar increase.[25] Clearly, in this production team significant results are reported - although nothing is said about increases in production costs which would be expected alongside more intensive grain production.

Mechanisation is also of great potential importance to grain production in Xuhuai. The availability of agricultural machinery can increase work efficiency, reduce agricultural costs and improve economic benefits.[26] In Shihuang brigade, Duqiao commune, Huaian county for example, the average expenditure for ploughing and harrowing one *mu* of cultivable land with an ox was calculated at 12 *yuan/mu*. In contrast, similar work with a 12 hp tractor cost only 1.2 *yuan/mu*. Additionally, such 12 hp hand-held (walking) tractors can be put to a variety of other uses including threshing, pumping and transportation.[27]

However, a closer inspection of the materials is revealing. While the oxen costs are well detailed the costs expended by the 12 hp tractors are not. No mention is given of purchase prices or running costs - fuel, lubrication, maintenance and so forth. Thus, the conclusions contain serious reservations, perhaps representing vested interests (political or otherwise) in increasing the extent of mechanisation.

Nevertheless, the utilisation of agricultural machinery in grain production does much to reduce the hazards of the tight planting schedules associated with double- and triple-cropping. In Huaiyin prefecture, before the mechanisation of grain production, summer harvesting and planting commonly took 45 days. After mechanisation this work could be done in only 27 days. Thus, peasants who had seen yields fall as a result of not being able to complete all the work to be done in the busy harvesting and planting season, were now able to reap bumper harvests from their responsibility fields.[28]

However, although in 1981 alone over 20 million *yuan* was spent on agricultural machinery within Huaiyin prefecture, the level of agricultural mechanisation in Xuhuai remains relatively low.[29] There is still a real need to increase the scale of agricultural mechanisation.

Concern is also expressed about the price-scissors which continues to exist between agricultural and industrial goods and also the price difference between grain and other agricultural produce. The problem remains of how to promote enthusiasm for grain production.

The introduction of production responsibility systems, in particular *baogan daohu* into the Xuhuai countryside is said to have done much to increase peasant enthusiasm, both for grain production and production in general. The introduction of *baogan daohu* within agriculture in Suining and Suqian counties in 1981, for example, is said to have been an important turning-point in the development of grain production in these two counties.[30]

In the 1970s, grain production in Suqian increased significantly from 280 million *jin* in 1969 to 680 million *jin* in 1974. Such an increase is attributed to the extensive agricultural projects in Suqian during that period, some 649,500 *mu* (65.6%) of cultivable land developed as stable high-yield land.[31] Given this base, the development shown above by Suqian county appears to be quite straightforward - increased incentive for production giving rise to increased output alongside continuing improvement in production techniques.[32]

Alternatively Suining, traditionally a backward county, had little of the advantageous production conditions available to producers in Suqian. However, after introducing *baogan daohu*, not only was enthusiasm for production aroused but it is claimed that the potential benefits of production under *baogan daohu* encouraged peasants within the county to undertake large-scale agricultural construction projects, in particular widespread irrigation of cultivable land.[33] Grain production was transformed. However, nothing is said about how such projects were financed.

Claims concerning the ability of *baogan daohu* to motivate peasants in Xuhuai to increase grain production are numerous.[34] But such claims often ignore, or at least understate, the importance of the agricultural resource base in determining the extent of grain production. *Baogan daohu* has increased peasant enthusiasm for grain production, but it cannot be thought that in the long-term, improvements in the resource base can be ignored. Real increases in agricultural output have been achieved. But at the same time, maintaining these increases and furthering rural production will require more than just management change; they demand real investments.

What of grain specialisation? Are units in Xuhuai able to offer the subsidies and incentives necessary for specialisation in grain production? The material for Xuhuai is sketchy on this point. Little is made of the recent upsurge of grain-producing specialised households. What reference is made to grain specialisation has only scant mention of subsidies for grain specialists.[35] Similarly, while there are numerous reports dealing with the establishment of commodity grain bases in Xuhuai - in Lianshui, Sihong, Shuyang, Donghai, Pi and Tongshan counties - again no mention is made of compensation to grain specialists.[36]

While the experience of grain specialists elsewhere in China, including Taihu, indicates the wide variety of incentives to promote specialised grain production and would suggest that some form of compensation must be in operation, in Xuhuai the lack of detail concerning compensation to grain specialists is probably a genuine reflection of the lack of specialisation within Xuhuai. If this is so, then production in Xuhuai's commodity grain bases must surely be restricted. Alternatively, in these commodity grain bases the state seems to maintain a greater degree of control than that exhibited in the Chinese countryside in general. Thus the state may prefer to keep subsidies hidden as it is inevitable that it cannot afford to maintain such subsidies at a national level.

This point may be linked to a final important element towards improved grain production in the current phase - increased use of scientific methods on the land.[37] Use of fine-seed strains, fertiliser, agricultural chemicals and so forth within a framework of rational management can have a significant impact upon per-unit grain yields. In Tongshan, Ganyu and Huaiyin counties for example, the popularisation of the rational application of ammonium carbonate fertiliser has in some instances increased agricultural production by 10 to 20%.[38]

The more recent policy emphasis upon intensive grain production replaces Maoist policy in Xuhuai which promoted - intentionally or otherwise - extensive grain cultivation (that is, increasing output through an increase in the area sown with grain crops) without necessarily improving per-unit yields. Intensification of grain production requires both the application of improved agricultural techniques and a trend towards more advanced agricultural production systems.

Initially at least, agricultural technicians in Xuhuai were reluctant to become involved in the promotion of advanced agricultural techniques within the grain economy. In Binhai county for instance, three fears were common among technical personnel: first, the fear of being made responsible for production losses; secondly, the fear that their skills were not up to standard; and thirdly, that the peasants for whom they were working would conceal the facts about output which would detrimentally influence technician incomes.[39] In response the Binhai county authorities implemented detailed responsibility systems among agricultural technicians to solve these problems. However, little detail is given and no comment is made on progress, if any.

This experience in Binhai notwithstanding, other counties in Xuhuai report considerable success in attempts to popularise advanced scientific techniques in agriculture. Materials for Suqian county note the use of fine-seed strains. The seeds are developed by brigade technicians and then supplied to the teams who cultivate seedlings. The seedlings are then distributed to individual households. This system has developed rapidly. In 1981, 16,500 *mu* of cultivable land in Suqian was planted with fine-seed strains; by 1984 this figure had reached 350,000 *mu*. Per-unit yields increased by 200 *jin/mu* on average.[40]

Similar improvements are noted for Panzhuang brigade, Machang commune, Shuyang county.[41] One peasant, Wu Zhendong, was responsible for introducing advanced agricultural techniques to 200 *mu* of paddy-rice fields in the spring of 1982. The results were impressive enough (a doubling of per-unit yields and total grain output[42]) to encourage the brigade to extend such techniques to the remainder of its responsibility land, with the expectation of substantial improvements in grain output.

However, the success of Panzhuang brigade in increasing grain production also raises some interesting questions. It must be asked whether the doubling of grain yields can be readily maintained. It would be expected that to maintain such a high level of per-unit yield inputs should increase and production costs rise. Many units have discovered that production costs increase at a quicker pace than income generated from increased output. This may well be so here.

Furthermore, it is difficult to understand why the brigade would want to continue concentrating its efforts on grain production. One explanation might be that the state is increasing its grain contracts with the brigade. Alternatively, grain production might be subsidised to some extent, or the brigade has opportunities to sell the grain privately to local industry (for use in brewing for example) at much higher prices. The success of Panzhuang brigade has encouraged neighbouring units - Yuelai, Yinping, Huidong communes among others - to develop similar seed-strains in order to improve their own yields.

Another example of this recent upsurge in the use of advanced agricultural techniques is given for Chenyan brigade, Zhanggou commune, Binhai county.[43] In this brigade, a peasant - Guo Zhengqiu - observed that many paddy-rice and wheat fields were overgrown with weeds and afflicted by insects. Upon enquiry, he discovered that many individual farmers did not know how to use pesticides correctly, and that fees charged for pesticide application were prohibitively high. In 1982, after purchasing agricultural chemicals and spray equipment, he signed contracts with 75 individual households to rid 20 *mu* of wheat fields of weeds and to clear 205 *mu* of paddy of insects. Upon completion of this work, yields in these 235 *mu* increased on average by 30%. This is not an isolated case.[44]

Reservations remain, however, about this kind of personal adventurism into advanced agricultural methods. For all the examples of success given above, instances of failure must also be found in the Xuhuai countryside. Failure of this kind, seldom reported, can be disastrous both for the individual who has to bear the financial losses and also for the producer who may lose his crop.

While the adoption of advanced agricultural techniques has obvious benefits, there is still much work to be done. Xuhuai lacks qualified agricultural scientific and technical personnel - a situation true for Jiangsu and China as a whole.[45] The adoption of advanced agricultural techniques, as well as higher levels of mechanisation within agriculture and effective agricultural capital construction, all require adequate levels of skill and experience among the peasants. The detrimental impact of the Cultural Revolution on education and science and technology remains a stumbling-block to development in the current phase. The state must urgently seek to improve skill levels and encourage the experience which does exist within the Chinese peasantry.

It can be seen that Xuhuai's attempts to adopt a development strategy which includes more large-scale agricultural capital construction, more agricultural mechanisation, greater incentives for specialist grain producers, and higher levels of agricultural scientific techniques is likely to lead to increased grain production thereby facilitating all-round development in the rural economy. However, each element of such a strategy has difficulties. The biggest obstacle, common to each element, is the availability of sufficient capital funds to finance the strategy and the means of production with which to implement it.

## Financing Xuhuai's development strategy: the role of the state

Xuhuai, unlike many areas in China, has been fortunate to benefit from considerable state investment in its natural resource base since liberation. However, Xuhuai can no longer rely on state finance for the widespread development which is still needed. The state has made clear that Xuhuai must depend on its own efforts to promote future farmland capital construction.[46] The only areas where the state will continue to invest for sure are the six commodity grain bases of Lianshui, Sihong, Shuyang, Donghai, Pi and Tongshan, evidence of continuing state commitment to grain production.[47]

In these areas, construction projects jointly financed by state and local authorities, are focused on improvement of present irrigation and drainage facilities, breeding of fine crop strains, popularisation of advanced agricultural techniques and other undertakings directly connected with grain production.[48]

Such state-local investment will be carried out under a series of joint state-local investment agreements whereby, between 1985 and 1990, the commodity grain bases annually deliver five *jin* of grain to the state for each *yuan* of state investment, in addition to normal grain delivery contracts.[49]

To circumvent previous difficulties when state investment did not result in increases in commodity grain supplies, these agreements purport to clarify responsibilities, powers and rights of both parties. They allegedly guarantee that special state funds for building projects in connection with the popularisation of agricultural techniques and superior seed strains and for building small farmland water conservation projects will be utilised only in that way. That is, they are specifically designated for grain production.[50]

Donghai county, one of the six commodity grain production bases in Xuhuai, was considered up to 1970 to be a backward county. Donghai is located in the extreme north of Xuhuai. To the west of the county are undulating, elevated and hilly areas constantly suffering from drought while to the east are low-lying alkaline beaches, the confluence of numerous streams and more often than not under floodwater. Throughout history grain output was both low and unstable. Over 600,000 *mu* of cultivable land in the county was considered to be of very poor quality, yielding less than 100 *jin/mu* of grain crops.[51]

In 1970 the county authorities decided to initiate a series of basic agricultural construction projects within Donghai. They reasoned that Donghai was endowed with a relatively large number of streams and had an annual precipitation of over 900 mm. Control of these water resources was crucial and accordingly, irrigation works were coordinated in order to combat floods, a longstanding difficulty in the region.[52]

This 'coordination' involved the construction of 250 km of canals; 100 km of drainage ditches; drainage and irrigation stations; the terracing of 70,000 *mu* of fields; the conversion of 400,000 *mu* of previously dry fields to paddy; large-, medium- and small-scale projects involving the moving of over 70 million cubic metres of earth and stone; sinking 4400 wells; and increasing the levels of agricultural mechanisation by 170,000 hp.[53] Though no figures are given, grain production in 1971 and 1972 was said to have increased by the equivalent to the total increase achieved in the preceding two decades.

Certainly by 1973 Donghai county was considered a 'granary'. Throughout the 1970s and especially since the 1978 reforms in agriculture the county has continued to make remarkable strides in grain production, grain output rising from 0.7 billion *jin* in 1978 to 1.29 billion *jin* in 1982 (with a 38.8% commodity rate).[54] By 1983, Donghai was one of 22 counties throughout China which supplied the state with over 500 million *jin* of commodity grain.[55]

In order to further grain production and to consolidate its status as a commodity grain base, considerable investment - from both local and state sources - is taking place in Donghai. In the first half of 1983 for example, 2.36 million *yuan* was spent to establish and popularise advanced agricultural techniques, in particular the adoption of fine-seed strains in wheat, maize, rice, soya bean and sweet potato production.[56]

Additionally, while the irrigation and drainage system in Donghai was extensively developed in the 1970s, a further 5.9 million *yuan* is needed to complete this system. Between 1983 and 1986 the county aimed to improve a million *mu* of cultivable land through a series of capital investments including irrigation projects (bridges, culverts, floodgates, electrically-powered pumping stations). These projects aimed to make available 280,000 *mu* of newly-irrigated land, draining a further 160,000 *mu*, in addition to improvements to 330,000 *mu* of existing irrigated land and 300,000 *mu* of existing drained land.[57]

With state and local investment, Donghai should be able to further improve grain production if the implementation of fine-seed strains is as successful as it has been seen to be in other areas, if the irrigation and drainage system being completed fulfils expectations in terms of the improvement in cultivable land resources, and if the incomes of the peasants involved in grain production are high enough to maintain enthusiasm for production (which must involve some degree of subsidy either of production inputs or directly of income).

Three points however, need to be made concerning state investment in Donghai. First, it is the improvement of grain production which is the main concern here. There is little doubt that state investment would not have been forthcoming had Donghai not been a commodity grain base and established as a 'granary'. Secondly, the element of risk involved in the investment which is taking place within Donghai was minimal given the productive conditions established in the 1970s. Finally, the state investment in Donghai was not only specific (for grain production improvements) but also localised. It is to be doubted if any wider spatial impact is felt outside Donghai. (Although the state will no doubt argue that in the long-term, a stable supply of commodity grain from counties such as Donghai, reduces the need for other areas to concentrate so heavily on grain production).

Elements of the grain production development strategy outlined earlier are clearly visible in Donghai county. The strategy is obviously workable. However, it is equally clear that away from the few favoured commodity grain bases such a strategy - either in part or as a whole - will not be possible unless local units can accumulate the necessary capital to finance investment in the agricultural resource base, production techniques, and most importantly to subsidise grain production. State finance for such areas will not be forthcoming.

Indeed, unless finance from whatever source is available to subsidise local grain producers, in the short-term Xuhuai may well be able to expand grain production and become an important commodity grain area, but it will remain in the high-output-poor trap. If peasant incomes remain low, eventually enthusiasm for grain production will suffer and the amount of commodity grain supplied to the state by Xuhuai must consequently fall. It is far from certain that Xuhuai will be able to solve this problem. But what is certain, is that for the most part, this problem must be solved by the localities themselves, independent of state help. For Xuhuai to break free of high-output-poor conditions, investment funds must be generated locally through the development of local industry and the diversified economy.

## Local finance: *rural industry*

The Xuhuai authorities do not have to look far to find a model of rural industrial development serving as the source of accumulation funds to support agriculture. Taihu agricultural district, Southern Jiangsu is a perfect example, with Wuxi county in particular being a model of rural industrialisation.

Before 1978, the contribution of small-scale rural industrial enterprises to the gross agricultural output value of Xuhuai was small. Inevitably any development financed by the accumulation of investment capital from the profits of such industrial enterprises would be limited and localised. Much of Xuhuai would be unaffected.

However, there are indications in the materials that rural industrial enterprises within Xuhuai have shown some degree of development in the current phase. In Ganyu county for example, there has been a sharp rise in commune- and brigade-run industrial enterprises in recent years; rising from 34 in 1976 to 1962 in 1980. Profits generated by these enterprises amounted to 14.6 million *yuan*.[58]

This sharp rise in the number of rural industrial enterprises reflects a change in thinking towards commune- and brigade-run industrial enterprises in Ganyu. Initially the county authorities invested several tens of thousands of *yuan* to establish large factories - including a rock crystal factory, a welding electrodes factory and a chemical plant - in the belief that large factories would produce large returns. However, more often than not, techniques in these factories were not up to standard, quality was low and products were over-priced. Recognising these shortcomings, the county authorities changed the orientation of their policy, taking Wuxi as their model (so they argued), and more numerous and smaller-scale industrial enterprises were started. These smaller enterprises were able to benefit, so it was claimed, from low levels of investment, quick returns and good economic benefits. In 1980, the average return to capital in Ganyu's commune- and brigade-run industrial enterprises was 21.3%. This compares well with a provincial average of 16.38%.[59]

Three broad areas of rural industrial activity can be identified as dominant in Xuhuai: the extraction industry; the construction industry; and the agricultural produce processing industry. Small-scale coal mining is well established in Xuhuai and has played an important role in local economies for some years.[60] In Xuzhou prefecture for example, there are 28 coal mines run by communes and brigades annually producing 7 million tons of coal, which might reasonably be expected to raise 20 million *yuan* for collective investment funds.[61]

Locally-mined coal not only provides fuel for domestic and industrial use, it is said to stimulate the expansion of small-scale plants producing chemical fertiliser, coke, iron and steel, farm machinery and bricks. Other materials including stone, sand, and limestone are all extracted locally - providing the basic raw materials for the construction industry.

The development of the construction industry is also important. In the current phase, this development reflects the fact that basic foodstuffs and clothing requirements seem to be assured and some level of prosperity is being reached. In Xuhuai, there has been a visible change in peasant priorities from 'first food, second clothing, third other household expenditure and fourth home improvements' to 'first home improvements, second clothing, third other household expenditures and fourth food'. Increasingly, peasants, dissatisfied with their old, cramped, poor-quality, grass-covered houses, are becoming more able to finance the construction of new, spacious, better-quality houses.

In Ganyu county for example, between 1978 and 1982, it is claimed that 195,000 new rooms have been built by the construction industry, almost one new room for every four people in Ganyu. Undoubtedly the extent of building should mean that collective units in Ganyu at least, are able to accumulate some amount of capital accumulation funds from the profits of construction undertakings. Two other points are also of interest. First, and most significantly, peasant investment in housing is almost certain to take up a substantial part of any disposable income thereby restricting available funds for the expansion of production.

Secondly, in some areas there is concern over the illegal accumulation and indiscriminate seizure of previously cultivated land to build new houses. This kind of illegal action has involved both rural cadres and ordinary peasants.[62] Given the amount of new building claimed in Ganyu alone - which may or may not be a reflection of Xuhuai as a whole - the problem could be quite significant.

The development of the agricultural produce processing industry in Xuhuai is also of great significance. Again, in Ganyu county, since 1978 30 small enterprises, including wine producers, noodle and starch processing factories have been established. Such enterprises not only helped satisfy local demand for wine, dried starch and noodles, but they also generated sales in Zhejiang, Anhui, Shandong, Henan and Hebei. Zhudu commune in Ganyu for example, established a wine and noodle processing workshop. Output was of a high quality and costs were low. Output value in 1980 was 470,000 *yuan* with net profits of 80,000 *yuan*. Furthermore, the by-products of many of the agricultural produce processing undertakings can serve as fodder for pigs thereby facilitating extensive pig-breeding.[63]

Similarly, in Haian county the milling industry has been developed to facilitate the expansion of animal husbandry. As a result of this development in milling, livestock fodder costs have been reduced thereby encouraging a rapid expansion in animal husbandry. The milling industry can thus increase the value of grain production and provide incomes higher than would be expected if grain production was simply sold to the state at above-contract prices.[64]

Thus, some development of Xuhuai's rural industrial undertakings has taken place in the current phase. Nevertheless, reservations remain. First, the scale of Xuhuai's rural industry is limited, both in numerical terms and volume of accumulation funds generated. Certainly in comparison to that exhibited by the more illustrious units of Southern Jiangsu, Xuhuai's rural industry - and the agricultural developments such industry can promote - remains very much second-best. Secondly, the materials available on rural industrial enterprises in Xuhuai are largely drawn from certain localities, in particular Ganyu county in the east of Xuhuai bordering Lianyungang. This may indicate that Xuhuai's rural industrial development remains, as yet, highly localised and thus can be expected at best to generate accumulation funds only for localised agricultural development and implies continuing polarisation of prosperity.

## Local finance: *the diversified economy*

Xuhuai has a potentially significant diversified resource base. Animal husbandry is well established; forestry reserves are substantial, accounting for a quarter of the provincial reserve; the coastal counties have ample potential for developing the fishing industry, Lianyungang being the major fish-port of Jiangsu; and a wide variety of cash crops can be cultivated including fruit, cotton, tobacco, and oil-bearing crops.[65]

In the years immediately prior to 1978 a variety of influences limited the exploitation of these diversified resources. These included the Maoist emphasis on grain, the view that diversification was a 'tail of capitalism' and something to curtail, and the paucity and inefficiency of commercial channels. Nevertheless, some units were able to develop the diversified economy significantly and raise collective accumulation funds in this way.

Dinglou brigade, Pi county was one such unit. In 1975, its developed diversified economy was reported as having made a significant contribution to collective accumulation funds which reached 500,000 *yuan*. With these funds 99 tractors and other farm machinery were purchased. Ploughing, threshing, transport and processing of agricultural produce were wholly or partially mechanised. Such mechanisation contributed both to the progress made by Dinglou's grain production and also to the all-round development of the brigade's rural economy.[66] In Dinglou brigade at least, the diversified economy has had an important role to play in rural economic development. Certainly the Xuhuai authorities can look to the experience of Dinglou brigade as a model for rural economic development in the current phase.

Examples of successful development in diversified undertakings are found throughout Xuhuai, for example, fish-breeding in Yuanji village, Huaiyin county.[67] Yuanji possesses 800 *mu* of fish ponds and 1250 *mu* of rivers upon which fish-breeding is being developed. Here, successful exploitation of resources has been achieved under the 'umbrella' of an aquatic produce company which has installed drainage equipment, prevented flooding in the area and developed facilities to breed fish-fry and improve survival rates. It provides individual households with nets, fishing boats and so forth. In return, under the terms of a contract, the peasants must hand over 10 *jin* of fish annually for every *mu* of water area contracted: 3 *jin* representing payment for 'management fees' and the other 7 *jin* contributing towards equipment purchase, installation, repair and management. Similar examples indicate development in forestry in Pi county;[68] and in Suqian county;[69] and also in livestock in Pei county.[70]

Presumably, if effectively and rationally exploited, the diversified resource base within Xuhuai could develop into a major source of capital investment funds, funds which would be used to further free Xuhuai from the traditional limitations of grain production. Indeed, if grain production is sufficiently developed, diversified undertakings themselves should be increased.

In Xuhuai, however, the difficulty remains of how to take advantage of the available diversified resources. The development of diversified undertakings requires initial investment capital, capital which is also needed to develop the agricultural resource base and so forth in order to further grain production. A conflict for capital resources is evident. Indeed, no doubt this conflict is exacerbated by rural industry's need for investment funds. In Xuhuai, however, the conflict is best illustrated in the materials concerning agricultural diversification.

From the materials it seems possible to distinguish three different types of rural diversified economies within Xuhuai: first, those areas which historically have been able to fulfil grain quotas with some ease and where the diversified economy is well-developed. Investment funds are more readily available. This would be expected in those areas peripheral to Xuzhou and Lianyungang, for instance the lowlands of Ganyu. The diversified resource base of Ganyu supports such cash crops as mushrooms, beans and tomatoes, asparagus, peppermint and mulberry plants. Pigs and rabbits also provide an important source of income, as does aquaculture.[71]

The second type of diversified economy is identified as those areas where, up to the present, attention has been focussed almost entirely upon grain production thereby restricting the investment funds available to the diversified economy and limiting the extent of diversification and all-round development. Much of Xuhuai would fall into this category.

The uplands in the north of Ganyu county, for example, in contrast with the lowlands, offer much less opportunity for diversified production. Though little more than 200 metres above sea level, diversification is limited to some orchards and tea-gardens, much less than that seen in the lowlands of the county.

The diversified economy of the Ganyu lowlands indicate high density populations, the availability of local markets (perhaps including Lianyungang), and surely an unusual degree of sophistication. The reverse is true for undertakings in the uplands. Income differences from such undertakings will also be found, with much more opportunity for high incomes in the lowlands.

The final type of diversified economy in Xuhuai is that found in the peripheral and backward areas where the agricultural resource base remains weak, grain production difficult and investment funds - if any - continue to concentrate upon improvements in grain production. Such areas remain within the low-output-poor trap.

It is the second type of diversified economy which dominates within Xuhuai. For most rural units grain production has improved but incomes remain low. The way out of the high-output-poor trap for such units rests with their ability to use the limited financial resources available to them to develop diversified undertakings sufficiently in order to generate accumulation funds. Such funds would then be used to reduce demands made by grain production upon land, labour and capital resources freeing them for further diversified or rural industrial development.

Yet, despite official optimism, examples of this kind of development are limited. One such example is Gangxi brigade, Gangshang commune, Pi county. This brigade, after years of relying upon the state for relief grain, had been able to improve grain production.[72] Incomes, however, remained low. The brigade had, it was reported, been able to accumulate 10,000 *yuan* - although no details were given as to how this was achieved. With this money, the brigade successfully developed poultry and cattle-breeding, although again, no figures were given to illustrate this success.

Similarly, there is the example of Xu Xiaotan, a peasant of Matou commune, Huaiyin county.[73] In 1981 Xu Xiaotan took out a bank loan of 310 *yuan* to develop goose-breeding. By the end of 1982 he had successfully repaid the loan and had an income of 2655 *yuan* (though it is not made clear whether this was gross or net). With this money he was reported to be further diversifying his undertakings to include pig-breeding.

Both of these examples are given to illustrate the kind of development which local commentators feel is both possible within Xuhuai and necessary for accelerated local economic development. However, it must be said that the materials, concentrating as they do on such small-scale individual examples, may be symptomatic of a lack of anything better to report. Furthermore, some comment must be made about the consequences of failure - something rarely reported in the media. Failure in either example offered above would give rise to a situation where future development of diversified undertakings would not only be hindered by a lack of available collective investment funds or bank credit, but also the consequences of rural indebtedness.

It is by no means certain that diversified undertakings in Xuhuai can be sufficiently developed to facilitate wider rural economic development. Some units may break free of the high-output-poor trap whilst others - the majority - will remain in it.

# Rural commerce

The commercial situation in Xuhuai will play a significant role in determining the depth of local economic vitality. The commercial system is not only the mechanism by which peasants sell produce, it also provides producer goods. In the development strategy outlined earlier for Xuhuai, availability of producer goods is obviously an important factor for future prosperity.

Xuhuai's commercial system suffered considerably under the Maoists. Indeed, as late as 1983, leftist influences continued to hinder commercial activity in several Xuhuai counties.[74] In addition to the officials who continue to block commercial reform, the Maoist legacy was perhaps most keenly felt in the absolute paucity of retail outlets and purchasing stations. These networks take time to reestablish. In Lianshui county, for example, the purchase of meat in townships was said to be 'very inconvenient' - a euphemism for rarely possible - because no retail outlets were to be found in the smaller production units.[75]

However, it is argued that the commercial channels are beginning to shake off the remnants of Maoist influence and become more efficient. In Xuzhou prefecture, for example, efforts have been made to increase the number of retail and purchasing outlets and personnel; to improve business skills and vocational training; to improve purchasing methods; and to improve distribution of goods to the countryside. However, no figures are given, suggesting that thus far, these measure have realised little concrete improvement.[76]

In Lianshui, the development of purchasing and marketing stations throughout the county - at various levels - is said to have done much to alleviate previous problems in buying and selling when official commercial channels were considered inaccessible. In all, 400 of these stations were said to exist in rural Lianshui in 1983 and their work was said to be excellent.[77] (This may represent approximately 13 stations per commune or a station in about 70% of all production brigades in the county.)

The emergence of individual commerce is also of potential importance in surmounting the blocks in the official commercial system which continue to exist. In Feng county alone for example, in 1982 and 1983, 2470 individual households established 1772 individually-managed retail outlets. In 1982, one such individually-managed retail outlet in Wangfuzhuang village was reported to have recorded sales of over 1 million *yuan*.[78]

However, two points emerge in the material from Feng county. First, these individually-managed retail outlets remain very much a complement to state- and collectively-run commerce and in this sense the effectiveness of official commercial channels in handling the increasing burdens being placed upon it remain of crucial importance. Secondly, the goods sold in individually-managed retail outlets appear to be mainly consumer goods - tobacco, wine, sugar, and salt - raising doubts about their ability to supply needed producer goods.

Similarly, Wangfuzhuang village illustrates a growing rural demand for consumer goods - no doubt in part a response to the lack of producer goods, but also reinforcing the argument that many peasants are concerned about taking advantage of increased incomes for short-term consumer gains rather than investing in their contracted resources to reap longer-term gains.

It would appear that official commercial channels are still unable to guarantee supplies of important producer goods. In Xuhuai supplies of synthetic fertiliser, diesel fuel, and small-scale walking tractors for example, all fell far short of actual demand, a sign both of commercial inefficiency and inadequate output.[79]

While it is reasonable to expect that progress is being made with the commercial system, this progress remains patchy and uneven. Access to urban markets is recognised as a marked advantage for local development.[80] Beyond these favoured areas, the progress that is reported has obvious limitations. Individual commerce for example, is said to be making a positive contribution, but, much of this contribution is limited physically by unmechanised transport (hand-pulled carts, horse and cart, and bicycle, for instance) and is thus restricted both by distance and cargo weight. This progress should not be ignored, but it does little to dispel conclusions already reached about development in Xuhuai: namely, that progress, remains for the moment at least, uneven and far from striking.

## Conclusions

An official report from Huaian county noted with some vigour, that Huaian county was a rural area with an intermediate level of development that was showing promising signs of 'speeding up' the development of its economy.[81] Huaian county, it stated, was a model for all those areas with a similar environment to follow. However, the experience of Xuhuai as a whole does not suggest a very optimistic interpretation of this 'speeding up'.

Development in Xuhuai remains patchy and uneven. To be sure some production units are experiencing real development in their economies but others remain backward. Another official statement concluded that some places are still very poor, particularly in the old liberated areas in the Northern Huai river area where a considerable number of communes and brigades do not really have any substantial resources and the peasants' living standard is still very low.[82] Certainly, the development exhibited by Xuhuai's rural economy continues to lag behind that of much of Southern Jiangsu.[83]

Localised development is possible and evident. The strategy of using collective accumulation funds, derived from the profits of rural industrial enterprises and diversified undertakings, to finance improvements in the agricultural resource base and fund local economic initiatives is sound. However, many production units in Xuhuai remain unable to adopt this strategy owing to the initial problems of establishing such enterprises and undertakings.

The ability of rural industry to support agricultural development has been well demonstrated in Southern Jiangsu. In Xuhuai, however, rural industry remains relatively weak; initial investment capital remains sparse; accessibility to established large-scale industry is limited, curtailing the possibility of 'putting-out' work - Southern Jiangsu after all includes the major manufacturing cities of Nanjing, Changzhou, Wuxi, Suzhou and Shanghai; and commercial difficulties are still present.

More might be expected of diversified undertakings - even if they generate far less profit than rural industry and are probably more administratively difficult to extract funds from. However, the development of such undertakings remains a problem: grain production still absorbs much land, labour and capital, thereby reducing the possible development of such undertakings; initial investment capital is difficult to find; no doubt some peasants continue to fear the return of a 'cutting-off the tails of capitalism' policy and resist calls to diversify production; and commercial problems still restrict the growth of the diversified economy.

Basic grain problems are said to have been solved through a gradual improvement in the last 15 years of the agricultural resource base and the application of advanced agricultural methods. Yet, for the most part the situation of low-output-poor has been replaced only by the high-output-poor trap. That is to say, grain production is now said to be relatively stable, basic needs are met, yet this does not mean that peasant income and living standards are greatly improved. Neither does this preclude the problems that many units continue to have in terms of their inability (because of a lack of land, labour and capital resources surplus to grain requirements) to diversify beyond grain farming.

Some units have been able - by virtue of longstanding relative wealth, successful investment of limited collective resources, superior location, and good use of bank loans - to step out of the high-output-poor trap. Through the accumulation of funds to promote intensive grain production thereby freeing resources for other production tasks, some units have been able to develop their economies in an 'all-round' way. As yet, however, most units still seem to be struggling to rid themselves of the restrictions of grain production, such restrictions being reinforced by the state's perception of Xuhuai as a potentially important source of commodity grain.

A further worrying aspect for development in Xuhuai is the lack of producer goods which has been reported. This could do much to limit enthusiasm for long-term economic development. If rural units accumulate investment funds but find themselves unable to buy the necessary production inputs, enthusiasm to develop production will inevitably wane. This lack of producer goods puts considerable pressure on the state not only to improve its commercial channels but also to increase output of such producer goods. This is something the state is only just beginning to focus its attention upon and something that will inescapably require considerable financial investment as well as managerial restructuring, and a much better commercial system whether public or private.

This however, is not a problem which should come as much of a surprise to the state. It has long espoused the use of advanced agricultural techniques and yet it seems unable to cope with the demand for the relevant producer goods now apparent in the Chinese countryside. Such a difficulty is symptomatic of two problems which continue to beset the Chinese economy. The first of these is the inefficiency of the Chinese bureaucracy. One set of departments outlines policy proposals but there is little coordination with other departments which have important roles to fulfil in the execution of such policies. Thus, while rural demand has been considerably stimulated in the current phase, producer goods remain in short-supply and difficult to purchase in the countryside.

The second problem is the short-term outlook which seems to dominate both official and unofficial economic thinking. Emphasis is continually given to the short-term restructuring of rural production management forms while only lip-service seems to be paid to the real and long-established problems which areas such as Xuhuai and the Chinese countryside as a whole face: soil erosion, insufficient water conservation measures, diminution of soil quality and so forth. The state cannot avoid these problems for much longer - although it must be open to question whether the Chinese bureaucracy can be sufficiently motivated and reformed to tackle them.

It comes as little surprise to discover that many peasants prefer to concentrate on building new homes and (where possible) buying consumer goods - bicycles, televisions, watches and so forth - rather than using any personal finances to develop agricultural production. Given previous instability in rural policy, the attractiveness of short-term consumer gains outweighs the rationale of long-term investments in agricultural production. To facilitate more personal investment, the state is attempting to create an atmosphere of stability in the countryside through decisions such as those allowing long-term contracts, and the passing of contracts from one generation to the next.

Yet, it remains to be seen whether such attempts will encourage peasants to invest in the land or simply to continue to translate what small gains they have been able to make in recent years into consumer goods.

In Xuhuai, conflicts between long-term and short-term interests, between grain and other sectors of the rural economy remain to the fore. While there is certainly a way out of the high-output-poor trap for rural units in Xuhuai, at present progress remains uneven. Skill and experience continue to be in short supply. The potential for economic development is certainly present, it has yet to be fulfilled.

# Notes to Chapter Six

1   *People's Daily*, 'Jiangsu's Haian county integrates agriculture with animal husbandry and transforms half of its grain output into meat, eggs and poultry', 29.11.1984 tr FBIS/DR/PRC 5.12.1984, K2-3.
2   She Zhixiang, op cit.
3   Ibid.
4   Shan Shumu *et al*, op cit.
5   She Zhixiang, op cit.
6   *Xinhua*, 'Disaster-stricken area in East China becomes important grain and cotton producer', 5.10.1974 in SCMP 1974 (43) pp 94-7.
7   *Guangming Ribao*, 'Our country's agricultural production reaps bumper harvest for ten years in succession', 1.1.1972 tr SCMP 1972 (3) pp 62-6.
8   *Xinhua*, 'China's great achievements in harnessing Huai river', 23.5.1971 in SCMP 1971 (22) pp 136-7. *Xinhua*, 'East China region extends paddy fields, reaps good harvest', 22.2.1972 in SCMP 1972 (10) pp 39-41. *Xinhua*, 'East China commune agricultural scientific experimental station', 5.6.1973 in SCMP 1973 (25) pp 26-7. *People's Daily*, 'Rapid transformation of backward features under the guidance of the "9th party congress"', 18.11.1971 tr SCMP 1971 (48) pp 80-2. *People's Daily*, 'Operate agriculture in a big way in keeping with the spirit of the general line', 26.2.1973 tr SCMP 1973 (10) pp 175-9.
9   *Xinhua*, 'East China party branch leads people in changing nature', 16.7.1972 in SCMP 1972 (30) pp 133-4.
10  *Xinhua*, 'Area north of Huai river makes big progress in agriculture', 22.8.1970 in SCMP 1970 (35) pp 18-19.
11  *Xinhua*, East China xian transformed by harnessing rivers', 15.9.1970 in SCMP 1970 (38) pp 181-2.
12  Dinglou brigade party branch, 'Build a new countryside in the struggle between the two roads', *Red Flag*, 1.1.1975 tr SPRCM 1975 (04) pp 99-104.
13  Dinglou brigade party branch, op cit.
14  *Red Flag*, 19.5.1981, op cit.
15  *Xinhua*, 15.9.1970, op cit; *Xinhua*, 22.8.1970, op cit; She Zhixiang, op cit; Shan Shumu *et al*, op cit; Liu Xigeng, op cit.
16  Shan Shumu *et al*, op cit.
17  *People's Daily*, 26.2.1973, op cit. *Xinhua*, 5.10.1974, op cit.
18  Shan Shumu *et al*, op cit.
19  She Zhixiang, op cit.
20  *Red Flag*, 19.5.1980, op cit. *Xinhua*, 5.10.1974, op cit.
21  She Zhixiang, op cit.
22  Xuzhou agricultural science research institute, 'A summary report on demonstration work in stable high output in Damiao, Dawu and Dayangshan communes', *Zhongguo Nongye Kexue* (*China's agricultural science*), 1965 (3) tr SCMP 1964 (467) pp 17-25.

23 Liu Xigeng, 'How agricultural output value can be doubled as seen from rural areas in Xuzhou prefecture', *People's Daily*, 24.2.1983 tr FBIS/DR/PRC 3.3.1983.

24 Xiao Lu, '"Dabaogan" brings about great change', *Xinhua Ribao* 13.1.1983, p 1.

25 Xiao Lu, op cit.

26 Wang Liang (a), 'The results of implementing comprehensive production responsibility systems in Huaiyin', *Xinhua Ribao*, 15.3.1983, p 1.

27 Ibid.

28 Liu Zheng (b), 'Huaiyin prefecture's commune members enthusiastically purchase tractors', *Xinhua Ribao*, 1.1.1983, p 1.

29 Wang Liang (a), op cit. Liu Zheng (b), op cit.

30 Su Linge, 'Observations on the survey of the rural areas of two counties in Northern Jiangsu', *Nongye Jingji Wenti*, 1984 (4) pp 33-6.

31 *Xinhua*, 23.10.1975, op cit.

32 Su Linge, op cit.

33 Hu Kangya & Xie Chengjin, 'After implementing the "Dabaogan" it is possible to improve agricultural field capital construction', *Xinhua Ribao*, 8.1.1983, p 2.

34 Hua Zhuanbao, Mao Duncheng, Wang Quiping & Wu Zhijun, 'Take a lead from people for whom reclaiming wasteland has led to wealth', *Xinhua Ribao*, 15.4.1983, p 2.

35 Zhu Xinzhong, 'Tongshan county grain-producing specialised households greatly develop', *Xinhua Ribao*, 28.4.1983, p 2.

36 Yu Aixiang & Xie Chengjin (b), 'Donghai county quickly establishes a commodity grain base', *Xinhua Ribao*, 9.6.1983, p 3. *Xinhua Ribao*, 'Lianshui, Sihong, Shuyang, Donghai, Pi and Tongshan counties are established as experimental commodity grain base counties', 22.3.1983, p 1. *Nanjing radio*, untitled 28.2.1983 tr FBIS/CR/A 6.4.1983, p 134. Ma Jifa & Liu Shoutang, 'Build Tongshan and five other commodity grain base counties, and agree upon and sign documents', *Xinhua Radio*, 11.5.1983, p 1.

37 Liu Xigeng, op cit.

38 Yu Meixian, 'Prevent nitrogen loss, promote increased agricultural production', *Xinhua Ribao*, 26.5.1983, p 2.

39 Zhao Shaolong & Lu Rongnan, 'Popularise agricultural technical responsibility; promote agricultural development', *Xinhua Ribao*, 12.6.1983, p 2.

40 Su Linge, op cit.

41 Wu Xuewen & Li Naiji, 'Wu "the large granary" is rewarded', *Xinhua Ribao*, 5.4.1983, p 2.

42 Wu Xuewen *et al*, op cit.

43 Xu Yiwen & Wang Xiangtou, 'School graduate Gu Zhengqiu establishes a crop protection team', *Xinhua Ribao*, 25.5.1983, p 2.

44  Mao Zongjie & Wang Baisen, 'Popularising agricultural scientific methods is not possible through "a single blow"', *Xinhua Ribao*, 25.5.1983, p 2.  He Yucai, 'Chen Tongyin establishes an agricultural skill-consultancy household', *Xinhua Ribao*, 22.5.1983, p 2.
45  Liu Xigeng, op cit.  *People's Daily*, 'Agricultural education must be geared to the needs of the rural areas', 10.2.1984a tr FBIS/DR/PRC 15.2.1984, K4-5.
46  Liu Xigeng, op cit.
47  *Xinhua Ribao*, 22.3.1983, op cit.  Yu Aixiang *et al* (b), op cit.  *Nanjing radio*, 28.2.1983, op cit.  Ma Jifa *et al*, op cit.
48  *Nanjing radio*, 28.2.1983, op cit.
49  Tian Jijin & Zhou Yichang, 'State, provinces to build commodity grain bases', *Xinhua Radio*, 24.3.1983 tr FBIS/DR/PRC 25.3.1983, K2-4.
50  Ibid.
51  *People's Daily*, 26.2.1973, op cit.
52  Ibid.
53  *People's Daily*, 18.11.1971, op cit.  *People's Daily*, 26.2.1973, op cit.
54  Yu Aixiang & Hu Xiaodong (a), 'Donghai county's grain and oil-bearing crops gross output doubles in five years', *Xinhua Ribao*, 4.2.1983, p 2.
55  Chen Qizhen, '22 counties of the country have sold more than 500 million *jin* of grain each', *Jingji Ribao*, 6.2.1984 tr FBIS/DR/PRC 15.2.1984, K8-9.
56  Yu Aixiang *et al* (a), op cit.  Yu Aixiang *et al* (b), op cit.
57  Yu Aixiang *et al* (b), op cit.
58  Jiangsu commune- and brigade-run enterprise department, 'Ganyu county suits the development of commune- and brigade-run enterprises to natural conditions', *Jingji Guanli*, 1982 (3) pp 69-70, 72.
59  Ibid.
60  *Xinhua*, 'East China province opens small coal mines', 11.12.1972 in SCMP, 1972 (51) p 103.
61  Liu Xigeng, op cit.
62  Shi Qingmin *et al*, op cit.
63  Jiangsu enterprise department, op cit.
64  *People's Daily*, 29.11.1984, op cit.
65  Chao Hai, Lu Yu & Nai Hua, 'Xuhuai comprehensive agricultural region's districts report on text', *Xinhua Ribao*, 31.5.1983, p 2.  Shan Shumu *et al*, op cit.
66  Dinglou brigade, op cit.
67  Pan Meizhong & Wang Xiangsheng, 'Yuanji xiang greatly develops river-course fish-breeding', *Xinhua Ribao*, 15.6.1983, p 2.
68  Zhao Yuangang, 'In Pi county, 1700 agricultural households raise tree seedlings', *Xinhua Ribao*, 1.4.1983, p 2.
69  Xiao Yunfu, 'Zhikou commune helps commune members choose the correct work-style and goods', *Xinhua Ribao*, 12.1.1983, p 2.

70  Zhang Shijun & Cui Chengzhu, 'Pei county rural cadres take the lead in diligent work-style', *Xinhua Ribao*, 29.6.1983, p 4.
71  Jiangsu commune and brigade-run enterprise department, op cit.
72  Xiao Chengjin, Shi Qingmin & Li Darong, 'Help commune members to develop the diversified economy', *Xinhua Ribao*, 6.4.1984, p 2.
73  Feng Zhengfang & Zhu Jian, 'Hardship households become conspicuous households', *Xinhua Ribao*, 21.2.1983, p 2.
74  *Xinhua Ribao*, 'Feng county authorities and government supports peasants engaged in trade', 4.2.1983, p 1.
75  Liu Zheng & You Buwen, 'Lianshui county foodstuffs company organises peasant purchasing and marketing', *Xinhua Ribao*, 23.3.1983, p 2.
76  *Xinhua Ribao*, 'Xuzhou prefecture tackles problems in buying, selling', 26.10.1982 p 1 tr FBIS/CR/A 28.2.1983, pp 46-7.
77  Liu Zheng et al, op cit.
78  *Xinhua Ribao*, 4.2.1983, op cit.
79  Liu Xigeng, op cit. Wang Liang (a), op cit. Liu Zheng (c), 'Huaiyin and other counties' peasants are not allowed to dry wheat straw upon main roads', *Xinhua Ribao*, 23.2.1983, p 2. Li Yang & Liu Zheng, 'The progress in Sihong's wheat harvest is both quick and of a high quality', *Xinhua Ribao*, 5.6.1983, p 2.
80  Wang Shouchang, Xie Chengjin & Zhao Shaolong, 'Shahe commune grain production and diversified economy reap bumper harvests', *Xinhua Ribao*, 14.1.1983, p 2.
81  *People's Daily*, 29.11.1984, op cit.
82  *Red Flag*, 19.5.1980, op cit.
83  *People's Daily*, 'Jiangsu projects more increases in gross industrial and agricultural output value', 16.3.1984 tr FBIS/DR/PRC 22.3.1984, O5-7.

# Chapter Seven

# Nenjiang Prefecture: Mechanisation and Intensification

## Introduction

Heilongjiang is the largest of the three provinces which comprise the Chinese 'North-East', the old Manchuria. The most northerly of China's provinces, Heilongjiang's principal physical characteristic is the severity of the winter cold, the frost-free period being as low as 120 days in some parts, compared to 250 days immediately to the north of the Yangzi and 180 days at Beijing.

In human terms, Heilongjiang is an area experiencing the full flood of Chinese colonisation. Broadly speaking, until this century, Chinese farm settlement was prohibited. As a result, gross population densities are lower than for China as a whole - 71 persons per square kilometre in comparison to 109 persons per square kilometre - while the amount of cultivable land per agricultural labourer is much higher than the national average - 26.3 *mu* per agricultural labourer in comparison to 5.8 *mu*.[1]

The combination of these physical and human characteristics, in conjunction with the state's perception of Heilongjiang as a major source of commodity grain, has had an important influence upon the development of the rural economy of the province. The purpose of this chapter is to outline and comment upon this development, with reference to one specific area of Heilongjiang: Nenjiang prefecture. Of particular concern is how local production units are responding to what is a potentially rich, yet also difficult, natural environment.

## Nenjiang prefecture: the setting

> It is rare for a province to have so rich and such a satisfactory variety
> of natural resources of farmland, forests, grasslands and water. To
> describe it as a 'golden bowl' is not an exaggeration.[2]

Nenjiang prefecture is located in the south of Heilongjiang, and as such, represents an area where settlement is relatively well-established. The prefecture itself is a vast plain generally less than 200 metres above sea level, though becoming more elevated towards the east. It contains the important city of Qiqihar, ten counties - Longjiang, Tailai, Gannan, Fuyu, Nehe, Lindian, Yian, Keshan, Kedong and Baiquan - and the autonomous county of Duerbote. The plain is bisected north to south by the Nen river and broadly east to west by a number of smaller rivers, including the Wuyur, Arun, Nemor, Yalu and Chaor. Railway lines follow a number of these river valleys (See Figure 10).

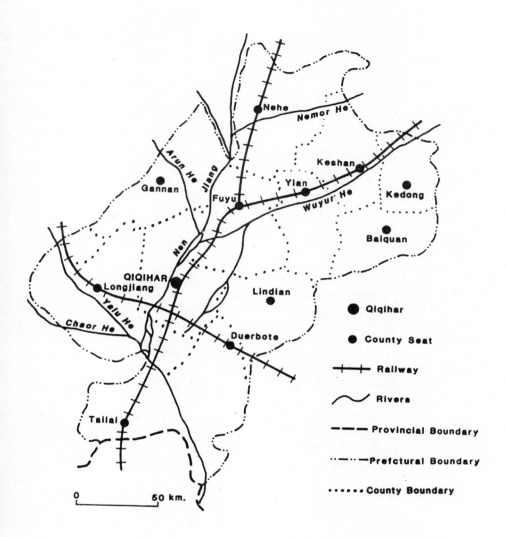

**Figure 10 Nenjiang prefecture: Qiqihar; county seats; railways; and major rivers**

In the main, soil conditions are good - black earths, calcareous and fertile. The frost-free period ranges from 120-150 days with the short summer period (June to September) generally hot. Rainfall is usually 370-540 mm.[3] The range of climatic conditions in Nenjiang is given as follows.

**Table 1  Nenjiang: climatic data of different weather stations**

| Station | Elevation (m) | Average temperatures: Annual | Average temperatures: January | Average temperatures: July | Frost-free days | Average annual rainfall (mm) |
|---|---|---|---|---|---|---|
| | | (degrees C) | | | | |
| Nehe | 203.9 | 0.8 | -22.8 | 21.4 | 121.7 | 436.7 |
| Kedong | 306.4 | 1.2 | -21.3 | 21.3 | 130 | 543.6 |
| Keshan | 236.9 | 1.3 | -21.8 | 21.5 | 124.8 | 468.6 |
| Baiquan | 230.7 | 1.2 | -22.1 | 21.4 | 122.8 | 471.4 |
| Gannan | 185.2 | 2.7 | -18.7 | 21.9 | n/a | 442.5 |
| Longjiang | 189.2 | 3.4 | -14.4 | 22.5 | 129.8 | 445.1 |
| Yian | 218.6 | 1.6 | -21.5 | 21.9 | 125.4 | 445.7 |
| Fuyu | 162.3 | 2 | -21 | 22.1 | 125.2 | 421.8 |
| Lindian | 154 | 2.3 | -20.9 | 22.7 | 118.4 | 398.5 |
| Qiqihar | 145.9 | 3.2 | -18.9 | 22.9 | 131.9 | 396.5 |
| Duerbote | 153.7 | 3.5 | -19 | 23.5 | 149.7 | 391.2 |
| Tailai | 149 | 4.2 | -17.1 | 23.4 | 137.8 | 366.8 |

Source: Shen Yuancun, op cit. (slightly adapted).

Apart from winter cold in general, the farm environment in Nenjiang faces two important practical problems: drought in spring and early frost in autumn. Spring drought results from the continuing continental conditions of winter in these northern latitudes into midsummer with very little rain until June. This creates obvious difficulties both for the germination and also for the growth of grain crops. These difficulties are intensified when the strong northerly winds which persist into spring are also considered. The combination of low spring rainfall and strong spring winds creates conditions where wind erosion of the top-soil is always a potential hazard. Frost early in autumn is obviously serious when the crops have not been able to make rapid growth in spring. It is disastrous when it comes in early-September when the grain is forming in the ears.

In spite of these difficulties, it is possible to see from Figure 11 why the natural resource base of Nenjiang could be considered an integral part of the 'golden bowl' of Heilongjiang. Figure 11 is abstracted from a broader study of the Nen river basin, based on Landsat data, and purports to show the diversity of land-use within Nenjiang.[4] (Landsat data are provided by earth-observation satellites. First launched in 1972, Landsat satellites - through multi-spectral imaging - can provide information on such subjects as the location of energy supplies, an assessment of food production, and large-scale environmental monitoring.)

From Figure 11, it is possible to identify a significant amount of 'wetland' in Nenjiang (concentrated along river valleys outlined in figure 10). This wetland is the result of poor drainage combined with the concentration of rainfall in the

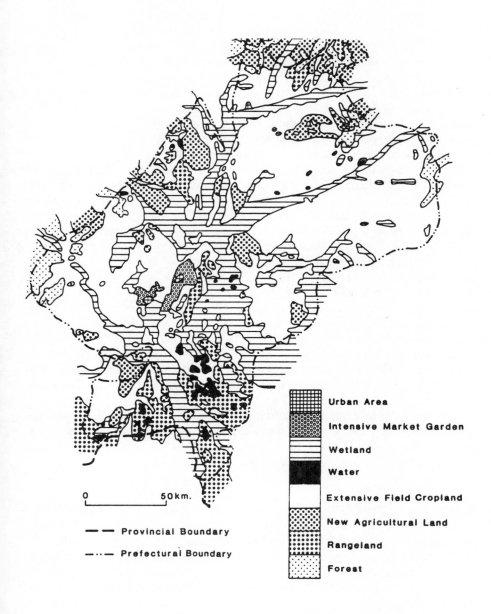

Urban Area

Intensive Market Garden

Wetland

Water

Extensive Field Cropland

New Agricultural Land

Rangeland

Forest

0          50km.

— — Provincial Boundary

—··— Prefectural Boundary

**Figure 11  Nenjiang prefecture: land use, 1976**

summer and low evaporation rates. Much of this wetland will serve as pasture during the dry periods of the year, and thus can possibly be classified as rangeland. Rangeland - steppe, scrubland and grassland - is currently being converted to cropland. What remains is concentrated in the south of Nenjiang and is characterised by rough terrain and/or poorly drained alkaline soils. However, there remains much scope for the development of animal husbandry.

The significant pockets of new agricultural lands throughout Nenjiang are reclaimed from rangeland, wetland, rough terrain or dry/saline soils. Reclamation involves much improvement of the natural environment through a variety of measures, including the construction of drainage ditches, irrigation channels, and shelter belts. State farms are often located on such lands.

The most important category of land-use is that of extensive field cropland which is predominantly found to the east of the river Nen. Extensive field cropland describes farmland traditionally cultivated for soybeans, corn, Chinese sorghum, wheat and millet. In Nenjiang, such farmland is characterised by regular farm patterns and relatively large field sizes (300 to 600 *mu* per field), both indicating that agricultural production is mechanised to a significant extent.

Of the other land-uses in Nenjiang visible from Figure 11 - urban, intensive market gardening, water and forest - little needs to be said. Nenjiang, in contrast to the Nen river basin as a whole, has only a small amount of forest area and this is confined to its periphery. Finally, an area of intensive market gardening is noted around several of the numerous identifiable urban settlements. However, with the exception of that around Qiqihar, it is unlikely that such intensive market garden areas have anything more than a marginal influence upon Nenjiang's rural economy. In total, Nenjiang has 23 million *mu* of cultivable land (17.6% of Heilongjiang's total) with 3.45 million *mu* (3.5%) of wasteland capable of reclamation for arable farming, of which 2.37 million *mu* is pasture.[5]

In terms of rural settlement in Nenjiang, in 1984, the resource base outlined above supported something over 900,000 rural households - a rural population of about 4.6 million.[6] Of these households, over 107,000 (12% of the total number) were classified as specialised or key households.[7]

## Commodity grain production - *mechanisation and intensification*

The state's perception of Nenjiang has long been as a source of commodity grain, yet the prefecture's performance in grain production has not matched the state's demands of it. While not ignoring the damaging impact of Cultural revolutionary policies upon the motivation of producers, much of the fault for this weak performance has been a failure over a number of years to make real progress with the creation of new farmland, with land improvements on the existing arable, or with the raising of levels of production technique which remain low.

In recent years, policy makers have been attempting to rectify the serious production problems of Nenjiang's numerous commodity grain bases in particular and grain producers in general. Eleven of the province's 13 commodity grain bases are situated in the Nen river basin, although it is unclear how many actually fall within the prefectural boundaries.[8] The development path taken by the prefectural authorities is one of mechanisation and intensification of production techniques allied to the adoption of a variety of the new production management forms available in the rural economy since 1978.

## *Mechanisation*

Given the farming characteristics of Nenjiang - the high amount of cultivable land available per agricultural labourer; spring drought; the short frost-free period; and extensive cultivation - it is unsurprising that agricultural mechanisation is important in the development of grain production. Under such conditions, mechanisation can ensure timely early sowing, preserve seedlings in the initial stages of growth, promote intensive and meticulous cultivation, and facilitate harvesting.[9]

Neither is it surprising to discover that mechanisation has been concentrated upon developing grain production. Almost 40% of the 2216 brigades in the Nenjiang river plain have been given priority to mechanise ahead of other brigades because they are the key suppliers of wheat and soybeans.[10] In Nenjiang and throughout the Nen river basin, the state's concern for large stable supplies of commodity grain is channelling mechanisation towards the development of grain production ahead of other areas of agricultural production.

The impact of mechanisation upon grain production can be illustrated by a number of examples. Liming brigade, Beilian commune, Keshan county has an interesting history. This brigade was established in 1956 by 250 people from Ju county in Shandong who came to Keshan as an organised migrant group to clear and settle new arable land.[11] They raised per-unit grain yields from a little over 100 *jin/mu* to 224 *jin/mu* in 1968. At this time, the question of mechanisation was first suggested, no doubt in an effort to combat the short frost-free period of 110 days.[12] At that time, the state tractor station was selling off machinery cheaply and Liming brigade purchased a Caterpillar tractor on hire purchase and then a plough attachment. Since then, the brigade has consistently purchased large-scale agricultural machinery. In 1978, the brigade had 8140 *mu* of cultivable land, of which 7420 *mu* was sown with wheat and soybean, and 720 *mu* with maize and millet. Wheat and soybean cultivation was completely mechanised while maize and millet cultivation was over 90% mechanised. Grain production in 1980 was impressive, with total production of almost four million *jin* and grain sales to the state of 2.3 million *jin* (a commodity rate of

153

almost 60%). Even more remarkably, the state commodity grain quota was set at only 0.5 million *jin*.[13]

Liming brigade is one of 11 brigades in Beilian commune and each brigade has, it has claimed, followed this path of agricultural mechanisation. In 1979 alone, each brigade spent over 100,000 *yuan* on the purchase of agricultural machinery with the county authorities contributing a further one million *yuan*.[14] The principal concern of these purchases was to raise the level of mechanisation in weeding and storage techniques for example, to that of ploughing, sowing, and fertiliser application. Indeed, by early 1980, agricultural production throughout Beilian could be considered virtually completely mechanised. Grain output in 1979 for Beilian commune as a whole was only marginally less impressive than that illustrated for Liming brigade.[15]

A similar example of development through mechanisation is given for Jianshe brigade, Keshan county.[16] Before 1979, Jianshe was considered a backward production unit, producing 1.13 million *jin* of grain. All cultivation was extensive, production organisation was incomplete and the labour force was insufficient to meet the production tasks placed upon it. At the beginning of 1979, the brigade purchased seven large- and medium-scale tractors, three complete harvesters and a complete set of agricultural implements. Many aspects of the production process were mechanised with the result that grain production increased to almost 4 million *jin* with grain sales to the state of 2.1 million *jin* (a commodity rate of just over 50%). Again, the sales to the state were well above the commodity grain quota of 0.6 million *jin*.[17]

However, the benefits of mechanised agricultural production illustrated in these two examples have not been universal. Criticism comes from some quarters that the cost of the promotion of mechanisation in terms of state investment loans, the commitment of goods and materials, and the prices paid by the peasants are not matched by the benefits that result.[18] The reasons for this disparity between the cost and the benefits include: first, the path of mechanisation has for too long been one of an 'isolated force penetrating deep into enemy territory'; that is, mechanisation has not been accompanied by agronomic, biological or engineering measures to improve the productive capacity of the soil.[19] Mechanisation alone has not been able to equate relatively high land and labour productivity. This situation is only now beginning to change.

Secondly, the composition of mechanisation is poor. The current allocation of farm machinery exhibits 'a big head and a small tail'; that is, great power but few complete sets of farm machinery.[20] For example, up to 1000 million *jin* of grain goes unharvested annually in Heilongjiang due to a shortage of combine harvesters. Significantly, only in 1979, a decade after beginning mechanisation in agriculture, was Liming brigade able to strengthen its harvesting capacity. Furthermore, the farm machinery is often inferior in quality. All of this adds up to a low utilisation rate for farm machinery, a narrow range of suitable uses and low benefits.

Thirdly, there is still a tendency to blindly mechanise irrespective of natural conditions and the availability of fuel supplies from the state. State supplies of petroleum, oil and lubricants are insufficient to meet the demands of agricultural machinery - a shortfall throughout Heilongjiang of 160,000 tons.[21] This seriously reduces the utilisation rate of the available agricultural machinery.

Finally, before the introduction of production responsibility systems into agricultural machinery work, management and service of farm machinery was contracted out either exclusively to farm machine brigades or jointly to farmland brigades and farm machine brigades. While this system was workable in large, sparsely-populated areas of monoculture, it was argued that in other areas crop variety and agronomic complexity tended to produce poor results.

Thus, major problems were to be found with agricultural mechanisation. It is significant that the examples given above from Keshan county seem to have avoided such problems. Equally significant, the Keshan county authorities have, it is claimed, coordinated the development of mechanised farm production with a policy of intensification and the introduction of production responsibility systems into agriculture.

## Intensification

Historically, agricultural production in Nenjiang has been based upon extensive cultivation, large areas producing low yields. Increases in total output were dependent upon increases in sown area. This was certainly true for land use in 1976 for example, as depicted in Figure 11.

However, future improvements in output are to be sought through intensification on the existing arable. In particular, it is hoped that a policy of intensification can contribute to reducing fluctuations in output which remain significant, as well as improving the ecological conditions of the natural resource base.[22]

The natural resource base of Nenjiang certainly seems to have suffered in recent years. The destruction of forest and grassland in order to reclaim wasteland for arable, the contamination of water, the indiscriminate excavation of mines and quarries have all seriously disrupted the environment.[23]

Soil erosion is becoming a serious problem and in some places the organic content of the soil has dropped to 2% from its original level of 8%. Baiquan county for example, a county known for its relative fertility, has seen 7% of its upland area degraded to loess hills and 30% of its land become alkaline.[24] Again, 25% of the cultivable land in Baiquan and Keshan counties suffers from soil erosion.[25]

There is little doubt that such a decline in the natural resource base is a major contributory factor to low grain yields. Furthermore, the effective irrigation area is very low, farmland water conservation work weak. As a result, the capacity for resisting natural disasters remains low.

In recent years, some production units have responded to the decline in the natural resource base through an intensification policy which encompasses a variety of measures to improve productive capacity. First, land inappropriately converted to arable under the Maoist drive for increased grain output has been returned to pasture. In 1980, Longjiang county for example, returned 40,000 *mu* of arable land to pasture contributing to a total of 400,000 *mu* of arable returned to pasture in Nenjiang in the the same year.[26]

Secondly, the implementation of a variety of techniques has aimed at reducing wind and soil erosion. Lianmin brigade, Xihe commune, Keshan county for example, is situated on a loess ridge. To reduce wind and soil erosion this brigade constructed shelter-belts, 'fish-scale' pits (pits arranged like fish-scales, dug on mountain slopes for holding water or planting trees) and terraces. Indeed, Nenjiang is just one prefecture in western Heilongjiang which is being aided by the state's 'Sanbei' shelter-belt construction project. This project aims to build sufficient shelter-belts to preserve 40 million *mu* of cultivable land in western Heilongjiang. In the year up to mid-1984, it is claimed that shelter-belt construction helped to preserve 8,010,000 *mu* of cultivable land, four times the amount that had been preserved by shelter-belt construction in the previous 26 years.[27]

Within the limits of this shelter-belt, it is said that it has been possible to reduce wind-speed by 20-35%; reduce water evaporation rates by 16-18%; increase the soil moisture content by 9%; increase temperatures by 0.9-1.4%; and extend the frost-free period by 2-6 days. If these claims are to be believed, ecological conditions - and therefore productive capacity - will undoubtedly improve in Nenjiang.[28]

Thirdly, increased applications of fertiliser - organic and inorganic - to improve soil fertility has been potentially of great importance. Lianmin brigade, for example, managed to increase the organic content of their soil from 2-4% by applications of fertiliser obtained from the development of pig-keeping.[29] This was an important factor in the improved grain yields achieved by Lianmin brigade between 1978 and 1980. Finally, crop rotation is also encouraged as a means of improving soil fertility.[30]

Production units are urged to capitalise upon such improvements in productive capacity by utilising advanced agricultural techniques - fine-seed strains, pesticides and so forth - to improve per-unit yields. Given Nenjiang's production characteristics, the use of early-maturing, drought-resilient seed varieties, for example, could do much to improve grain yields.

The adoption of such a broad set of intensification measures alongside agricultural mechanisation is clearly important in the development of Liming and Jianshe brigades. Liming brigade for example, benefited from the utilisation of high-yield varieties of seed developed by the Keshan agricultural scientific station as well as increased applications of fertiliser and agricultural pesticides.[31]

The improvement in grain production in Liming and Jianshe brigades has already been noted. However, it is also clear that the improvement is localised. While per-unit yields in Liming brigade in the early 1980s were approaching 400 jin/mu (double that of the 1970s), per-unit yields in the Nen river basin were a little less than 300 jin/mu, and in Keshan county under 250 jin/mu.[32]

While grain yields in Nenjiang are certainly above the provincial average (slightly over 200 jin/mu), they are still below the target figure for the province, set at 400 jin/mu. Clearly there is still a need for more widespread utilisation of intensive agricultural production techniques alongside agricultural mechanisation.

## Production responsibility systems

It is interesting to note that Liming brigade for example, in addition to coordinating intensive and mechanical agricultural production, was also quick to utilise a variety of production responsibility systems. As with units throughout China, it is claimed that the introduction of such systems into Liming brigade, was an important motivational factor behind the improved grain production displayed in Liming after 1978.[33]

By 1984, 98% of all production teams in Heilongjiang had implemented *baogan daohu*. However, within this framework much variety of detail is noted.[34]

For example, there is the 'four unifications and four fixes' system. This involves the implementation of unified management alongside assigning production quotas to individuals or work groups. Production teams draw up unified farming plans, unified management of farm machinery, vehicles and draught animals, a unified plan for production costs and unified accounting and distribution. The four fixes comprised fixed plots, fixed output, fixed penalty and bonus and one other which was not made clear.[35]

The extent of mechanisation in Nenjiang heightens the importance of systems whereby output quotas are set for farm machine operators or groups. Once again there is much variety in detail illustrated in the literature and two examples will be given.

First, farm machinery teams undertake assignments on a contract basis, and payment is calculated on the basis of work performed. Contracts between the brigade and the farm machinery team arrange work quotas, and work points are calculated on the basis of work performed with unified distribution of payment.

Secondly, the farm machinery team becomes an independent accounting unit and signs contracts with the production team which requires the work. Nevertheless, interdependence between manual and mechanised production remains inevitable. Some teams in Baiquan county for example, assign production quotas to households and individuals who are responsible for field management while collectively-owned farm machinery is still used to plough the arable. However, by distinguishing the role of farm machinists and acknowledging and rewarding their particular skills, this should not only arouse their enthusiasm for production, but also increase enthusiasm amongst those peasants involved in manual labour by the improved livelihoods - as well as eased workloads - which mechanisation can bring about.[36]

In some localities farm machinery has become individually managed. Three villages in the Shuanghe district of Keshan county for example, began selling previously collectively-owned large-scale agricultural machinery to individuals. After six months of individual management it is claimed that machine productivity rates had increased and service quality was improved. As a result, a further eight villages in Shuanghe sold 24 Caterpillar tractors and 126 pieces of large-scale agricultural machinery to individual peasants. While this represents a significant move on behalf of the collective, it should also be noted that control over such farm machinists - through local cadre groups and contracts - remains strict.[37]

There seems little doubt from the literature that the implementation of production systems within agriculture - with subsequent developments and modifications - not only arouses peasant enthusiasm for production, but also can complement the growth in mechanisation and intensification of agricultural production in Nenjiang. This combination of production responsibility with mechanised and intensive production is said to have already done much to promote bumper grain harvests within Nenjiang in recent years.[38] In 1983, for example, Nenjiang's grain harvest was the third largest in history despite severe storms, low temperatures and waterlogging which hindered production. Grain sales to the state amounted to 1.12 billion *jin*, 388 million *jin* above the 1982 figure and 9.1% above the figure in the state plan.[39] Furthermore, stability of current agricultural policy should, it is argued, enable Nenjiang to overcome natural difficulties, achieve stable yields and thereby improve supplies of commodity grains to the state.[40]

However, numerous questions remain to be asked: first, how commodity grain producers can overcome the negative effect of low state prices; secondly, how mechanisation and intensification policies are financed; thirdly, how to employ the surplus labour force created by mechanisation and the widespread introduction of production responsibility systems; fourthly, how effectively the commercial system can withstand the increased burdens being placed upon it; and finally, how widespread is rural development in Nenjiang.

# Foundations for mechanised and intensive production

To best answer the questions framed above, four aspects of the rural economy in Nenjiang need to be investigated: state prices and investment; rural industry; diversified undertakings; and commerce.

## State prices and investment

A contradiction continues to exist between the importance of grain production and the relative state prices for grain and other economic crops. This contradiction is reflected in concern about the desirability of equalising incomes between peasants involved in grain production and those who are not. Peasants farming grain must be able to achieve profits equivalent to those possible from planting economic crops. Without this kind of parity, there is little incentive to produce grain.[41] This concern is especially pointed within commodity grain base areas.

The state's attitude to grain prices is unlikely to change. However, the state will encourage grain production in commodity grain base areas through direct investment. Although Nenjiang is not specifically mentioned, commodity grain bases in Heilongjiang are amongst those signing joint state-local investment agreements outlined earlier for Xuhuai.

It is doubtful, however, if such levels of state investment will be sufficient to promote development beyond a localised level. Certainly, it will do nothing to change the fact that state grain prices remain low. Indeed, in Nenjiang, just as in many other areas of China, it is the local production unit which finds itself increasingly subsidising grain production, either directly through income subsidies, or indirectly through the subsidy of the costs of production.

Yangfa brigade, Pingyang commune, Tailai county for example, is developing commodity grain production through grain-producing specialised households - 70 in 1984 from nine the previous year - and is implementing six measures in order to safeguard increased grain production and incomes: first, supplying 34,000 *jin* of high quality seed strains; secondly, supplying 80,000 *jin* of fertiliser; thirdly, alleviating seasonal shortages in investment funds; fourthly, supplying agricultural machinery services to guarantee the autumn harvest; fifthly, encouraging the transfer of knowledge from other grain specialists in Keshan and Longjiang counties, for example; and finally, organising transport and marketing of the grain.[42]

While such measures may provide one answer to the problems caused by low state grain prices and the absence of more widespread state investment, they still beg the question as to how this local subsidy is financed. The answer rests with the development of rural industry and diversified undertakings, together with the ability of the commercial system to market the produce of these sectors of the rural economy.

*Rural industry*

Generally speaking, it is rural industry which both provides the initial finance - through accumulation funds - for mechanisation and intensification of agricultural production, and is also a major contributor - again through accumulation funds - to the subsidies more recently made available to grain specialists. It is true that there is some evidence to suggest that the financing of mechanisation and intensification is possible through farming income alone. In the Maoist model of Taiping brigade, Zhongxing commune, Gannan county, for example, considerable investments in agricultural machinery seem to have come from farming income with little mention made of industry.[43] However, other examples point to the importance of industrial finance. Given the longstanding difficulties of purely farming units in raising accumulation funds, rural industry seems to be the most likely source of significant local funds.

In Jianshe brigade, a wide variety of industries - including a galvanised iron plant, tile-yard, distillery and foodstuff processing workshops - contributed to accumulation funds which were used to purchase farm machinery.[44] In addition, the distillery would create a demand for grain at a price above that paid by the state, thus directly rewarding grain production.

Similarly, the importance of industrial finance in the development of Liming brigade is well detailed.[45] Between 1970 and 1979, brigade-run industrial enterprises - including a canning factory and a confectionery plant - contributed over 500,000 *yuan* to collective investment funds which had subsequently been used to purchase agricultural machinery.

Such industrial enterprises - along with diversified undertakings - also provide an important source of employment for those labourers displaced from farming through the establishment of mechanised production. In Liming brigade, only 20% of the labour force of 550 was employed in farming.[46] In Jianshe brigade the figure is one-third. Clearly, both brigades enjoy a level of rural industrialisation capable of providing significant amounts of rural employment and income opportunities.

However, some doubt remains as to how widespread such industrial enterprises are throughout Nenjiang. It has already been indicated that mechanised and intensive farm development is still very much localised. Evidence concerning the spread of rural industry within Nenjiang seems to confirm this view.[47]

Only recently have peasants begun to consider using personal funds to establish small-scale industrial undertakings. Of late, this small-scale, localised individual entrepreneurship is becoming more common.[48]

Certainly there appear to be numerous opportunities for small-scale industrial development. Eight commune members of Changsheng brigade, Youyi commune, Fuyu county, for example, invested 15,000 *yuan* of personal funds to purchase the necessary machinery to establish an oil-extraction mill. Previously, peasants in the area had had difficulty obtaining edible oil because there was no available oil mill. Within three months of commencing operations, these eight commune members had earned a favourable reputation for their work and their net per capita incomes between January and March of 1984 reached 820 *yuan*.[49]

There is also some evidence to suggest that, in more well-established rural industrial enterprises, it was not until the recent introduction into such enterprises of a well-defined responsibility system that profitability was achieved and expansion possible. In Duerbote county, between 1980 and 1983, responsibility systems in industrial enterprises were not clear cut, penalties were unclear. Losses by light industrial enterprises for example, amounted to 258,000 *yuan* over the four year period. Only after the implementation of well-defined responsibility systems assessing output values, taxes, and profits did production and profits improve.[50] Similar arguments are put forward to explain recent success in county-run industry in Longjiang and state-run industry throughout Nenjiang.[51]

To sum up, although there is evidence to suggest that financial contributions from rural industry to agriculture - via collective accumulation funds - might reasonably become more widespread in the future, it is perhaps too early to expect that such enterprises play anything more than a marginal, localised role in the provision of funds for mechanised and intensive farm production, subsidies to grain producers and as employers of surplus farm labour. However, as demonstrated in Liming and Jianshe brigades, where rural industry is developed, it is a powerful driving force behind the development of agricultural production in general, and grain in particular.

## Diversified undertakings

> Our objectives were to build our province into the following sorts of base area: a modernised agricultural base concentrating on production of commodity grain, and including the overall development of economic crops and diversified operations.[52]

Despite the models of agricultural development through diversification presented in the media at that time, it is now claimed that under the Maoists, diversified undertakings throughout Nenjiang were severely curtailed.[50] During the Cultural Revolution, those peasants who engaged in diversified production were labelled capitalists and faced often quite severe discrimination. In this kind of political environment, the diversified economy was understandably weak.[53]

Not until 1978 did diversified undertakings began to be reestablished in many areas - although it is significant that some brigades including Liming and Jianshe, in the 1970s at least, seemed able to diversify without apparent condemnation.

There is clearly much potential for diversification in Nenjiang. Although confined to the peripheries, forestry is an important source of local wealth. Similarly, the development of the fishing industry and orchards are said to have much potential.[54] However, animal husbandry is undoubtedly the dominant sector of the diversified economy. Nenjiang prefecture has an estimated 15.3 million *mu* of grasslands to complement its cultivable area and there has been a steady increase in the number of cattle kept in the current phase.

Similarly, great claims are made for the sheep-breeding industry especially in Longjiang and Gannan counties. Nevertheless, even in these prominent sheep-breeding areas, problems still remain. Xingshan township, Longjiang county, for instance, an area of extensive grasslands highly suited to the development of sheep-breeding, up until 1984 had no sheep-dipping facilities. Disease was common and the breeding of sheep suffered.[55] In Gannan county, the number of sheep at hand at the end of 1983 was down 15,000 on the previous year. Upon investigation, county, township and village authorities discovered that sheep-breeders were faced with shortages of fodder, and herding difficulties.[56] Clearly, there is still room for improvement.

Pig-breeding has also developed in Nenjiang through the implementation of a variety of measures. These can perhaps be best summarised in the 'four priorities' and 'three guarantees' adopted by Baiquan county to encourage pig-breeding. The four priorities relate to the provision of loans, the supply of fodder materials, the supply of construction materials for the building of pig-sties, and the marketing and transport of goods and materials. The three guarantees refer to technical work, the availability of fine breeding strains and insurance work.[57]

Furthermore, six counties of Nenjiang - Kedong, Baiquan, Keshan, Yian, Nehe and Longjiang - have had an integrated pig semen system established within them. Provincial authorities have invested heavily to establish artificial insemination stations, and to purchase fine strains of boar from Hangzhou, Zhejiang province. Certainly, within Kedong county at least, such insemination centres were beginning to have a favourable impact upon pig production.[58]

Nevertheless, pig-breeders still face numerous problems, especially the availability of fodder supplies. There is however, evidence to suggest that this problem is being overcome in a number of ways: first, through the allocation of fodder land to breeders according to the number of pigs supplied to the state; secondly, by allocating fodder supplies on the same basis; and thirdly, through the establishment of certain small-scale industries - bean-curd plants and distilling plants - where the by-products and residual materials can be utilised by pig-breeders.[59] In addition, the development of pig-breeding also offers opportunities to grain farmers to sell grain profitably.

Animal husbandry must be considered a major source of income along with the diversified economy in general. Furthermore, in the current phase the diversified economy is being vigorously promoted, not least the utilisation of specialised production forms.[60] Yet, despite all the claims being made for diversified production, not least as a source of employment and income for the rural population, the full potential for diversified production on the Nenjiang resource has yet to be realised.[61] Though less so than in rural industry, opportunities for employment in, and income from diversified undertakings, still appear limited and localised.

## Commerce

> Rural production and marketing are directed by 14 different government agencies. Sometimes the production of one variety of grain is under the jurisdiction of several government agencies. They usually do not agree with one another and argue endlessly. Unnecessary duplication of links in one chain of distribution hinder the flow of agricultural products. The system should be reformed gradually.[62]

The effectiveness of the commercial system in Nenjiang is a key determinant to growth in the rural economy. Without an effective commercial structure, industrial and diversified undertakings cannot fully develop, thereby limiting the accumulation of collective funds for mechanised and intensive farm production and subsidised grain production, and reducing employment and income opportunities for surplus farm labour. Thus, peasant enthusiasm for all aspects of rural production becomes depressed.

Significantly, Li Lian, the secretary of the Heilongjiang provincial CCPC, in a number of articles is scathing about the commercial organisation within Heilongjiang. In particular, he notes the 'gradual strangling' of buying and selling. Bureaucratic control, he argues, is too tight. Prices are also too tightly controlled. Shortly after this criticism, the state relaxed its monopoly over the purchasing and marketing of certain agricultural products. Media reports on the commercial system were immediately much more favourable.

The supplies of industrial goods for daily use, as well as non-staple food, including meat, fish and eggs all improved. Indeed, many products previously rationed, were said to be in unrestricted supply.[63] (More recently, this situation has again reversed, supplies of pork in particular being once again rationed. This indicates the very fragile nature of agricultural progress in Nenjiang and many parts of China).

The truth of the matter is that it remains difficult to gauge how much improvement has been made within the commercial organisations. Certainly in the literature from Nenjiang there are numerous examples of apparent commercial efficiency. In Yian county for example, the county vegetable corporation planned to completely sell the expected bumper harvest of potatoes in that county in 1984 not only in Heilongjiang, but also through sales to southern China.[64] Contracts guaranteeing quality, quantity and timing of delivery/purchase were signed by producers and consumers with the vegetable corporation purchasing bagging materials and providing transport.[65]

Similarly, there is also the emergence of allegedly sophisticated commercial organisations such as the integrated agricultural and commercial company of Lindian county, based on existing supply and marketing cooperatives and about 1000 specialised households.[66] This company not only provides technical services to a wide-range of producers, but more significantly guarantees the marketing and transport of produce. The stability provided by this company has encouraged commodity production to develop, with the variety of commodity produce increasing from 29 to over 150 goods.

Yet, despite such examples of efficiency, conflict between what the commercial organs want to purchase and what the rural producers have to sell remains. Even in grain production it seems, surpluses have no guaranteed buyer. In 1984 for example, Fuyu county produced 200 million *jin* of grain. After sales to the state, amounts retained for personal needs and existing fodder requirements, a significant surplus remained unsold. This prompted the peasants to greatly expand animal husbandry.[67]

However, if grain production fell, it is easy to see how a conflict between animal husbandry, fodder requirements and state grain demands would arise. (Indeed, the question of feed-grain supplies is expected to grow in significance in the future, as absolute demands on grain increase.) More significantly, if grain surpluses are not effectively utilised - unlike the example of Fuyu - enthusiasm for grain production will inevitably be reduced. It is difficult to understand how the state can expect to develop commodity grain bases under such commercial conditions.

When official commercial organs fail to market goods effectively, individual traders often emerge in an attempt to fill the breach. Yongfa brigade, Yongfa commune, Longjiang county, for example, has as its most important sideline undertaking the production of whisk brooms. In 1984 however, the local SMC decided to reduce its purchase quotas, leaving many peasants with large surpluses of brooms. One peasant, Lin Changwen, seeing this situation, travelled to Dandong city in the South-East of Liaoning and signed contracts with a local company to sell 30,000 surplus brooms in Dandong and the surrounding area.[68]

Individual traders, however, are limited in number and scope and realistically cannot be expected to dramatically influence local rural development. Despite claims about the improving commercial situation, commercial organisational rigidities - so forcefully noted by Li Lian - must remain an important block to rural development. An investigation of the commercial infrastructure within Nenjiang reveals three key difficulties: first, the insufficient grain storage capacity; secondly, the relative inconvenience of road transport; and thirdly, the paucity of the means of transport.

The problem of insufficient grain storage capacity is common throughout Nenjiang.[69] The state, it would appear, has encouraged commodity grain bases to increase grain production without a concomitant development of storage capacity. Consider, for example, the problems of grain storage at the Nehe county grain depot.[70] The grain depot annually receives 62 million *jin* of grain, yet capacity remains only 14 million *jin*. Forty-eight million *jin* of grain is therefore stored in the open air and becomes subject to inevitable losses from the climate, vermin and theft. While efforts have been made to improve storage conditions, it remains a major problem. Indeed, it must be said that if such storage problems are found with grain crops in an area which purports to be a major supplier of commodity grain, like problems for diversified produce must also be large.

Opinions as to the state of Heilongjiang's road network differ. According to one commentator, the road network is both dense and well developed. Alternatively, another notes that the lack of transport facilities is a major hindrance to agricultural production.[71]

Even though the road network in Nenjiang might be considered relatively dense, much of it is seasonally impassable and in disrepair. Efforts are being made to repair roads to make them passable all year, but there is still much work to be done in this regard.[72] Until such time as these substantial improvements are made it is inevitable that those units with access to convenient roads will prosper ahead of more peripheral and less accessible units. Indeed, reports of road improvement all too often dwell on the construction of major highways. While necessary, it should not be thought that these roads would dramatically alter market access for the majority of peasants who live well beyond these highways.[73]

Finally, there is the problem of access to the means of transport. Even in those units where the peasants are able to diversify and produce goods for sale above quota requirements, and where road routes are convenient, it appears the means of transport are often unavailable. To combat this problem, two developments are noteworthy: first, an improvement in public transport; and secondly, the emergence of individual households specialising in the transport of goods.

An improvement in public transport was noted in Longjiang county, for example. Recent improvements include the rescheduling of buses between Longjiang county seat and Qiqihar (50 kilometres away), so that they arrive in Qiqihar early in the morning instead of at noon, allowing peasants to carry more commodities onto the buses, and extending passenger transport routes. In this way, it is claimed, peasants are now more able both to sell their produce at the city markets and to purchase the means of production - such as inorganic fertiliser, fine seeds and small-scale implements.[74] If such flexibility is shown by public transport authorities throughout Nenjiang, a significant number of peasants may benefit - although of course, numbers remain limited by accessibility to public roads. Indeed, more pertinent examples of road transport away from the main road - which would be expected between a county seat and the most notable city in the prefecture - would constitute a greater step forward for the bulk of Nenjiang's peasantry.

In the immediate future, the emergence of households specialising in the transport of goods is considered more significant. Such households can be expected to increase in number given the growing inability of the official transport organs to handle the increasing burdens being placed upon them by the development - albeit slow and uneven - in Nenjiang's rural economy. Indeed, the extent of the wealth displayed by such households in the examples below indicate both the abundant potential and pressing need for individual transporters in Nenjiang.

In Nehe county for example, 150 specialised transport households were able to transport 31.85 million *jin* of surplus potatoes for sale in a variety of localities, including Shandong, Jiangxi, Hebei, Shanxi, Liaoning, Shaanxi, Jilin and Tianjin.[75] This earned the producers 1.2742 million *yuan*, with the transport households earning 532,000 *yuan* (an average of 3546.66 *yuan* per household - this figure is probably gross income, although nothing is said).

Similarly, in Xiangyang village, Kedong county 37 households engaged in specialist transport work - a total of 68 labourers, or 29% of the labour force.[76] These households - both individually and combined with other households - had three major impacts upon the rural economy of Xiangyang *tun*: first, by leaving the land, landholdings were able to increase from 17 *mu* per agricultural labourer to 24 *mu*. Secondly, they complemented public transport which was previously insufficient to meet peasant needs. In 1983, they transported goods and materials with a value of over 1 million *yuan*. Finally, by easing transport difficulties and improving access to markets, they contributed to increased peasant income as well as reaping large incomes themselves. The net income of each household engaged in transport in Xiangyang in 1983 was estimated at 3162.16 *yuan*.

However, the emergence of such households - certainly in the examples given above - is closely linked to convenient access to road and rail links. Thus, initially at least, those units with convenient access to markets - through state and/or private commercial activity - will develop ahead of other units. Again, this is consistent with arguments outlined earlier concerning the localised development of rural industry and diversified undertakings and hence of rural economic development in Nenjiang.

The differentiation of local development is matched both by differences in per-unit yields (as noted above) and also for rural per capita incomes. As in other examples, the figures for units at the smaller spatial levels - in particular the brigade/village and even more so the household - are much higher than larger spatially-aggregated units. Liming and Jianshi brigades, already noted above as being progressive units, saw incomes rising rapidly in the late 1970s, reaching 300 *yuan* per capita in 1980, 50% higher than that of the province as a whole. Rural per capita incomes in Nenjiang prefecture and Heilongjiang did

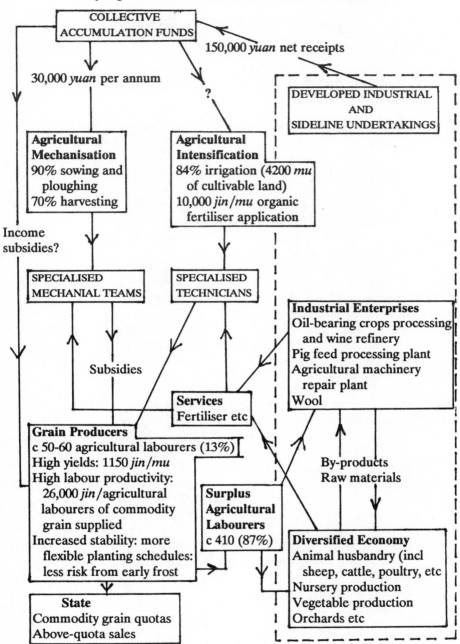

## Nenjiang Prefecture: Mechanisation and Intensification

**Figure 12  A simple development model of agricultural production through mechanisation and intensification: Xingshisi brigade, Gannan county, 1978**

not reach 300 *yuan* until 1983, by which time, some units in the area were reporting average per capita incomes in excess of 500 *yuan*.[77]

Figures for individual households are even higher - as high as 10,000 *yuan*.[78] Until all producers have equal access to markets, both to sell produce and purchase producer goods, this differentiation will continue and economic development within the rural economy will inevitably remain localised.

## Conclusions: a model of agricultural development - Xingshisi brigade, Gannan county

A synthesis of previous arguments concerning the mechanisation and intensification of farm production is given in Figure 12, using material for Xingshisi brigade, Yinhe commune, Gannan county. This brigade had, in 1979, 5000 *mu* of cultivable land, an agricultural population of over 700, and an agricultural labour force of about 470.[79] Mechanised and intensive farm production set against a backcloth of numerous production responsibility systems had, it is claimed, transformed the brigade's agricultural output and all-round development (see Figure 12 for detail). Certainly incomes in 1979 were high, with average per capita incomes approaching 400 *yuan*.[80]

Xingshisi brigade exemplifies what local authorities hope can occur throughout the rural economy of Nenjiang. As such, Xingshisi can serve as a model for the development of agricultural production in the Northeast environment. It represents a distinct shift from the 'small but complete' Maoist models of the past.

Furthermore, in detail, it represents a model which is perhaps unique to the Northeast environment. While a dual strategy of mechanised and intensive farm production is well-suited to developing agricultural production in Nenjiang and in the Northeast in general, elsewhere different environments will promote different agricultural development strategies.

Nevertheless, Xingshisi - like Liming and Jianshe brigades - remains an example only of localised development. As emphasised throughout, in no way is such brigades' development representative of the more gradual development displayed by Nenjiang's rural economy in recent years. While economic growth has undoubtedly occurred in Nenjiang, farm production is neither as developed nor as stable as that claimed in the models. Similarly, the extent of rural industrialisation and diversification is much more limited. As yet, Xingshisi brigade and others like it are simply models upon which it is hoped a more widespread economic development can be based. In the meantime, income and output differentiation continues to be large.

In Baiquan county for example, large discrepancies in income have prompted some peasants to sabotage the production of their wealthier neighbours.[81] Clearly, in the long term, it is important to reduce the extent of such differences, though without resorting to the egalitarian policies of the

Maoists, which did so much to dampen peasant enthusiasm for agricultural production. Currently the only answer to this problem seems to be to encourage production in the poorer units to match that of the prosperous producers. However, as stated above, this remains difficult given local differences in productive capacity, resources and accessibility to markets.

It is also clear that commercial improvement - both organisational and infrastructural - must accompany the development of agricultural production. Already numerous contradictions have arisen in commerce which have hindered rural development. Indeed, when Nenjiang has been able to produce the commodity grain which the state has always sought from the area, the official commercial system has proved incapable of handling the quantities of grain awaiting delivery. Little wonder that the marketing and transport of other rural produce remains difficult and a major block on development.

The growth of individual commerce to complement official organs may prove to be an important element in the development of Nenjiang. However, such a growth in individual commerce and in the absolute quantity of commercial activity has prompted a significant amount of corruption - in the form of profiteering, swindling, theft, and favouritism towards individuals and units in the provision of supplies or in access to facilities - at all levels of the commercial bureaucracy as well as amongst individual traders.[82] Such corruption may prompt the state to strictly regulate individual commercial activity, further overburdening the official commercial system and reducing rural economic activity.

The Northeast environment provides the context for a more basic development problem than that found in more environmentally-favoured (though more densely-populated) areas. The basic problem remains of how to create wealth in a challenging natural environment and thus facilitate capital accumulation. This problem is compounded by the state's perception of the area as a major grain base. Income and employment opportunities are limited and development is localised. It remains to be seen if all production units in Nenjiang and throughout the Northeast can emulate the example provided by Xingshisi brigade and other advanced units.

# Notes to Chapter Seven

1   *Statistical Yearbook of China, 1986*, (Beijing) 1986.
2   Yang Yichen (a), 'Problems in development strategy for Heilongjiang agriculture', *Heilongjiang Ribao*, (*Heilongjiang Daily*), 15.9.1981 tr FBIS/DR/PRC 26.10.1981, S1-13.
3   Shen Yuancun, 'Basic features of natural zones in the Nenjiang area and their agricultural development', *Dili Xuebao*, 1982 37 (3) pp 281-9.
4   R Welch, H C Lo & C W Pannell, 'Mapping China's new agricultural lands', *Photogrammetric Engineering and Remote Sensing*, 45 (9) pp 1211-28.
5   Dai Xu & Zhao Songqiao, 'An analysis on the land condition of Heilongjiang province and Hulunbeier league as related to its building into a commodity grain base', *Dili Xuebao*, 1984 39 (1) pp 65-73.
6   Liang Yuxiu & Pei Shouju, 'Nenjiang prefecture's cadres thoroughly implement Document no 1', *Heilongjiang Ribao* 2.3.1984, p 1.
7   Pei Shouju, 'Nenjiang area's "five industries" simultaneously generate popular feeling', *Heilongjiang Ribao* 3.1.1984, p 1.
8   Bing Yushu, 'Inquiry into building commodity grain bases in Heilongjiang province', *Nongye Jishu Jingji*, 1983 (4) pp 6-10, tr FBIS/CR/A 7.9.1983, pp 70-8.
9   Yang Yichen (b), 'Problems concerning the development of the rural economy in Heilongjiang province', *Jingji Guanli*, 1981 (12) pp 3-6.
10  *Beijing Review*, 'Heilongjiang - a mechanised granary', 27.10.1980 23 (43) pp 23-4.
11  Yu Quanyu, Ren Yongda & Bao Quan, 'Liming brigade through their own efforts implement agricultural mechanisation', *People's Daily*, 4.6.1979, p 2.
12  Yu Quanyu, 'Walk the path of self-reliance to promote agricultural mechanisation', *People's Daily*, 4.6.1979, p 2.
13  Yu Quanyu *et al*, op cit; Yu Quanyu, op cit; Li Tianxing *et al* (b), op cit.
14  Jing Bo & Mou Weixu, 'Raise production efficiency, speed up wealth', *People's Daily*, 12.3.1980, p 3.
15  Ibid.
16  Li Tianxing & Jing Bo (a), 'Centre on mechanisation to improve management', *People's Daily*, 23.11.1980, p 2.
17  Li Tianxing *et al* (a), op cit.
18  Xu Bu, 'Examination of a few questions on the promotion of agricultural mechanisation in Heilongjiang', *Nongye Jishu Jingji*, 1983 (6) pp 19-22, tr FBIS/CR/A 26.1.1984, pp 58-63.
19  Ibid.
20  Ibid.
21  Bing Yushu, op cit.
22  *People's Daily*, 'Gannan county achieves bumper harvests in grain and oil-bearing crops', 25.1.1980, p 2.

23  Yang Yichen (b), op cit.

24  Bing Yushu, op cit.

25  Dai Xu *et al*, op cit.

26  Yang Yichen (b), op cit.

27  Shen Jiken & Wang Yang, 'The western part of our province's shelter-belt forest construction begins to take shape', *Heilongjiang Ribao*, 23.8.1984, p 2.

28  Ibid.

29  Yang Yichen (b), op cit.

30  Yang Yichen (a), op cit.

31  Yu Quanyu *et al*, op cit.

32  Yang Yichen (b), op cit; Yu Quanyu *et al*, op cit; Yu Quanyu, op cit; Bing Yushu, op cit, p 74.

33  Li Tianxing, Zhang Wuhou & Jing Bo (b), 'Implement specialised production contracts and formulate agricultural, industrial and sideline all-round development', *People's Daily*, 17.12.1980, p 2.

34  Liang Yuxiu *et al*, op cit.

35  *Heilongjiang radio*, 'Heilongjiang's responsibility systems examined', 16.8.1981 tr FBIS/DR/PRC 17.8.1981, S1-2.

36  Heilongjiang social science research institute (b), 'Implementing the contract responsibility system with agricultural mechanisation - an investigation into several commodity grain base counties', *Xuexi Yu Tansuo (Study and Investigate)*, 1984 (3) pp 17-20.

37  Chen Qing and Jiang Yongde, 'Shuanghe's large-scale agricultural machines and tools are all sold to the peasants', *Heilongjiang Ribao*, 13.8.1984, p 1.

38  Pei Shouju, op cit.  Zhao Guo & Du Zixin, 'Jianhua production brigade guides peasants to pay attention to economic benefits', *Heilongjiang Ribao*, 7.6.1984, p 2.

39  *Heilongjiang radio*, untitled, 29.11.1983 tr FBIS/CR/A 12.1.1984, p 56.

40  Li Lian (a), 'Efforts should be made to develop a new situation in the initial prosperity of the province's rural areas', *Heilongjiang radio*, 19.1.1984 tr FBIS/CR/A 20.1.1984, S1-3.

41  Bing Yushu, op cit.

42  Zhang Haishan, 'Specialised grain households purchase fertiliser and fine seed strains without having to leave the brigade', *Heilongjiang Ribao*, 24.2.1984, p 2.

43  *People's Daily*, 'Taiping brigade relies on collective strength for agricultural mechanisation', 26.8.1971 tr SCMP 1971 (36) pp 136-41.  Heilongjiang revolutionary committee, 'Fight the great task of speeding up realisation of agricultural mechanisation', *People's Daily*, 7.8.1980 tr SCMP 1970 (33) pp 83-9.

41  Li Tianxing *et al* (a), op cit.

45  Li Tianxing *et al* (b), op cit.  Yu Quanyu *et al*, op cit.

46  Ibid.
47  Li Tianxing *et al* (a), op cit.
48  Guan Defeng & Pang Zhongliang, 'Seven peasants combine to establish a pulp mill', *Heilongjiang Ribao*, 8.4.1984, p 2.
49  Pang Zhongliang (a), 'Eight commune members combine investment funds to establish an oil mill', *Heilongjiang Ribao*, 8.4.1984, p 2.
50  Jin Fengshan & Zhang Lijie, 'Eight household enterprises are rewarded, two household enterprises are penalised', *Heilongjiang Ribao*, 7.8.1984, p 2.
51  Wang Lijuan, 'Longjiang light industry scales even greater heights', *Heilongjiang Ribao*, 4.4.1984, p 2. Tong Yongda & Wang Ruigang, 'Nenjiang prefecture's industry makes up deficits and commerce increases surpluses', *Heilongjiang Ribao*, 26.8.1984, p 1.
52  Yang Yichen (c), 'Take the road of co-ordinated development of agriculture, industry and commerce', *Red Flag*, 1.11.1982 tr JPRS/CR/RF No 21, pp 59-67.
53  *Xinhua*, 'Northeast China production brigade develops agriculture in an all-round way', 31.5.1971 in SCMP 1971 (23) pp 171-2. Yang Yichen (a), op cit.
54  Yang Yichen (b), op cit.
55  Lin Shufan, 'Longjiang's Xingshan area's villages build a sheep-dipping vat', *Heilongjiang Ribao*, 18.6.1984, p 2.
56  Zhang Ruigang, Sun Yingjie & Pei Shouju, 'Gannan county sheep-breeding changes', *Heilongjiang Ribao*, 30.8.1984, p 2.
57  Provincial and county animal husbandry survey, 'Baiquan county pig-breeding industry develops more quickly than last year', *Heilongjiang Ribao*, 18.6.1984, p 2.
58  Wang Jingzi & Li Jizhong, 'Kedong and six other counties purchase a lean meat variety of boar', *Heilongjiang Ribao*, 26.7.1984, p 2. Gui Chen, 'Kedong county pig breeders turn defeat into victory', *Heilongjiang Ribao*, 31.5.1984, p 2. Zhang Xueju, 'Xiangyang village has 29% of its labour force engaged in the transport industry', *Heilongjiang Ribao*, 2.5.1984, p 2.
59  Provincial and County survey, op cit. Li Tianxing & Zhang Xiang (c), 'Lianmin brigade has a new development in breeding pigs', *Heilongjiang Ribao*, 1.1.1984, p 2. Bai Chunwen & Yang Ruigang, 'Give specialised households preferential supplies of fodder', *Heilongjiang Ribao*, 1.8.1984, p 2.
60  Pang Zhongliang (b), 'Fuyu county greatly develops processing and breeding industries', *Heilongjiang Ribao*, 11.10.1984, p 1. Wang Shucai & Ma Yuren, 'Keshan agricultural and commercial contracts are well administered', *Heilongjiang Ribao*, 4.3.1984, p 1.
61  Han Xuejian, 'Extend an open policy to find places for surplus labourers, *Heilongjiang Ribao*, 24.7.1984, p 1.
62  Li Lian (b), 'Call for further reform of China's rural economy', *China Daily*, 29.3.1984 in FBIS/CR/A 1.5.1984, pp 49-51.

63  *Heilongjiang Ribao*, 'Heilongjiang Ribao on economic achievements', 1.10.1984 tr FBIS/DR/PRC 19.10.1984, S1-2.
64  Li Yinghua, op cit.
65  Li Yinghua, 'Yian estimate that the whole of the potato yield will be sold', *Heilongjiang Ribao*, 16.8.1984, p 1.
66  Liu Jianxi, Gao Shude & Pei Shouju, 'Three villages combine to create an agricultural and commercial unified management company', *Heilongjiang Ribao*, 14.6.1984, p 1.
67  Pang Zhongliang (b), op cit.
68  Ge Zhongliang, untitled, *Heilongjiang Ribao*, 31.5.1984, p 2.
69  Feng Qian, 'After a bumper harvest of wheat, how is the recent grain to be harvested?', *Heilongjiang Ribao*, 9.8.1984, p 2.
70  Yuan Guoshan, 'Nehe grain depot adopts four measures', *Heilongjiang Ribao*, 13.2.1984, p 2.
71  Bing Yushu, op cit. Zhan Wu, op cit. Shi Yanjiang, 'Repair the roads well, come close to new sources of grain', *Heilongjiang Ribao*, 1.8.1984, p 2.
72  Zhang Qiang, 'Kedong repairs over 200 km of rural roads', *Heilongjiang Ribao*, 21.7.1984, p 2.
73  Wang Liancai, 'An integrated network of public roads has been tentatively completed within the province', *Heilongjiang Ribao*, 26.5.1984, p 1.
74  Zhao Tieshang & Li Dong, 'Longjiang passenger transport station makes it even more convenient for peasants to transport commodities and sell them in the city', *Heilongjiang Ribao*, 8.3.1984, p 2.
75  Wang Ruigang, 'Nehe transport and commercial specialised households sell overstocked potatoes', *Heilongjiang Ribao*, 27.7.1984, p 1.
76  Zhang Xueju & Wang Rui, 'Kedong integrates the supply of pig semen strains', *Heilongjiang Ribao*, 2.5.1984, p 2.
77  Li Tianxing *et al* (a), op cit; (b), op cit; Han Qiang, op cit; Pei Shouju, op cit; Yang Yichen (c), op cit; *Heilongjiang Ribao*, 15.5.1983, op cit; Li Lian (b), op cit.
78  Fu Xigui, 'Yu Renxia spurs on half the households in her village to breed rabbits', *Heilongjiang Ribao*, 23.2.1984, p 2.
79  Mou Weixu, 'Each agricultural labourer produces over 26,000 *jin* of grain', *People's Daily*, 20.1.1979, p 2.
80  Mou Weixu, op cit.
81  Zhou Wei, 'Let specialised households feel rest assured when taking the road to wealth', *Heilongjiang Ribao*, 22.9.1984, p 1.
82  *Heilongjiang Ribao*, 'Continue to deal severe blows at serious economic crimes'. 21.1.1984 tr FBIS/DR/PRC 16.2.1984, S1-2. *Heilongjiang Ribao*, 'Heilongjiang on dealing blows to economic crime', 29.1.1985 tr FBIS/DR/PRC 14.2.1985, S1.

# Chapter Eight

# Yanbei Prefecture: Specialised Production

## Introduction

The 1978 reforms prompted the emergence of numerous production management forms throughout China, including a variety of specialised production units. In Yanbei prefecture it is possible to distinguish in the literature one management form - the grain-producing specialised household - which, it is claimed, is emerging to have a dominant influence both upon the shape of the prefecture's rural economy and also upon the direction in which it is headed. The development, influence, and practical difficulties associated with the grain-producing specialised household, will therefore form the heart of this discussion upon the rural economy of Yanbei prefecture.

## Yanbei prefecture: the setting

Yanbei prefecture is situated on the Saiwai plateau in the north of Shanxi province. The prefecture is made up of 13 counties - Tianzhen, Yanggao, Guangling, Lingqiu, Hunyuan, Datong, Huairen, Ying, Shanyin, Zuoyun, Youyu, Pinglu and Shuo - and also includes the industrial city of Datong (see Figure 13).

Yanbei has traditionally been a backward area. Grain yields have for many years been low, peasant livelihood difficult. Average annual temperatures are low, the frost-free period is short, severe wind storms are frequent, annual rainfall is only about 400 mm, vegetation cover is lacking, and ecological conditions are considered poor.[1]

Much of Yanbei consists of an unbroken chain of undulating mountains. An estimated 74.7% of the prefecture's total land area - 25.51 million *mu* - is considered mountainous.[2] Much of the prefecture lies between 1000 and 2000 metres above sea level. The only significant area of lowland (land below 1000 metres above sea level) is the plain of the Sanggan river (see Figure 13).

Against these inhospitable physical conditions, Yanbei can boast two aspects of superiority: the first is the wealth of coal resources, ten of the counties possessing significant coal reserves;[3] and secondly, the relative abundance of land. The total land area of Yanbei is just over 34 million *mu*, three-quarters of which is classified as 'mountain area'. Cultivable land per capita of agricultural population is 4.37 *mu*.[4] Although the amount of cultivable land per capita of agricultural population is considerably lower than the figure of 8 *mu* for Shanxi as a whole, it compares favourably with that for most other provinces.

174

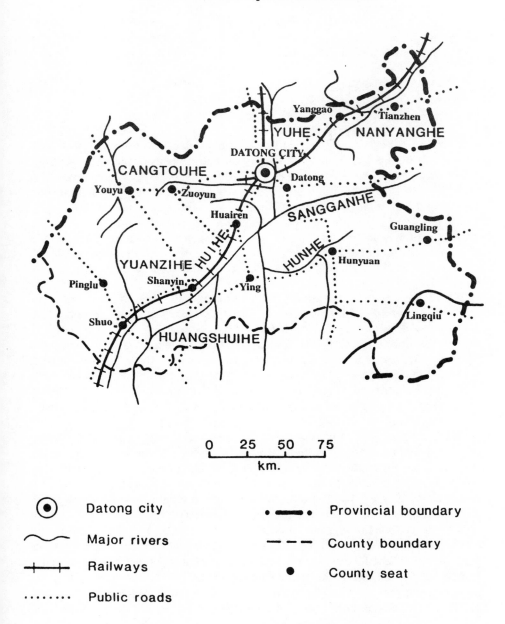

**Figure 13  Yanbei prefecture: major rivers, railways and public roads**

Despite this relative abundance of land and the existence of excellent coal reserves, before 1978 Yanbei remained backward. However, in the current phase, much progress has been reported. How this progress has been achieved is the main concern of this chapter.

## The grain problem and grain specialists

The most important aspect of the current development of Yanbei's agricultural production has been its ability to increase grain production. For many years the province of Shanxi had to depend upon grain deliveries from the state. During the 26 years between 1953 and 1978, the province showed small net exports of grain in only five years and in the other years was a net grain importer, averaging 1 billion *jin* per annum.[5] It would not be unreasonable to suppose that in the same period Yanbei was not a major exporter of grain.

Production problems in Yanbei were numerous. Wheat production, for example - the dominant grain foodstuff - faces longstanding, common problems, such as drought, infertile soil, careless ploughing, and a lack of drought-resistant crop varieties.[6]

This inability to consistently produce sufficient quantities of grain was seen as a major stumbling-block to the all-round development of the economy of Yanbei as well as that of Shanxi. It has been recognised by regional authorities that future development in the region will be built upon its important coal reserves. With this development of coal and subsequently of heavy industry, especially the chemical industry, there will also be a sharp increase in the non-agricultural population. Thus, the region's ability or otherwise to produce more grain becomes a key factor determining the pace of growth of key state industrial construction projects.[7]

Since 1978, grain production in Yanbei has undoubtedly improved. While there is clearly no room for complacency, at the same time there does appear to be some basis for cautious optimism. Grain production in 1978 was around 1.5 billion *jin*, with commodity grain sales of 209 million *jin*, a commodity rate of 14%. By 1982, grain production was up to over 2 billion *jin*, with commodity grain sales of 520 million *jin*, a commodity rate of over 25%.[8]

This improvement in grain production can be attributed to a variety of sources. The success of the production responsibility systems in improving peasant enthusiasm for production, including grain production, is widely noted.[9] Equally important, were the good climatic conditions of the early 1980s, in particular the regular precipitation levels. This is a point which is rarely made by Chinese commentators - most preferring to concentrate on the impact of administrative changes - but carries great weight in determining agricultural performance.[10]

Furthermore, crop rotations have been rationalised, fertiliser applications have improved both in quantity and quality, and many aspects of production are now subject to the use of advanced agricultural techniques.

Yet despite these improvements, two important reservations remain. First, numerous problems continue to beset agricultural production. In Yanbei's wheat production for example, many spring wheat varieties are predominantly planted on dry land where wheat production is essentially, from planting through to harvest, a chancy proposition. Where rotten and diseased roots occur, output is seriously reduced. Furthermore, extensive cultivation is the norm, and per *mu* yields often do not exceed 100 *jin*. In essence these are the same noted earlier as being longstanding problems in wheat production. Obviously there are few signs of progress here.

The second reservation is that in spite of the improvements fostered by the introduction of responsibility systems into agricultural production, all too often the mere fulfilment of state grain targets is only sufficient to meet the basic demands of the state for grain. This point is made very clearly - unusually so - in the following lengthy but revealing passage:

> For the past few years the responsibility system has greatly motivated the productive energies of the masses. At the same time, the state has adopted various measures to aid grain production, and brought about outstanding results in both grain production and purchase. But the grain sold by the vast majority of peasant households was still only the remainder left after satisfying their own needs. Although the commodity rate has gradually risen, due to the influence of various factors such as amount of land managed and productivity, generally speaking the commodity rate for grain is still quite low, and basically we still do not have commercialised production. Consequently sales to the state of commercial grain are still not very secure, and the quantity level is not stable either. Moreover, in recent years some areas have squeezed out cultivated land by blindly expanding cash crops and large-scale construction of homes etc, so that the grain-growing area has shrunk.[11]

In many ways such a state of affairs is not unexpected. Yanbei's natural conditions as outlined above mean that agricultural production is always difficult and much long-term as well as short-term investment is needed before yields can substantially increase. Given that in 1978, per capita incomes in the mountain areas which make up the bulk of Yanbei were only 30.4 *yuan*, it is not surprising to discover that such investment has not been great up to the present.[12] In such harsh conditions, it is difficult to persuade peasants that investment in the land from household incomes is a worthwhile proposition. This is especially true for grain producers.

To overcome these varied problems, many commentators advocate the widespread use of grain-producing specialised households. Yanbei, they argue, should plan to come to rely on specialised grain production households to fulfil state grain purchase targets for the prefecture.[13]

The advantages of such a development are said to be numerous. The most significant is that such a move helps to guarantee that the state obtains a sufficient supply of commodity grain. This is because of the high marketing rates claimed for such grain specialists. By the mid-1980s, there were 22,000 grain-producing specialists in Yanbei (that is, households with sales of over 10,000 *jin* of grain to the state). These 22,000 households represented less than 4% of total rural households, yet they sold 340 million *jin* of grain to the state (almost two-thirds of total grain sales) and had an average commodity rate of over 75%, three times the average rate in Yanbei.[14]

This obvious superiority in the grain output characteristics of grain specialists, so the argument runs, makes a reliance upon such households for commodity grain supplies an attractive proposition to the state. Not only, it is claimed, will grain supplies be stable, but because the households which supply a large amount of commodity grain are a very small proportion of the total number of peasant households, the implementation and supervision of commodity grain sales contracts is easier. There can be little doubt that the state prefers to keep grain production under strict state regulation - though, as yet, relationships between grain specialists and the state remain unclear.[15]

Several questions must also be raised about a grain production strategy based upon a small number of specialist producers as envisaged above. First, there is the problem of dependence upon a small number of households responsible for producing the bulk of Yanbei's commodity grain requirements. If too much reliance is placed upon these grain specialists, any shortfall in their production from adverse weather conditions for instance - not improbable in this part of China - could have significant repercussions.

Again, there is the matter of insisting that grain specialists adhere to contracts. If grain specialists do not fulfil production targets agreed upon in their contracts then the system will falter. Some specialists in Yanbei are reported to have only partially fulfilled contracted obligations.[16] This is clearly an unwelcome situation and one which the state cannot allow. It must exert what authority it has upon grain specialists to ensure that contracts are adhered to (although, of course, sometimes contracts are unrealistic).

Nevertheless in the minds of most commentators, such doubts are outweighed by other advantages. It is argued that grain specialists benefit the promotion of diversified undertakings and increased specialisation of production beyond grain.[17] Their ability to supply Yanbei with much of its commodity grain requirements allows other households to reduce grain commitments or even cease grain production entirely. Thus, diversification becomes easier, some households specialising in another form of agricultural production or even 'leaving the land' to specialise in undertakings other than farming. By 1983, in Ying county for example, 4060 households were considered to have 'freed themselves from the land', 6.9% of the total number of peasant households in the county.[18]

Those households which either leave farming or diversify from grain production can in turn assist grain specialists. Households which turn to concentrate on livestock-breeding, for instance, can supply fertiliser in return for fodder grain; households which develop a specialist knowledge of certain agricultural techniques can help increase yields; and households which concentrate on commercial activities can assist in the marketing of grain.[19] Numerous interactions between a wide range of households can be developed. This represents a distinct change in attitude from the 'small but complete' Maoist production models which had previously prevailed, whereby each individual production unit was responsible for producing a certain amount of grain foodstuffs, including that for personal consumption. It is this kind of interaction which represents a clear shift from previous rural thinking, and of course, which makes a return to previous policies all the more difficult.

In neighbouring Xinxian prefecture, immediately to the south of Yanbei, is Hengshan brigade, Dingxiang county.[20] Hengshan has witnessed specialisation of production develop to a marked degree throughout the whole brigade. Almost a third of the households are considered grain specialists, with a similar number engaged in cash crop production. Ten percent concentrate on sideline occupations - rural industry, forestry and herding. A smaller number provide a variety of specialised services - including irrigation work, commerce, and transport. The remaining households are non-specialists.[21]

Many commentators see Hengshan brigade as the model for development which Yanbei should adopt - that is, a small number of grain specialists, with other households specialising in other agricultural and non-agricultural production tasks and yet more households catering for the service needs of those households involved in production. In this way a mutual link is established between the growth of grain specialists and other specialised forms, in particular the specialised household. While, initially the expansion of grain production by specialists was a response to the greatly increased needs of other types of specialised households for food and fodder grains, more recently a reciprocal relationship has begun to emerge.

A further advantage claimed for grain specialists is that they can promote the use of advanced agricultural techniques and so increase yields.[22] In Datong County, for example, grain specialists farm on average 11 *mu*, compared to 8.3 *mu* for non-grain specialists. Their investment in the land is also higher (34.5 *yuan/mu* compared to 16 *yuan/mu*) as is fertiliser application (130 *jin/mu* to 58 *jin/mu*). Use of fine seed strains among grain specialists is 23.6% higher than non-grain specialists, with disease prevention techniques also more widespread among grain specialists.[23]

The motivation for using such techniques is increased yield and higher incomes to offset the higher investment costs, - although it must also be said that grain specialists may have better access to such limited producer goods than ordinary households.

Grain specialists often contract out certain production tasks involving modern agricultural techniques to specialised service households and companies. In Datong county, for example, detailed contracts are drawn up between grain specialists and the county technical service departments. In these contracts, compensation arrangements are made for grain producers, should correct utilisation of advanced agricultural techniques not produce estimated yields. Under these agreements, the technical departments would compensate for 50% of the households' shortfall. Alternatively, if the households exceed the agreed yields, the technical department would collect 20% of the surplus.

As it reads however, such agreements appear fraught with difficulty. In the event of adverse weather conditions for instance, it is unclear who - if anybody - will take the responsibility for any shortfall in output. Furthermore, what is considered 'correct utilisation' of techniques remains vague.

A final advantage claimed for grain production by grain specialists is the economic benefit to specialists. Consider the following data again drawn from Datong county.

**Table 1 Datong county. A comparison of income and yield data for grain production by grain specialists and non-specialists. 1983**

|  | Grain specialists | Non-specialists |
| --- | --- | --- |
| Average per-unit yields (*jin/mu*) | 371.0 | 256.4 |
| Average per-unit net incomes (*yuan/mu*) | 37.1 | 29.07 |
| Average workday values (*yuan*) | 3.37 | 2.9 |
| Average net income (*yuan*/capita) | 407.0 | 350.0 |

Compiled from materials in Datong county party committee and people's government, op cit.

It must be said that the production conditions found in Datong county are comparatively favourable: soils are fertile; there is a comparative abundance of water; and a relatively good infrastructure. Nevertheless, while production and income levels may be above average for Yanbei as a whole, there is no reason to doubt that the comparative benefits of producing grain by specialised households are found consistently throughout the prefecture.

Before any of the advantages claimed above can come into play, however, certain conditions must be met. The most important condition seems to be satisfying the grain specialists' demands for land.[24] It is clear that the average land holdings of grain specialists are greater than those of non-specialists. In this way, they are able to reap economies of scale and fully utilise their expertise in grain production. Given the longstanding problem of land shortage in China, where is this land likely to be found?

The Datong county authorities were confronted with exactly this problem.[25] In 1984, they needed to increase the contracted area allotted to grain specialists by 11,000 *mu*. To do this they utilised five different sources of land: reserve land (4200 *mu*); land transferred from other specialised households under the supervision of the collective (1500 *mu*); land recalled from other households (3600 *mu*); private transfers of land from other specialised households (1200 *mu*); and 'wasteland' (500 *mu*).[26]

A number of points emerge from this list. First is the importance of holdings of reserve land as a source of land for grain specialists. Yanbei is fortunate in this respect that land is comparatively abundant. In other more densely populated areas it is questionable whether such large reserves of land are available. How such large reserves of land actually came into being is, however, open to much speculation.

Secondly, there is the recall of land from a variety of sources where there is insufficient labouring ability to effectively carry on cultivation. When this recall takes place, numerous guarantees including the maintenance of the quantity and quality of the grain ration have to be made and effectively kept.

Finally, the importance of land transfers from other specialised households - both privately and through the collective - is also apparent. Interestingly, in 1983, of 32,000 *mu* of additional land contracted to grain specialists in Datong county, only 249 *mu* came through transfers from other specialists.[27] The reason for this change in 1984 is unclear. It may be an indication of the significant shift towards specialisation in non-farming activities by a greater number of households who subsequently relinquish some of their landholdings. Nevertheless, given the importance attached to grain production, and the need in Yanbei to make grain specialisation work, 'commandism' cannot be excluded.

Further to the actual amount of land allotted to grain specialists, it is also clear that such land, where possible, is to be concentrated.[28] Normally, a household would expect a number of small parcels of land of varying fertility. Such dispersed landholdings are inconvenient and unsuitable for the type of production envisaged for grain specialists. The authorities in Yanbei have therefore taken steps to ensure that grain specialists have relatively concentrated holdings of land. Using the slogan 'those with a lot of capacity, contract a lot; those with a little capacity, contract a little; and those with no labour capacity, contract nothing', land has been concentrated.[29] Such a slogan relates to the amount of labour power usually found in a grain-producing specialised household.[30]

The key measure adopted in Yanbei to consolidate land holdings has been to encourage households to transfer land through the collective and not to undertake private transfers. Not only does this enable the collective to ensure that land is distributed to those grain specialists who need it and to maintain some level of concentration in such a distribution, it also reduces the practice of illegal 'rent payments' for the use of land. Little is said, however, about the precise nature of such 'encouragement'.

There is little doubt that the landholdings of some grain specialists are becoming very large indeed, with some holdings reaching as much as 600 *mu*.[31] Given such landholdings, it is not surprising to discover that in 1983, 16 grain specialists in Yanbei were each able to produce more than 100,000 *jin* of commodity grain in addition to the more than 22,000 selling more than 10,000 *jin* of commodity grain.[32] Small wonder that much is expected from the development of grain specialists.

Given that, in the current phase, the land area sown with grain is falling, and in the foreseeable future the imbalance between population and land resources will continue, the importance of claims concerning the ability of grain specialists to improve per-unit yields through the adoption of advanced agricultural methods is paramount. Yet, it has also been noted that the application of advanced methods requires both a relatively high level of investment and also the availability of producer goods.

A considerable number of grain specialists in Datong county in 1983 for instance, spent over 5000 *yuan* on production inputs.[33] With low state prices for grain this expenditure might be surprising were it not for the claimed level of economic benefits for grain specialists. However, it must be said that such economic benefits hide within them a significant amount of priorities, rewards and subsidies. In Yanbei, the problem of the price differential between grain and economic crops has, of necessity, given rise to a situation whereby grain specialists are compensated for growing grain.[34] This compensation takes several forms.

There is, for example, a variety of priorities to be considered. It has already been shown that grain specialists receive priorities both in the distribution and packaging of land. They also receive priority when applying for loans for capital investment. Such loans have three sources: agricultural banks; commune or brigade funds; and grain departments who can advance up to 30% of the basic payment expected for fulfilment of signed contracts.[35]

Of greater significance are such priorities as: prior claim to the means of production, that is supplies of fertiliser and diesel oil; priority in the allocation of technical services, that is irrigation, drainage and mechanical repair; and finally, priority in the marketing of grain in such areas as grain inspection, bagging materials and transport.[36]

There appear to be two principle forms of reward in operation in Yanbei. The first form is a reduction in the price of producer goods if a grain specialist exceeds quota rates, the reductions increasing as excess quantities grow larger. The second form involves a more straightforward reciprocal approach whereby an amount of supplied commodity grain in any one year is rewarded by the prefecture, county or commune authorities with a particular item. In Datong county for example, 1000 *jin* of commodity grain is rewarded with a like amount of ammonium carbonate, with larger amounts of ammonium carbonate available for even higher sales. Sales of 100,000 *jin* of grain can mean a half-price four-wheeled tractor.[37] Overall a wide range of subsidies can be identified.

First, the means of production - fertiliser, agricultural chemicals, agricultural machinery, water, and electricity - may be available to the grain specialists at lower prices irrespective of total production. This could amount to a considerable overall saving in total production costs.

Secondly, there is subsidised capital investment to improve the agricultural resource base available to grain specialists. In Liaohuozhuang brigade, Zuoyun county, for example, 60,000 *yuan* of the 200,000 *yuan* brigade income from industrial and sideline occupations in 1982 was used as supplemental aid in the building of 6000 metres of irrigation ditches, three irrigation stations and the levelling of 6000 *mu* of land primarily intended for utilisation by grain specialists.[38]

Thirdly, there is a system of equalising income operating within Yanbei. Under this system, it is intended that an equal amount of labour expended by different occupations within a given collective unit will receive financial rewards that are approximately equal. This basically amounts to giving supplemental help to grain producers from the relatively high incomes obtained by those engaged in diversification and rural industry.

In 1984 alone, Yanbei used two to three million *yuan* from the financial resources of the prefecture, county and commune, to subsidise grain specialists in a variety of ways.[39] No doubt when brigade and team subsidies are also taken into account - as argued below - the actual level of subsidy is much higher, a point which worries some commentators. They warn against reliance on the expansion of subsidies. Some production units, they argue, award material incentives to grain specialists in addition to lowering state quotas and required accumulation contributions. This is considered excessive.[40]

Whether the combination of these various incentives to grain specialists actually represents an excess or otherwise is open to debate. The need for incentives does, however, reflect low state purchase prices for grain. They also throw a different light upon the benefits claimed for this mode of production. Clearly, the economic results are not as good as indicated after potential subsidies are considered.

Nevertheless, if after the utilisation of a variety of incentives, grain production becomes sufficiently attractive to prompt the emergence of specialist grain producers who can amply fulfil state grain contracts at the same time as freeing other producers from growing grain other than for subsistence (if that), the state will allow such incentives to continue; and localities will continue to try and finance them.

Some commentators are still concerned that adverse income differentials continue to exist, preventing the spread of grain specialists. Yet, while this point is debated, all agree that the preferential treatment which is accorded to grain specialists (to whatever degree) can lead to difficulties. Some specialists have been guilty of fraudulently accepting preferential treatment. In other cases, the distribution of land is prejudiced towards friends and relatives of local cadres. Indeed, given the system of subsidies, priorities and rewards, local cadres inevitably have much opportunity for corruption.[41]

Specialists are also accused of selling subsidised fertiliser supplies at higher prices. Others sell grain privately before fulfilling agreed state sales targets. It seems, however, that the state will not - unofficially at least - be too concerned about such practices while supplies of commodity grain are maintained.

Given the importance of incentives of various types, it becomes crucial to discover how production units can finance them. As with other units in China, rural industry and agricultural sideline occupations are the major source of investment funds. The dominant industry in Yanbei is coal mining, and it is income from coal mining which provides the bulk of funds for the financing of subsidies for grain specialists.

In other more favourable areas, Southern Jiangsu for example, there is less dependence upon a single sector of the economy to provide funds for agricultural development, income being derived from a whole range of undertakings, industrial and agricultural. In Yanbei, coal is the economic mainstay. In Zuoyun county in 1983 for example, county-, commune- and brigade-run mines produced over three million tons of coal with an output value of 62.6 million *yuan* of which the commune- and brigade-run mines contributed 26.87 million *yuan*. Of this 26.87 million *yuan* - 39.4% of the county's gross agricultural income - 5.8 million *yuan* was retained for agricultural capital investment funds.[42] Similar reports are found for other parts of Yanbei.[43]

Throughout the prefecture, it would not be unreasonable to expect that commune- and brigade-run coal mines contribute as much as 50 million *yuan* per annum to collective investment funds, a significant amount of this total undoubtedly being used to promote specialised grain production.

The stability which income from coal provides the rural economy of Zuoyun is well illustrated below.

**Table 2 Zuoyun county: domestic supplies of commodity grain, oil-bearing crops and coal. Total revenue**

|  | Commodity grain (mn *jin*) | Oil-bearing crops (mn *jin*) | Coal (mn tons) | Total net re-venue (mn *yuan*) |
|---|---|---|---|---|
| 1980 | 1.12 | 2 | 0.726 | 5.555 |
| 1981 | 0.53 | 0.59 | 1.018 | 8.102 |
| 1982 | 10.47 | 2.41 | 1.31 | 11.473 |
| 1983 | 27.75 | 11.13 | 1.4 | 13.542 |

Source Yan Zanyao *et al*, op cit.

Table 2 shows that, while in 1981 the supplies of commodity grain and oil-bearing crops were much reduced compared to 1980, total revenue was maintained by income from coal. At the same time as stabilising total revenue, the income from coal production in Zuoyun provided investment funds for the construction of 137,000 *mu* of stable high-yield agricultural land. The availability of this land is reflected in the commodity grain and oil-bearing crop production figures for 1982 and 1983. Additionally, the significant rise in commodity grain supplies must in part be attributed to local subsidies for specialist producers, subsidies provided for mainly from the income of coal sales.

Yanbei prefecture, then, is adopting the use of grain specialists in an effort to improve its grain output. Some authors move beyond the level of individual specialists to comment upon more integrated production networks and county-level commodity grain bases consisting of larger numbers of individual grain specialists and the corresponding service households.[44] However, little detail is given and it is the individual grain specialist around whom the rural economy of Yanbei is currently being shaped.

## Specialised production: the way forward in Yanbei prefecture

It is envisaged that Yanbei, having freed itself from the traditional limitations of small-scale grain production through the development of grain specialists, can go on to further develop all aspects of production. In such a development, it is envisaged that specialised production management forms will feature prominently, in particular the specialised household. A model of all-round specialisation of a local economy has already been noted in Hengshan brigade, Xinxian prefecture. Yanbei authorities, utilising the specialised household as the main building-block, envisage similar all-round specialisation at the prefectural level.

The proportion of specialised households, for example, in Yanbei, 23.8% of total households (of which one-fifth are grain specialists), compares well to a national average of 13%.[45]

This is surprising given the relatively poor natural conditions said to exist in Yanbei. Yet, it must be said that the prefectural authorities are promoting specialisation of production with considerable energy - bolstered by financial resources from coal production. It is also claimed that in some instances, the harshness of terrain can itself stimulate specialised production. Nanyulin commune, for example, is a remote mountainous production unit in Shuo county, Southwest Yanbei. It has 3400 *mu* of cultivable land, most of which is dry-slope land. Even after the introduction of production responsibility systems, although some improvement occurred in output and income, the scale of this improvement was small. Grain production was limited by low temperatures, inadequate rainfall and sandy soils. Taking the advice of an agronomist it was decided that the commune should specialise in the production of a crop of Chinese Yams, more suited to the natural conditions than the grain crops being grown by Nanyulin peasants. Initially there was much resistance to this move. Commercial and processing problems remained. However, with the purchase of processing machinery by the commune, most peasants began to specialise in yam production and incomes rose.[46]

Thus, it would seem that specialisation of production can occur in areas of inhospitable as well as hospitable terrain, although it is difficult to gauge how far the above example can be taken as a model for specialisation in backward areas. Yanbei may well be a special case, and the local authorities trying to prove a point. Nevertheless, in Yanbei, the number of specialised households alongside other specialised production management forms such as commodity production bases, combinations of specialised households such as the 'Sanjiacun', and specialised villages, all indicate a significant degree of specialisation.[47]

However, if this numerical abundance of specialised production management forms in Yanbei is to be translated into a functioning specialised economy a number of conditions must be met: first, commodity grain supplies must be guaranteed. As already discussed, it is hoped that grain specialists can fulfil this condition. Secondly, the use of specialised management forms must be rational. Thirdly, adequate service levels - assisting in the application of advanced agricultural techniques - must be achieved. Fourthly, processing industries and all aspects of the commercial system must be relatively efficient. Specialisation of production implies increased commodity relationships between numerous production units over a wide spatial area. Such relationships can only occur if the commercial system is effective. If it is not, specialisation will be limited. Finally, some amount of capital investment in the agricultural resource base must take place.

Turning first to the question of rationality in the use of specialised production management forms. No exact details are available in the Yanbei materials as to the requirements necessary for specialised households to be recognised as such, yet it would appear that there are some examples of households being called 'specialised households' before they have really established themselves as specialist producers. Whilst claiming that the vast majority of specialised households are rationally based, it is admitted that throughout Yanbei some specialised households pay little attention to economic results.[48]

There are really two main areas of concern. The first is that many so-called specialists are by no means experts in their chosen fields of production. A whole series of accusations can be made against some specialised households including that they pay no attention to product quality, have little idea of cost, engage in blind investment and production, have limited managerial expertise and do not understand market information. It is difficult to see how these households can be considered 'specialists' in anything other than name given these complaints.[49]

In a number of cases it would appear that in the wave of enthusiasm for production and willingness to adopt new production management forms which followed the 1978 reforms, local cadres - partly no doubt in an effort to promote personal political ambitions - blindly pushed specialised households irrespective of local conditions and experience. Take, for example, the case of the household of Ma Daxiang, Xinpu brigade, Libazhuang commune, Huairen county.[50] The commune lent Ma Daxiang 1060 *yuan* to buy 1000 chicks in order that he might establish the county's first poultry-breeding specialised household. Neither Ma Daxiang nor any of his household had any knowledge of the techniques involved in poultry-breeding, and after three weeks 550 of the chicks were 'half-dead'.

The second area of concern involves subsidies to specialised households of all types and not simply grain specialists. The granting of subsidies and loans to specialised production management forms in all kinds of agricultural production appears to be commonplace in Yanbei. Usually, such loans and subsidies are accompanied by measures to ensure as far as possible effective utilisation and a reasonable rate of return. In Zuoyun county, Hangeta brigade for example, a forestry specialised household contracted 3500 *mu* of responsibility land for ten years. In the contract the household had to give 2000 *yuan* per annum to the brigade for collective accumulation funds. However, in the first year there was a shortfall of 1000 *yuan*. The brigade decided to subsidise the household for five years, with 800 *yuan* being given to them from collective accumulation funds every year. This subsidy was conditional upon the household improving its production record, especially timber survival rates. Given the subsidy of the brigade, in this example the household increased survival rates and prospered.[51]

The exercise of similar control is also well illustrated in Shiyu county. Shiyu has a large fodder capacity and is considered to have excellent characteristics for the development of animal husbandry. However, when the county initially encouraged specialisation in animal husbandry, households in Houzhuangwang brigade, Xihuangjiayao commune for example, were more concerned with the employment of surplus labour capacity than with the economics of livestock breeding. Thus, when Shiyu county authorities directly invested 150,000 *yuan* to purchase cattle to develop specialisation in cattle breeding, they laid down precise guidelines as to the characteristics of households which were to become specialised producers. These guidelines included the number of cattle to be held, the quality of enclosure facilities, and accessibility to fodder supplies. It was hoped that this would ensure successful breeding and a worthwhile utilisation of county investment funds.[52]

However, despite the controls over subsidies and loans illustrated above, on some occasions such funds are undoubtedly misused, for instance subsidies being allocated with vested interests in mind.[53] This should not be too surprising. In Zuoyun county, as in many rural areas, specialised households are established to utilise what were previously collectively-run undertakings.[54] Not only is this an area in which the personal interests of local cadres can often shape the actual distribution of such undertakings, but it is also seen by some as being detrimental to the general collective interest as undertakings which previously benefited all now appear to benefit only a number of households. (While this is almost inevitable, Chinese commentators have ignored the issue in discussions of specialised households based upon previously collective undertakings, either not recognising it or, more likely, not admitting it.)

In Yanbei, it would appear that in some cases the swift emergence of specialised households may have been a little too hasty. Some reassessment must take place and in the meantime efforts are being made to firmly control the development of specialised households in order to reassure the state that any problems are short-lived. As commentators note with some alarm, state policy concerning specialised production forms must not be changed because of a minority of ill-conceived ventures.[55] There is much - in terms of increased rural income and employment opportunities - at stake here.

A further condition for the full development of a specialised rural economy in Yanbei is an effective agricultural service sector, that is the efficient provision of advanced agricultural production methods. Numerous examples of the development of such a service industry are found in the Yanbei material.[56]

However, the materials offer little detail as to the exact nature of the services offered throughout Yanbei. In numerical terms, technical contract agreements between agricultural technicians and peasant households in 1983, were said to number between 356,850 and 400,000 households.[57] Both figures represent a significant proportion - c 64.5 to c 71.5% - of the total number of households within Yanbei, and not simply the number of specialised households.

Against the figures for contracts signed were contrasted much lower figures for the actual number of technical personnel working in Yanbei in the same year. Estimates ranged from 731 to over 6739.[58] In some senses, the discrepancies in the available figures make any conclusions tentative if not meaningless. They offer a spread of 1:53 to 1:547 in terms of the ratio between agricultural technicians and those households signing contracts for technical work. The first figure of 1:53 is clearly quite a reasonable ratio, while the latter would indicate that the level of technical services for many households is at best superficial. The truth is probably somewhere between the two.

The development of a specialised economy also requires the existence of effective processing industries and commercial channels. For the most part, commentators throughout China appear typically confused on this issue. Much praise is heaped upon the effectiveness of the processing industries and the commercial system, yet, at the same time, the need for substantial improvements is also noted. The material from Yanbei is no different in this respect.

Commercial problems can be divided into two broad categories: organisational and infrastructural. The problem of organisation is essentially that of inefficiency within the commercial bureaucracy. Even with the implementation of managerial responsibility systems, the work of commercial departments and supplementary collective commercial organisations remained weak. Practices such as arbitrarily increasing grain sales prices, the use of inferior materials and short weight are just some of the problems peasants face.[59] Furthermore, peasants complain bitterly that consumer and producer goods are all too often not available in the countryside.[60]

Yanbei's infrastructural problems primarily consist of a lack of road accessibility within the prefecture. Although most of the county towns are reasonably connected, off the major road routes communication is very inconvenient. This is not surprising given the nature of the terrain. Up to 40% of the mountain brigades are still dependent upon carrying goods upon their backs to reach markets. There is clearly a need to construct new roads as well as to repair the established routes to ensure convenient traffic flows.[61]

Processing facilities in Yanbei are also considered inadequate. In Shiyu county in 1982, 100 million *jin* of potatoes were produced. Only 95 million *jin* were needed to fulfil contracts, satisfy seed, fodder and foodstuff requirements. Of the surplus of 5 million *jin*, only 4 million *jin* was taken up and processed by households because they lacked sufficient processing capacity, 1 million *jin* going to waste. Furthermore, of the original 95 million *jin*, 6 million *jin* of potatoes ultimately went to waste because processing facilities were insufficient to meet the demands placed upon them and potatoes began sprouting and rotting. As a result of these problems, the county invested over 97,000 *yuan* in processing machinery to establish 150 processing specialised households. Although this satisfied demands for potato processing facilities in the county, numerous other difficulties remained.[62]

These are just some of the commercial problems which confront units in Yanbei in their current efforts to develop their local economies. One possible solution often offered to these problems is the SMC (Supply and Marketing Cooperatives) organisation. The Yanbei commentators are quick to mention these organisations for their prefecture.[63]

In 1983, 178 communes - about two-thirds of the total number of communes in Yanbei - had some form of SMC organisation, although no details are given. Furthermore, it is claimed that seven counties have some form of integrated commercial system. The Lingqiu county SMC for example, offers four key services: first, solving producer marketing difficulties; secondly, solving problems in the purchase of producer goods; thirdly, encouraging integrated management between households, that is linking production, processing, marketing and transport functions; and finally, making available market information.

While accepting that the mere existence of such SMC organisations may not be translated into solutions on the ground, they are clearly expected to shape future expectations from the Yanbei economy.[64]

Finally, something must be said about the need to improve the agricultural resource base and establish a significant amount of stable high-yield land. The rural economy of Yanbei cannot develop, certainly not along the lines of specialisation as is desired, unless agricultural production is stable. The inability of the state to invest to any significant extent in agricultural capital construction in order to establish stable, high-yield land, means the burden falls upon collective investment funds and the individual households themselves.

In this respect, as noted above, Yanbei is fortunate to possess considerable coal reserves. Income from coal production together with that derived from other rural industry, the diversified economy and sideline undertakings is crucial in the improvement of the agricultural resource base.

Collective investment funds, in themselves, are not sufficient to support the depth of specialisation anticipated for Yanbei given the level of incentives, rewards and priorities which appear to be given to grain-producing and other specialists. Individual households are clearly encouraged and expected to invest in the land. While per capita incomes are much increased in the current phase (323.4 *yuan* being the average in the mountain area of Yanbei), for much individual investment to occur, the state must convince the peasants that current policies are stable and that contractors will continue to be responsible for their contract land in the foreseeable future. This is especially true for those households which are developing the 'four wastes' - wasteland on hills, slopes, in gullies and unused water surfaces - where returns on investment will not be immediately forthcoming.[65]

The Yanbei authorities wish to develop the rural economy along the path of increasing specialisation upon a basis of stable commodity grain supplies provided by a small number of grain specialists. Clearly though, numerous problems exist to place limitations upon such development and the future is by no means assured. Only if these problems can be overcome can specialised production, as envisaged by the Yanbei authorities, be considered plausible.

## Conclusions

There can be little doubt that much improvement has occurred in Yanbei since the 1978 reforms. Grain production has increased, the economy has diversified and to some extent specialised. Yet, Yanbei's economy is still a rural economy in transition and it remains to be seen if this improvement will in reality presage the specialised economy envisaged by the authorities.

Furthermore, given the priorities adopted for the development of the rural economy in Yanbei since the 1978 reforms, other questions will come to the fore. One such question will be how much flexibility the state is prepared to allow the local authorities in order to enliven the rural economy. At some stage, wider political concerns can be expected to bring pressure upon too much liberalisation in the countryside. Concern has already been expressed over illegal rent payments and the hiring of labour, yet such phenomena arise out of the need to increase land holdings and make optimal use of them. That is to say, economic rationale is encouraging unwelcome phenomena but it is also providing the state with supplies of commodity grain in particular and agricultural produce in general. For the moment the state is prepared to put political concerns aside in pursuit of economic prosperity; at some stage, however, it may try to reinforce them.

Again there is the question of differential development and the possibility of income differentials which might also arise. This is particularly true when focussing attention on larger spatial units such as counties and prefectures. At this level, local physical characteristics are likely to have much influence on economic development. Thus, it is not surprising to discover that amidst the general development reported from Yanbei, backwardness is still found.[66]

In many cases, such backwardness results from poor natural conditions and the inability of such production units to generate investment funds to improve the agricultural resource base. While the prefecture as a whole may develop and to some extent prosper, there is no guarantee that the necessary investment funds will reach backward units. Indeed, increased prosperity through specialisation, which seems necessarily to involve widespread incentives being made available to specialist producers, appears to keep investment funds within the control of local production units, especially production brigades and teams.

In the current phase at least, there is little hope of a more equitable distribution of investment funds throughout a large spatial administrative unit such as the prefecture. Indeed, at present, when conflict over investment funds is evident between grain specialists and other specialist producers, it is almost inevitable that the ordinary households will suffer. This is potentially a destabilising situation and one which may cause the prefectural authorities to modify their current development path.

What is clear is that the 1978 reforms in agriculture have promoted development in the rural economy which has brought some prosperity to the peasants. Specialisation of production and the development of a commodity economy, even if somewhat experimental and limited in scope, has begun to occur. However, if further development is to take place, not only are more reforms needed but also a careful balance between economic and political objectives has to be maintained.

# Notes to Chapter Eight

1    Lin Zili & Tao Haili, 'An important advance in renewing rural production patterns - a survey of households specialising in commodity grain in Shanxi's Yanbei prefecture', *Nongye Jingji Wenti* 1983 (9) tr FBIS/CR/A 7.2.1984, pp 71-81.

2    Yan Zanyao & Feng Zigui, 'The fairly rapid development of commodity production in mountain areas of Yanbei prefecture', *Nongye Jingji Wenti*, 1984 (5) pp 15-19.

3    Huo Shilian & Li Ligong, 'Promote reforms and invigorate the rural economy in an overall way - enlightenment gained from Yanbei prefecture's increase in output and income', *Red Flag*, 16.5.1983 tr JPRS/CR/RF No 10, pp 1-8.

4    Yan Zanyao *et al*, op cit; Huo Shilian *et al*, op cit.

5    Zhao Mingzhu & Zhang Zhiyu, 'The important role played by households specialising in grain in promoting rural economic prosperity', *Nongye Jishu Jingji*, 1983 (11) tr FBIS/CR/A 11.7.1984, pp 89-93.

6    Liang Tongfang & Guo Mingyi, 'An analysis of the wheat production situation in our province', *Shanxi Nongye Kexue (Shanxi Agricultural Sciences)* 1982 (9) tr FBIS/CR/A 7.1.1983, pp 59-65.

7    Li Xiuren, 'Shanxi province must greatly develop specialised grain households and key grain households to transform the grain production situation and guarantee key state construction projects', *Chinese Peasant Journal*, 9.6.1983 tr FBIS/CR/A 7.2.1984, pp 68-70.

8    *Shanxi Ribao (Shanxi Daily)*, 28.10.1982, op cit; Lin Zili *et al*, op cit.

9    *Shanxi Ribao*, 'Yanbei prefecture increases agricultural output on a large scale', 28.10.1982 tr FBIS/CR/A 14.1.1983, pp 72-4.

10   Liang Tongfang *et al*, op cit.

11   Li Xiuren, op cit.

12   Yan Zanyao *et al*, op cit.

13   Li Xiuren, op cit. Huo Shilian, op cit.

14   Datong county party committee and people's government, op cit.

15   Lin Zili *et al*, op cit.

16   Han Jianmin, 'Several questions concerned with the sound development of commodity grain specialised households', *Shanxi Ribao*, 20.8.1983, p 2.

17   Lin Zili *et al*, op cit. Wang Tingdong, 'Great hopes for the development of specialised commodity grain households', *Shanxi Ribao*, 7.10.1983 FBIS/CR/A 4.5.1984, pp 79-86.

18   Zhou Qiren *et al*, op cit.

19   Zhang Licai, 'Discussions on matters common to grain-producing specialised households and other specialised households', *Shanxi Ribao*, 19.7.1983, p 2.

20   Zhao Mingzhu *et al*, op cit.

21   Ibid.

22   Wang Tingdong, op cit.
23   Datong county party committee and people's government, op cit.
20   Zhao Mingzhu *et al*, op cit.
25   Datong County, op cit.
26   Ibid.
27   Lin Zili (c), op cit.
28   Shanxi provincial government research office, 'A new way of developing commodity grain production', *Shanxi Ribao*, 13.7.1983, p 3.
29   Lin Zili *et al*, op cit.
30   Zhou Qiren *et al*, op cit.
31   Wang Tingdong, op cit.
32   Lin Zili (c), op cit.  Li Ligong, 'Li Ligong praises grain specialised households', *Shanxi Radio*, 13.2.1984 tr FBIS/DR/PRC 16.2.1984, R2.
33   Zhou Qiren *et al*, op cit.
34   Huo Shilian *et al*, op cit.
35   Shanxi research office, op cit.
36   Zhao Mingzhu *et al*, op cit.
37   Lin Zili *et al*, op cit.
38   Ibid.
39   Ibid.
40   Wang Tingdong, op cit.
41   Ibid.
42   Yan Zanyao *et al*, op cit.
43   Xu Liding & Wang Yuexiang, 'Huairen county makes great efforts to consolidate and improve specialised and key households', *Shanxi Ribao*, 5.7.1983, p 1.
44   Wang Ze, 'Commodity grain specialised households establish an integrated production network', *Shanxi Ribao*, 5.7.1983, p 2.
45   *Red Flag*, 21.10.1984, op cit.  Zhang Xikui *et al*, 'Yanbei prefecture supports the development of processing industry's two households', *Shanxi Ribao*, 26.9.1983; Lin Zili *et al*, op cit.
46   *Shanxi Ribao*, 'How mountain area peasants become rich by accepting advice', 15.7.1983, p 2.
47   Yan Zanyao *et al*, op cit.  Xing Zhiqiang, 'The decentralisation of the agricultural population is favourable to the development of production', *Shanxi Ribao*, 6.7.1983, p 2.  Tong Xunzu, 'Tianzhen county supports the development of specialist villages', *Shanxi Ribao*, 22.8.1983, p 1.
48   Zhao Xingzhong & Li Yue, 'Ying county helps the "Two Households" heighten economic benefits', *Shanxi Ribao*, 17.9.1983, p 2.  Shou Xiang, Wen Fu & Zhi Dong, 'Developing specialised and key households should not serve as a stopgap', *Shanxi Ribao*, 7.8.1983, p 2.  Lu Sheng, Yu Tianrong & Ma Dianfu, 'In Shiyu county on average each household has over one head of large livestock', *Shanxi Ribao*, 5.9.1983, p 1.
49   Zhao Xingzhong *et al*, op cit.

50   Xu Lidong *et al*, op cit.
51   Zuoyun county CPC, '"Support" not "burden"', *Shanxi Ribao*, 1.9.1983, p 2.
52   Lu Sheng *et al*, op cit.
53   Shou Xiang *et al*, op cit.
54   Zuoyun County CPC op cit.
55   Shou Xiang *et al*, op cit.
56   *Shanxi Ribao*, 'Xiaopingyi commune establishes a labour service industry', 13.8.1983, p 2. Zhao Xingzhong *et al*, op cit.
57   Wan He, Xue Qing, Duan Yu & Jia Hua, 'The increasing tendency in Yanbei prefecture to rely on scientific methods to strive for high yields', *Shanxi Ribao*, 26.7.1983, p 1. *Shanxi Ribao*, 'Spring farming preparations under way early in Yanbei rural villages; production responsibility systems stable; peasant zeal for production high', 7.3.1983 tr FBIS/CR/A 16.5.1983, pp 46-7.
58   *Shanxi Ribao*, 7.3.1983, op cit.
59   Pei Qiuheng, 'Strengthen vocational training. Safeguard consumer interests', *Shanxi Ribao*, 9.9.1982, p 2.
60   Ma Dianfu & Chen Jianjun, 'Shiyu county supports peasants planting grass seeds', *Shanxi Ribao*, 10.8.1983, p 2.
61   Yan Zanyao *et al*, op cit. Feng Qinxue & Xu Yali, 'Provincial transport development enthusiastically begins a new phase in road construction', *Shanxi Ribao*, 26.8.1983, p 1.
62   Liang Fengwu & Yang Cunren, 'Shiyu county invests to help specialised households purchase grinding machinery', *Shanxi Ribao*, 21.8.1983, p 1.
63   Yan Zanyao *et al*, op cit. Pei Qiuheng, op cit. Jin Xin, Jing Xi & Huang Fu, 'Yanggao county supply and marketing cooperative promptly delivers market information', *Shanxi Ribao*, 21.8.1983, p 2.
64   Yan Zanyao *et al*, op cit.
65   Ibid.
66   Bai Yulong, Zhang Wei & Zhang Lairen, 'Party members support common wealth amongst backward households', *Shanxi Ribao*, 26.7.1983, p 2.

# Chapter Nine

## Mountain Development:
## Examples from Southern China

## Introduction

It is estimated that mountains and hills make up approximately two-thirds of China's total area, with 2330 counties - 69% of the total - considered to be mountainous or semi-mountainous.[1] There seems to be no standard definition of 'hills' and 'mountains'. In this chapter, it is proposed to define hills as being between 200 and 500 metres above sea level, and mountains as being over 500 metres above sea level.[2] It is recognised that such definitions do not adequately convey details of relief, and where possible the text will clarify the nature of the terrain. The mountain areas contain one-third of China's population, produce one-third of the total grain output and possess 40% of China's cultivable land.

However, as the Geographical Society of China points out, for many years the state has concentrated much of its agricultural capital investment funds in developing production on the plains, ignoring the mountains. Indeed, the Society considers the state's consistent neglect of mountain areas and their development to be a major policy fault.[3] Certainly, Maoist exhortations for the mountains to 'learn from Dazhai' and rely on their own resources for agricultural development met with only limited success.[4]

In recent years, there seems to be some evidence to suggest that the state is prepared to do more to encourage the development of mountain areas. This chapter proposes first to outline in general terms the problems which mountain areas face, and to comment upon the possible solutions to these problems which have been put forward using materials drawn from the mountains of Southern China; and secondly, to look at developments in the rural economies of two specific areas within Southern China.

From the outset it should be noted that these materials are concerned with 'intermediate' rather than what might be called 'pure' mountain areas. These intermediate mountain areas are relatively low-lying (mainly under 2000 metres) and often contain some flat land (mountain valleys and plains). While various difficulties limit the potential economic development of intermediate mountain areas, this potential remains much greater than that of pure mountain areas.

A further distinction should be made about the materials presented here. The environmental conditions of the mountains in Southern China are favourable in comparison to the mountain ranges of Northern China and it would appear inevitable that the relatively advantageous natural conditions of the Southern China mountains will offer greater opportunities for development. Thus, while the problems outlined below may be found in any mountain area of China, it is doubtful if the proposed solutions can be so universally applied.

# The mountains of southern China: the setting

These mountain areas are in the nine provinces of Fujian, Guangxi, Jiangxi, Hunan, Guangdong, Guizhou, Hubei, Zhejiang and Anhui. The region has a sub-tropical or temperate climate with long daylight hours.[5]  However, inevitably there is considerable variation in temperature and rainfall in the area as a whole, not least being variation by elevation as illustrated below.

**Table 1 Southern Hunan. Variations in temperature and rainfall with elevation**

| Height above sea-level (m) | Average temperatures: January | August (deg C) | Annual | Frost-free days | Rainfall (mm) |
|---|---|---|---|---|---|
| 200 | 6.6 | 28.5 | 18.3 | 298 | 1400 |
| 400 | 6 | 26.4 | 16.7 | 273 | 1600 |
| 600 | 4.8 | 25.4 | 15.7 | 255 | 1800 |
| 800 | 4 | 23 | 14.9 | 225 | 2000 |
| 1000 | 3.6 | 21.3 | 13.5 | 201 | 1900 |
| 1200 | 0.1 | 20.3 | 11.3 | 175 | 1850 |

Source: Cheng Weimin (a), op cit, (slightly adapted).

The rural economy of the Southern China mountain areas in comparison with that of the north is relatively prosperous, with well-developed agricultural and industrial undertakings.  While there is no denying - as will be discussed below - that numerous problems do exist in the Southern China mountain areas, there seems to be little doubt that the resource base of the area offers a potential for development less evident in northern mountain environments.

# Problems, solutions and progress

The basic problem in China's mountains is that, on the one hand the state promotes all-round development of the five farming sectors of the rural economy (crops, livestock, aquatic production, forestry and sidelines), emphasising the need to suit development to local conditions, yet on the other hand, mountain economies have had to expand production of grain crops because of the shortage of foodgrains.  The expansion of grain production has often taken the form of improper reclamation of wasteland, inappropriate expansion of the area sown with grain, and irrational increases in multi-cropping.  Mountain areas have suffered tremendous ecological problems as a result - soil erosion, silting-up of lakes and ponds, and loss of forest cover.  Mountain economies fall into a vicious circle from which they struggle to escape, for as farmland fertility drops and water and soil are lost from the slopes, arable land becomes 'desert' and the environment is destroyed. Thus, increases in food grains slow, then stagnate, forcing a further expansion of the grain crop acreage which in turn depletes the environment still more.[6]

This policy offers the mountain economies little relief after the damage inflicted upon them and their environment by the Maoist grain policy. The forced extension of grain fields - often through wholesale destruction of forest resources - and multi-cropping into areas unsuitable for grain production gravely undermined the ecological balance of the mountain areas.

The clearance of forest areas together with the extension of grain production to land with slopes greater than 25 degrees inevitably led to increases in soil erosion. In China as a whole, an estimated area of 1.8 million square kilometres - one-fifth of the total land area - suffered from soil erosion in 1980, an increase of 0.64 million square kilometres since 1949.[7] Mountain areas were a significant portion of this total. Some counties in Hunan's mountains, for example, face soil erosion problems on 50% of their total land area.[8]

While the emphasis on grain production is less pronounced than it was, the mountain areas have been unable to reduce grain production sufficiently to repair the damage done previously. The main reason for this is the requirement that these areas still produce substantial amounts of grain to support basic needs - amounts which the resource base struggles to provide. Thus, not only are local economies and resource bases feeling the impact of ecological difficulties created by previous policy, they are not in a situation to do much to rectify it.

Consider the following details for Yongshun county in western Hunan.[9] Yongshun is a county of some 5.7 million *mu*. Fifteen percent is cultivable land (split roughly equally between paddy and dry fields), 60% is forest, 20% is pastureland. There are also some small lakes.[10] It would be expected that the rural economy of Yongshun county would reflect the importance of its forest and pasture. However, the attention given to grain production has resulted in the rural economy becoming unbalanced.


**Table 2  Yongshun county. Contributions to gross agricultural income. 1982 (%)**

| | | | |
|---|---|---|---|
| Grain foodstuffs | 69.0 | Forestry | 17.8 |
| Diversified undertakings | 5.6 | Sideline undertakings | 9.6 |
| Animal husbandry | 2.2 | | |

Compiled from materials in Chen Qilei *et al*, op cit.
The figures given above indicate that there is still an over-emphasis upon grain production in Yongshun, to the detriment of animal husbandry and the diversified economy in particular.

Recent capital investment of 29.81 million *yuan* (22.451 million *yuan* of which was state investment) in the county's agricultural fields, for example, came at a time when there was an urgent need to control river flows to curb soil erosion and losses in soil fertility. Soil erosion affects 1090 square kilometres of Yongshun's land, 28.6% of the total land area, with soil loss exceeding 1.41 million tons per annum. The decline in soil fertility is also quite startling, the lack of essential plant nutrients such as phosphorus and potassium being of particular concern. Similarly, 131,219 *mu* (34.3%) of Yongshun's paddy fields have extremely shallow plough layers.[11] To be sure, increasing grain production is a prerequisite to allowing local economies to develop other production undertakings, but county authorities must be aware of all the county's problems and not just those of grain production. Though, to be fair, the scale of the problem may be such that they are using what reserves they have to consolidate basic foodstuff production - or more likely, the state insisted that the funds were spent on grain production.

In addition to the grain question, mountain areas face a number of other pressures on their land resources which influence ecological stability. Deforestation, for instance, is a significant problem in any of the southern China mountain areas.

Simple population increase since liberation has resulted in deforestation due to increased pressure upon limited cultivable land resources.[12] But equally important is the concomitant growth in the demand for firewood. Of course this is less of a problem in southern China than it is in some of the northern mountain areas where firewood is usually in short supply for 3-4 months and occasionally as long as 8-10 months.[13] Nevertheless, some deforestation has resulted from the felling of timber for firewood, as well as for other uses such as building materials. This is acknowledged as a serious problem.[14]

While China has historically suffered ecological problems, it is now being argued that recent forest cutting has greatly hastened erosion. In Hunan between the mid-1950s and the mid-1970s, forest acreage declined by 22.83 million *mu*, with the percentage of plant cover falling from 41% to 31.9% and the extent of barren slope-land increasing to some 75 million *mu* - said to be 32% of Hunan's total mountain area. Consequently, the amount of land in Hunan which suffered from soil erosion rose from 12% to 27% of the total land area and river flows increased by 39.7%.[15]

These increases in soil erosion rates and river flows and the loss of vegetation cover, provide one explanation for the increasing frequency of natural disasters in Hunan in recent years. Between 1501 and 1950 there were 41 recorded instances of drought, on average one every ten years, whereas between 1951 and 1977 there were nine instances of drought, one every three years. Similarly the incidence of flooding in recent years has increased from one in ten years on average to one in five years.

Numerous efforts are being made to restore forestry resources in the mountains. First, there have been regulations to curb arbitrary logging of trees.

The State Council adopted a variety of regulations to curb this logging including: forestry production plans to be strictly implemented at all levels; the state monopoly in the purchase and marketing of timber and bamboo to be strictly enforced, with all timber and bamboo free markets in forest areas being closed; improving the management of timber logging and timber transport; and finally, severely punishing any peasant guilty of illegally felling trees, or profiteering on timber and bamboo.[16]

It is difficult to know how effective these regulations have been but it must be doubted if the state can completely prevent the arbitrary logging of trees unless it can be seen to remove effectively the continuing shortages of wood for fuel and building materials, especially in the light of its insistence upon a continued monopoly on the purchasing and marketing of timber and bamboo.

To complement measures preventing the unauthorised felling of trees, it is claimed that the state has also promoted afforestation in resolutions such as the State Council's 'Resolution on a nationwide voluntary tree-planting campaign', this nationwide voluntary tree-planting campaign being a 'major measure' in the general promotion of afforestation throughout China.[17] Such afforestation can be very successful where appropriate planting takes place, for example on those hills which became barren as a result of the drive to expand grain fields.

Nevertheless, while in itself this voluntary tree-planting campaign is laudable, the fact that it seems to occupy such a major part in the overall afforestation drive, indicates that the state finds itself unable to finance afforestation to any significant extent. Indeed, while commentators call for increased state investment to promote afforestation and the general development of the mountain economy, the Geographical Society of China makes the telling comment that mountain areas should not expect to rely on state investment funds in their development.[18] Given the many calls on the state's financial resources, it is this latter argument which appears to be more realistic, with local areas encouraged to accumulate their own investment funds and utilise available bank loans to develop forest resources.

Aside from the preservation and extension of the forest resource base, many authors express the view that existing forest resources could be better managed. The enclosure of forest areas, a balancing of planting and felling, and the development of nurseries as a source of saplings are all aspects of forestry management which require attention. This attention is critical. In the current phase, with growing emphasis on afforestation and (more crucially) the utilisation of forest resources, weak management represents a stumbling block to real improvement. The number of young trees planted remains insufficient. Survival rates are low. Logging too often occurs before trees reach maturity. Concern for immediate gains and quick profits still outweighs long-term considerations.[19]

In Hunan, while significant afforestation is now taking place, the structure of the forests that are constructed is irrational. In the 1950s, the amount of 'pure' forest (that is forest consisting of one type of tree) in relation to the total forest area was small. At present, however, in afforested areas, China fir makes up 74% of total tree stock. Such a large proportion of China fir pure forest, not only reduces the natural productive capacity of the forests, but also increases the instability of ecological conditions.[20]

It must also be said that state prices for timber are low in comparison to those of other cash crops. Peasants complain that 'selling timber is not as profitable as selling firewood'.[21] In other words, state prices for timber are low but 'private' prices for firewood are high. Given such a price discrepancy, it is not surprising that few peasants wish to develop timber forests and that their effective management remains a difficult proposition.

With effective management of forestry resources remaining a problem, it is unclear how much progress can be made to afforest mountain areas, for example, in an effort to control the serious ecological problems they face. In addition, while other possible solutions to these problems - such as controlling water flow through the construction of reservoirs and check dams, and the terracing of mountain slopes - are mentioned in the materials, there is little sign that such measures have thus far been implemented to any significant extent, no doubt partly because of heavy investment costs.

Solutions to the kinds of basic agricultural problems experienced by mountain communities are not easy. The state believes that the 1978 rural reforms offer much to stimulate peasant enthusiasm for production. The evidence suggests that, despite some difficulties in their implementation, the reforms have been well received in the mountains.[22] But in the mountains, perhaps more obviously than elsewhere in China, management reforms will in themselves do little to offset ecological problems. Solutions to these problems require major capital construction projects and substantial investment.

Currently, the state seems able to offer only the standard solution to the local improvement of the resource base and economy: develop your local income and employment opportunities to finance local capital improvements. In this equation, as for most local economies in China, grain production is the dominant variable.

There is much dispute as to the place of grain production in mountain regions. The Geographical Society of China maintains that grain production is an important prerequisite in the rural economy of mountain regions.[23] All too often mountain areas remain dependent on the state for grain, which does nothing to facilitate economic growth.[24] Indeed, in many mountain areas, the inconvenience of communications makes reliance upon the state for both edible and fodder grain foolhardy. Some commentators suggest that mountain areas be exempt from state grain contracts. The state is sympathetic to the needs of the poorest mountain communities, but it does not - and cannot - go so far as to advocate exemption from grain contracts.[25]

Perhaps the problem faced by the state is that any relaxation of grain requirements in mountain areas may lead to similar changes in other more favoured environments where the state expects large supplies of commodity grain to be forthcoming. The state's view is unlikely to change because nationwide, grain surpluses are at best a marginal proposition.

There is also considerable debate about the best way local mountain units might develop diversified production. Consider animal husbandry, for example. Most commentators argue that the development of livestock is a natural adjunct of mountain economies. Yet, some leading ecologists feel that 'obtaining meat from grass mountains' - not least to increase supplies of meat to offset shortfalls in grain foodstuffs - is not a suitable strategy for many mountain areas in Southern China.[26] They argue that the nutritional value of much of the grass in Southern China is poor and unable to sustain a large animal population. To improve grass quality would involve ploughing up hillslopes which would only encourage further soil loss. It would also create greater demands for fodder grain supplies in the winter months. In addition, the animal products themselves would have to be transported over long distances at high cost to participate in the commodity economy.

Commercial difficulties in the mountain areas remain a major obstacle to economic development. Aside from the usual problems of bureaucratic inefficiency, the quality and flexibility of transport networks is weak.[27] Access to major markets remains difficult with commodity and information flows restricted. Additionally, the frequency of natural disasters in the mountain regions - ranging from localised land-slips to widespread flooding - does much to disrupt the transport networks and impede commodity circulation.

While current reforms have to a certain extent resolved difficulties arising from previous rural policy, the development which has taken place is very uneven, with backwardness and poverty still evident. Crucially, it is unclear from this general review of materials how local economies can develop beyond grain production in order to finance the major investment projects needed to prevent further destruction of the rural resource base. Too many units cannot finance needed improvements to grain fields. The resultant instability in grain production in turn restricts development of other production undertakings.

In order to illustrate how local mountain economies can move beyond grain production, material from two mountain economies - northern Guangdong and southern Hunan - will be investigated.

## The example of Northern Guangdong

The mountain range of Northern Guangdong is made up of 14 counties - Yuechang, Renhua, Nanxiong, Shixing, Ruyuan, Lian, Lianshan, Liannan, Yangshan, Yingde, Fogang, Qingyuan, Wenyuan and Qujiang - and Shaoguan city (see Figure 14). The mountains - forming the southern section of the Nanling mountains - are, by Chinese standards, relatively low-lying between 600-1000 metres above sea level, with a maximum elevation of 2000 metres (see Figure 15). The region is some 35,645 square kilometres, with a population over

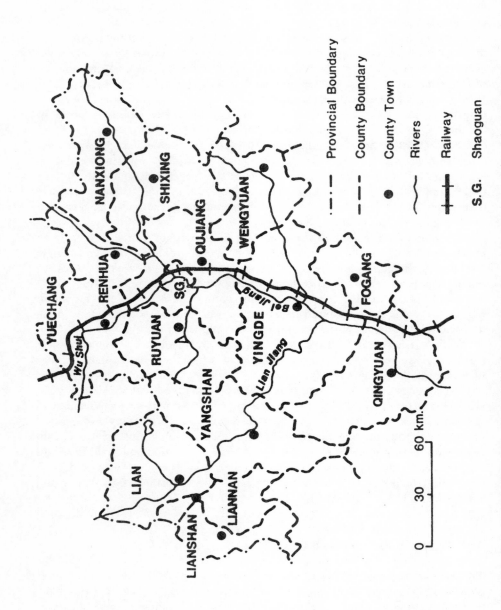

**Figure 14  The mountain region of Northern Guangdong**

five million. It contains almost 5 million *mu* of cultivable land, or a little over one *mu* per capita.[28]

In comparison with much of Guangdong which has seen dramatic development since 1978, not least because of its proximity to Hong Kong, the mountain area to the north remains backward. However, its potential for development remains quite positive in comparison to other mountain areas. This is a relatively low-lying mountain region, with numerous large and small river valleys and basins suitable for cultivation distributed throughout the area. Furthermore, the mountains themselves act as a 'protective screen' from typhoons and excessively cold weather although the region is still affected by monsoons, principally in the lowland regions. Compared to other mountain regions, Northern Guangdong has a favourable ecological system with dense forest cover protecting both upland and low-lying areas from excessive soil erosion. Climatic conditions are also favourable, with average annual temperatures of between 18.8 and 21.6° C, and 10 to 15 inches average annual precipitation.[29] Biomass levels exceed 450-600 tons per hectare, with high levels of micro-organic activity. It would appear that, for the most part, agricultural production conditions are good.[30]

Furthermore, mineral resources are abundant, with reserves of lead, zinc, silver and tungsten for example. Marble, limestone, quartz and China clay are locally quarried, and coal and iron ore are locally mined. It is not surprising therefore, that the industrial base of the mountain region is comparatively advanced, especially with respect to the metallurgical industries: in refining for example, zinc, silver, aluminium and tin; and in the production of coke, pig iron, steel and rolled steel products.

The mountain region also contains a rich variety of water resources, with almost every county capable of developing hydroelectric power stations. Tourism could also be developed, building on the area's natural beauty: interesting sandstone landforms, limestone caves and associated features as well as numerous hot springs.[31]

Finally, and perhaps most significantly, it is claimed that the Northern Guangdong region has relatively developed transport networks. Indeed, it appears to be the hub of the communications network between Guangdong and Hunan and Jiangxi. Almost every county has a major river flowing through it (although this still limits access to river margins) and most county towns are located on or near rivers (see Figure 14). Road transport is relatively developed, with a network of about 7000 kilometres of roads - although no comment is made upon their quality or distribution. While accepting that the communications network is still backward in comparison to southern Guangdong, it is considered better than that typically found in a mountain area. Consequently, commercial difficulties are not what they might be.

The local economy is troubled by four basic issues: first, the population of the area continues to expand upon a finite resource base. Although no comment is made in the materials, it would not be surprising to discover that the

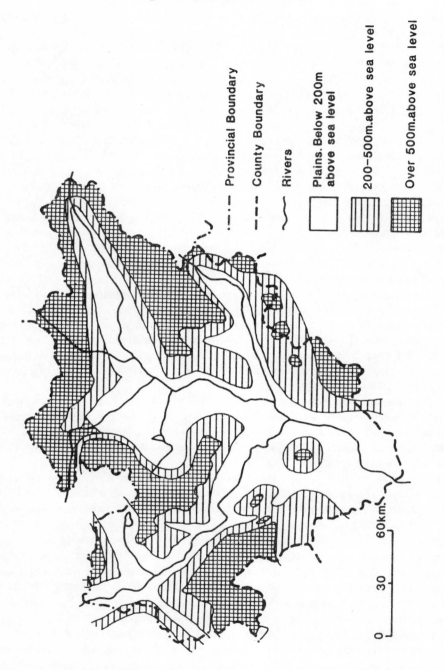

**Figure 15  The mountain region of Northern Guangdong: a sketch map of relief**

current 'one-child' policy is difficult to implement in the mountain regions, even in one as accessible as Northern Guangdong.

Secondly, there are numerous ecological problems to be faced, with natural disasters still commonplace. In May and June of 1983 for example, flooding occurred in numerous counties of Northern Guangdong following torrential rain throughout the mountain area. Qingyuan, one of the region's more low-lying counties, suffered much damage as a result. In May 1983, communes throughout Qingyuan experienced flooding and tornadoes which left one person dead, 12 injured, 832 houses either destroyed or damaged and over 60,000 *mu* of agricultural land inundated.[32]

A month later, in June 1983, further flood damage was reported in Qingyuan after yet more torrential rain - 460 mm in 48 hours.[33] On this occasion 7300 homes were destroyed or damaged with 11,000 people reported homeless. Over 200,000 *mu* of agricultural crops were inundated with at least 11,000 *mu* of crops totally destroyed. Communications and transport networks, electricity supplies and so forth were severely disrupted. Similar problems were reported for neighbouring Yangshan county.[34]

The problems of 1983 followed even more severe flooding in 1982 when 450,000 people were affected and 985,000 *mu* of farmland was inundated throughout Qingyuan, Yingde, Yangshan and Lian counties.[35]

Thirdly, the utilisation of the land resources available in Northern Guangdong is poor. Production levels remain low and the potential for development as yet unrealised. Given the previous low levels of peasant enthusiasm for production and standard of living, much is written about stimulating the local economy through a more efficient utilisation of the available resources, with little said about important issues such as population control and ecological improvement. This is a significant indication that long-term problems of population increase and ecological difficulties will remain and even intensify - especially given the cost of possible solutions.

Finally, grain production remains a significant problem. In 1982 gross grain output of the Northern Guangdong mountain area was 3.96 billion *jin*, an amount considered to be insufficient to meet local needs fully.[36] The state had to supply over 600 million *jin* of grain foodstuffs (16.6% of total needs).

The state had expected much from the introduction of responsibility systems into the region, and initial success with the new production management forms was reported.[37] It was hoped that renewed peasant enthusiasm for production could bring the region to grain self-sufficiency, but enthusiasm is only a single variable in the rural equation here.

Beyond grain production, development in the region has followed the standard path of development of diversified undertakings and rural industry. Before 1978 the diversified economy was weak, limited in extent and depth.[38] Since the 1978 reforms local specialties have reasserted themselves. Local fruit production has developed, pear production in Yangshan, plums in Wengyuan, sand pears in Shixing and mandarins in Lian. Similarly, silkworm production has gathered pace in Qingyuan, Yingde, Wengyuan and Yangshan.[39]

Forestry work is also improving. Responsibility systems have also been implemented in forestry work in an effort to repair the environmental damage caused by earlier excessive clearance of forest when average annual net depletion rates in the Northern Guangdong mountain region reached 400,000 cubic metres.

In Northern Guangdong, authorities have also recognised the importance of forestry work, and the fact that it is an occupation which often does not yield immediate profits, by guaranteeing grain rations to peasants who become involved in forestry. Take the example of Zhao Mujiao of Yaozu production team, Yaoan brigade, Yaoan commune, Lian county. This household, with a labouring ability of six, signed contracts with the brigade forestry centre to establish nurseries (for which it would receive subsidies) and develop forestry paths as well as being responsible for 1000 *mu* of forestry land. The brigade was responsible for supplying a sufficient quantity of grain for subsistence and all income derived from the contracted land went to the household, 10,685 *yuan* in 1982.[40] Similar examples are given for other counties, and obviously it is hoped that widespread forest development can take place.[41]

The development of aquatic production is also important. 390,000 *mu* of water area exists in Northern Guangdong, of which 270,000 *mu* could be used in the development of aquatic production. Breeding fish requires little investment and involves few costs but can yield quick and high returns as Liu Xueyuan of Maoping production team, Chengjiao brigade, Chengjiao commune, Shixing county discovered.[42] In 1982, from 24 *mu* of contracted fish-breeding pools, along with ancillary production of pigs and poultry, this household was able to earn a net income of 15,515 *yuan*.

Aside from agricultural production, the need to fully develop local industrial undertakings is also recognised. Local industry, for example, is developing using investment funds from two sources, household funds and provincial/county funds. In Qingyuan, one household was said to have established a copper refinery which in 1983 had a gross output value of over 970,000 *yuan*, 58,000 *yuan* going to the state as taxes with the household net income being 90,000 *yuan*.[43] On a larger scale, county authorities in Yangshan have developed large cement and phosphate fertiliser plants funded by provincial investment funds. Such plants have not only yielded good economic returns, but have also provided employment opportunities for surplus rural labour.

However, it must be said that the industrial development outlined above remains, in the former case, somewhat exceptional, and in the case of the Yangshan cement and phosphate fertiliser plants, an example of external investment which not every county can expect.[44]

Easily the most notable - and widespread - illustration of rural industry in Northern Guangdong is that of hydroelectric power generation. In Liannan county, for example, the authorities note how their county has developed 78,000 kw of a potential production capacity of 149,000 kw. Currently, the county network of small-scale hydroelectric power stations annually supply 200 million kwH of electricity, 45 million kwH of which goes outside the county, for instance to neighbouring Yangshan.[45]

The benefits that have derived from this development of hydroelectric power have been fourfold. First, through the channelling of profits into other industrial undertakings, it has facilitated the development of an industrial base at county and lower levels. The growth of commune- and brigade-run agricultural produce processing industries has been especially helped in this way. By 1982, the commune- and brigade-run industrial undertakings of the region enjoyed a gross industrial output value of 9.51 million *yuan*, more than the gross industrial and agricultural output value of 1970.

Secondly, this industrial development has in turn facilitated an increase both in collective accumulation funds (from 195,000 *yuan* in 1970 to 697,000 *yuan* in 1982) and peasant per capita incomes (from 70 *yuan* to 182 *yuan* respectively).

Thirdly, this increase in collective funds in turn promotes agricultural development. Of the 54,000 *mu* of cultivable land in Liannan county, some 33,000 *mu* was constructed (in Liannan this probably refers to the terracing of hillslopes) from collective accumulation funds obtained from hydroelectric generation. Similarly, certain advanced agricultural techniques can be implemented more readily if power supplies are available, for example electric irrigation-and-drainage pumps.

Finally, peasant livelihoods have improved as a result of the increased availability of electricity. In Liannan county 80% of all households have electricity - although it must be noted that 20% remain without even though Liannan supplies electricity outside of the county.

The rural economy of the Northern Guangdong mountain area is displaying some sure signs of economic vitality. Progress is being made in both diversified production and rural industry. However, this optimism must be tempered by the considerable difficulties which the peasants of the region still face.

The material on commercial activity, for example, is noticeably concentrated upon the activities of individual households.[46] Yet, the contributions of these households to the commercial activity of the region remain bound to points of access to local markets. Even in a mountain environment as favoured as this one, it is inevitable that most progress will be found in the relatively low-lying plain land as well as those units closer to the major urban market of Guangzhou or lesser urban centres such as Shaoguan.

For example, much material appertaining to quite pronounced rural development is offered for Qingyuan. But Qingyuan has a high proportion of plain land, and is only 60 kilometres from Guangzhou with - at least - good river and rail links to the provincial capital. No doubt these favourable conditions combine with recent policy changes to allow significant growth in the rural economy, even encouraging a relatively high degree of specialisation,[47] this in spite of problems it has encountered with flooding. Neither would this kind of development be unexpected in Qujiang or Yingde, for example. But, it cannot be considered as typical for more peripheral counties to the north, northeast and northwest, counties which contain much less low-lying land. For these counties, commercial and production difficulties are encountered which prevent much beyond localised development.

Furthermore, it is difficult to believe that these peripheral economies will be able to develop beyond grain production. Production units must expect to be at least self-sufficient in grain before they can exploit what other income opportunities are open to them. Grain supplies are insufficiently stable to expect significant development of the commodity economy. Widespread specialisation must be considered unlikely. Obviously, the local subsidies available to encourage grain production in favoured environments, are also absent, the local mountain economies ill-equipped to provide them.

In addition, because high incomes are more difficult to attain in the mountain environments, individual success often breeds resentment and discontent. In Yingde, for example, 60 *mu* of fish ponds remained unused even though contract terms offered to cultivate these fish ponds were favourable, only 100 *jin* of fish each year being required by the authorities.[48] (The example from Shixing county given above has already been seen to produce 13,350 *jin* of fish from only 24 *mu* of fish-ponds. Although pond quality may be different, a quota of 100 *jin* annually seems very reasonable indeed).

Two explanations were offered for the reticence displayed in Yingde; first, the fact that peasants have found that contracts have been arbitrarily amended by local cadres. In Yingcheng town, Yingde county, four households jointly contracted 800 *mu* of water area to develop fish-farming. The contract was valid for two years. They were required to hand over 2000 *yuan* to the local authorities in each year of the contract. Having made 1500 *yuan* profit after fulfilling the contracted profit quota, certain cadres - jealous of these high household profits and incomes - tried to raise the profit quota higher. As a result, the four households did not renew the contract.

Secondly, there is much theft of the produce of contracting households. Land in Yuechang, Yingde, Qujiang and Yangshan counties has been unused because peasants are afraid that any produce they develop will be stolen. A further reason for this reticence could be intimidation. In one example from Qujiang county, a peasant earned a net income of 11,000 *yuan* by contracting a 14.5 *mu* fish-pond and a 13 *mu* orchard. At the year end, jealous neighbours urged local cadres to divide these resources equally in contravention of signed contracts. The cadres refused, but when the peasant put his income into more fish-ponds on unused land, his neighbours (including some local officials) sabotaged construction.[49] Clearly, the state cannot tolerate such behaviour, but, with its decision to extend production contracts, it must expect it to continue.

To sum up, the Northern Guangdong mountain region must be considered a favourable mountain environment. In comparison to other mountain environments its development potential appears considerable. As yet, however, development is very much localised, predictably being concentrated on the more low-lying lands within the region where production possibilities are large and commercial difficulties less apparent. Significantly, the question of ecological difficulties and possible solutions to them are little mentioned. In the long-term, it will be these difficulties which must be overcome in order to sustain and further development in the mountain economies.

# Conclusions

> The distribution of rich counties and poor counties makes one uneasy... Poor counties are concentrated in regions where the natural resources and ecological equilibrium have been destroyed. And this destruction of natural resources and environment has to date not yet stopped. If it continues, the number of poor counties will increase further.[50]

Mountain regions - as defined by the Chinese - include the bulk of China's poor counties, counties where the natural resources and ecological equilibrium have been severely depleted. When added to their commercial difficulties, long-standing neglect from the state and an inability to generate capital investment funds, it is clear that the mountain regions of China, even the relatively favourable mountain environments of Southern China, experience severe development difficulties.

This does not preclude recognition of the fact that some progress has been made in the mountains since the 1978 reforms. Material compiled from a survey of households in 800 mountain counties throughout China, notes a rise in per capita incomes and livelihoods between 1978 and 1982.[51]

However, as already noted, the selection of 'mountain counties' in these surveys may well be misleading. Clearly, in interpreting materials on mountain economies in China, it is important to consider potential diversity in mountain counties and the production possibilities within them. Inevitably generalisations in interpretation of material are made, but as has been indicated, ultimately such local factors as relief, land quality and proximity to major urban centres make vital contributions in determining the scale and degree of development which might be possible within the rural economy of a mountain - or indeed any - area in China.

It seems possible, however, from a review of the development experiences of local mountain economies in this chapter, to place grave question marks against the extent of economic growth which might be possible in the mountains, especially in the more remote areas.

The issue of grain remains paramount in any discussion of mountain regions, just as it does elsewhere. The state's perception of mountain regions is that of being at the very least self-sufficient in grain. As long as the mountain economies are self-sufficient in grain, it is unlikely that the state will do much to actively develop them. Only if they remain grain-deficit areas might the state be tempted to invest capital construction funds - if any are available which is unlikely - and then only to increase grain production. As a result, what development occurs must essentially be internally generated, inevitably uneven and certainly slow. Such state attitudes are little different to those shown towards the mountains by the Maoists.

It is however, perhaps inevitable that the state's attitude should be such. If it relaxed grain policies in the mountain areas, not only would the state have to continue to carry the burden of making good the shortfalls in grain supplies - difficult if not impossible given the poor commercial conditions - such policy relaxation would almost certainly be taken up in areas which the state sees as major suppliers of commodity grain leading to reductions in total grain output.

Thus, current state attitudes towards grain production condemn many local mountain economies to continue a struggle towards grain self-sufficiency, a struggle which requires much land, labour and investment, and limits production possibilities. It is this official attitude to grain production which condemns many mountain economies to the low-output-poor, a trap from which they will struggle to emerge.

This is especially so given the lack of real effort by both the state and local units to combat the serious ecological problems which continue to afflict mountain areas. Without such effort, the economic development that has been possible in the current phase, will most certainly be unsustainable in the long-term. The evidence presented here is not promising. The awareness of ecological difficulties is all too often found only in academic materials and official pronouncements at the national level. Local production units continue to concentrate on short-term gains. This contradiction casts much doubt upon the possibility of long-term economic development in China's mountain areas.

210

# Notes to Chapter Nine

1    Li Zhuchen, 'Some problems of the utilisation of China's mountain areas', *Jingji Dili*, 1984 (2) pp 107-11.

2    Cheng Weimin (a), 'Some questions on the rational utilisation of land in Southern Hunan', *Jingji Dili*, 1982 (1) pp 26-32.

3    Geographical Society of China, 'Comprehensive development and management of China's mountainous areas', *Jingji Dili*, 1984 (2) pp 83-5.

4    Luchuan county revolutionary committee, 'Make a success of farm mechanisation in hilly and mountainous regions', *Red Flag*, 4.12.1971 tr SCMM 1971 (12) pp 57-64. *Guangming Ribao*, 'Vigorously make a success of water and soil conservation, develop agricultural production in mountain areas - typical experience of mountain areas in the middle reaches of the Yellow river in storing up water, conserving soil, and developing mountains and small valleys', 6.2.1971 tr SCMP 1971 (07) pp 134-41. Ba Shan, 'Speed up agricultural construction in mountainous areas', *Red Flag*, 1.12.1973 tr SCMM 1973 (12) pp 61-6.

5    Wang Youchen, 'A discussion of forestry construction in the mountain areas of Southern China', *Jingji Dili*, 1984 (3) pp 191-4.

6    Shi Shan, 'Where is the breakthrough in our nation's high speed development in agriculture?', *Nongye Jingji Wenti*, 1980 (2) pp 33-6 quoted by V Smil, *The bad earth - environmental degradation in China*, (London 1984).

7    Geographical Society, op cit.

8    Cheng Weimin (b), 'Problems of rational utilisation of hilly areas in Hunan province from the ecological viewpoint', *Jingji Dili*, 1984 (2) pp 112-16.

9    Chen Qilei, Wang Zhuxi, Yang Shenghua & Yang Lihua, 'On comprehensive development of the hilly area in Yongshun county', *Jingji Dili*, 1984 (2) pp 92-7.

10   Chen Qilei *et al*, op cit.

11   Ibid.

12   Li Zhuchen, op cit.

13   Wang Xinhua, 'Bring into full play the role played by commune-run commerce in the sphere of circulation', *Nongye Jingji Wenti*, 1984 (3) pp 41-3.

14   *People's Daily*, 'State council forestry circular', 6.12.1980 tr FBIS/DR/PRC 24.2.1981, L19-20.

15   Cheng Weimin (b), op cit.

16   *People's Daily*, 6.12.1980, op cit.

17   *Xinhua*, 'Resolution on a nationwide voluntary tree planting campaign', 12.3.1981 in V Smil, op cit.

18   Wang Youchen, op cit. Geographical Society, op cit.

19   Wang Youchen, op cit.

20   Cheng Weimin (b), op cit.

21  Wang Youchen, op cit.
22  *People's Daily*, 'Carry out strict forestry management and protection while relaxing the policy on forestry', 1.9.1984 tr FBIS/DR/PRC 10.9.1984, K14-15. *People's Daily*, 'Let the peasants be masters of wooded and hilly lands', 19.10.1984 tr FBIS/DR/PRC 26.10.1984, K6-7. Li Guifang, 'Guangdong's Wuhan county sternly handles a case of destroying forests in Rongfu township', *People's Daily*, 1.9.1984 tr FBIS/DR/PRC 10.9.1984, K14. Wang Youchen, op cit.
23  Geographical Society, op cit.
24  Wang Shaoju, 'Poor hilly areas hope that special policies will be implemented to help them get rid of poverty and attain prosperity', *People's Daily*, 24.6.1984 tr FBIS/DR/PRC 29.6.1984, K5-6.
25  Ibid.
26  Hou Xueyu, 'On the direction of exploiting the mountainous and hilly areas in Southern China', *People's Daily*, 9.12.1984 tr FBIS/CR/A 1.2.1983, pp 36-40.
27  Mao Zhiyong, 'Speech', *Hunan Radio*, 24.2.1984 tr FBIS/DR/PRC 27.2.1984, pp 5-6.
28  Wu Yuwen (b), op cit.
29  Ibid.
30  Wu Yuwen, 'Comprehensively develop mountain areas and the promoting of the local economy in Guangdong province', *Jingji Dili*, 1984 (2) pp 102-6.
31  Ibid.
32  He Shibing & Fu Jinbo (a), 'Qingyuan locality torrential rainfall becomes a disaster', *Nanfang Ribao (Southern Daily)*, 14.5.1983, p 1.
33  He Shibing (b), 'Qingyuan and Longhua counties rush to prevent flooding', *Nanfang Ribao*, 19.6.1983, p 4. He Shibing (c), 'In the light of the serious disasters in Shitan and Baiwan communes, Qingyuan county, the county committee and authorities have already appointed people to aid the stricken masses', *Nanfang Ribao*, 20.6.1983, p 1.
34  *Nanfang Ribao*, 'Torrential rain in Northern and Eastern Guangdong becomes a disaster', 17.6.1983, p 1.
35  *Guangzhou radio*, 'Figures on damage cited', 14.5.1982 tr FBIS/DR/PRC 17.5.1982, P1. *Guangzhou radio*, 'Additional damage figures', 15.5.1982 tr FBIS/DR/PRC 17.5.1982, P1-2. *Guangzhou radio*, 'Death toll hits 349', 16.5.1982a tr FBIS/DR/PRC 17.5.1982, P2-3. *Guangzhou radio*, 'Further antiflood measures', 16.5.1982b tr FBIS/DR/PRC 17.5.1982, P3.
36  Wu Yuwen, op cit.
37  Qiu Fusheng, 'In Qujiang county, over 70 households sell in excess of 10,000 *jin* of grain', *Nanfang Ribao*, 17.1.1983.
38  Wu Yuwen, op cit. Liang Rencai, ed, 'An Economic Geography of Guangdong', tr JPRS/DC-389, 21.11.1958.
39  Wu Yuwen, op cit.

40  Li Qingyu, Wu Liguan & Huang Kuang (b), 'Forestry centre work is on the verge of "eruption"', *Nanfang Ribao* 9.4.1983, p 2.
41  Guan Jian & De Ming, 'Nanxiong mountain area conveys a much-told tale', *Nanfang Ribao*, 20.4.1983, p 2.
42  Zhu Zuzhou, 'Mountain area fish-breeding has bright prospects', *Nanfang Ribao*, 17.5.1983, p 2.
43  He Shibing & Huang Jinchi (b), 'Ye Jinyang initiates a household copper-refining factory', *Nanfang Ribao*, 17.9.1984, p 1.
44  Bai Shanhua, 'Yangshan county accelerates the development of the mountain economy', *Nanfang Ribao*, 7.5.1983, p 1.
45  Liannan county authorities, 'Take advantage of the favourable natural conditions of mountain areas to greatly develop rural hydro-electric power', *Nongye Jingji Wenti*, 1984 (3) pp 44-6, 20.  Li Qingyu & Shi Dexiang (a), 'From now on Liannan county's surplus electricity capacity will be transferred out of the county', *Nanfang Ribao*, 3.4.1983, p 2.
46  He Shibing *et al* (a), op cit.  He Cheng, 'Within the mountains people are buying motor vehicles', *Nanfang Ribao*, 1.6.1983, p 2.
47  He Shibing (a), 'Qingyuan's town and country markets are greatly flourishing', *Nanfang Ribao*, 29.5.1983, p 2.
48  Li Qingyi & Shao Tiao, 'Why are large numbers of fish ponds and orchards in Northern mountainous Guangdong not put on a contract basis?', *Nanfang Ribao*, 16.10.1983 tr FBIS/CR/A 7.11.1983, pp 42-3.
49  Ibid.
50  Shi Shan, op cit.
51  Tian Jijin, 'Agricultural production speedily develops in more than 800 counties in the mountain areas throughout the countryside', *Economic Daily*, 21.11.1983 tr FBIS/CR/A 12.1.1984, pp 19-20.

# Chapter Ten

# Conclusions

We should see that the agricultural base is still very fragile and that
the real momentum (for agricultural reform) has only just begun.1

The impact of the 1978 reforms in the Chinese countryside has - by Chinese
standards - been dramatic.  For many peasants incomes and livelihoods have
improved in a relatively short period of time.  The relative success of the rural
reforms has also generated the momentum for further agricultural reform,
instilling enthusiasm and a sense of expectancy into China's peasantry.

However, as the quote above concedes, the agricultural base of much of
China's countryside remains fragile.  This fragility results from wider problems
such as dependence upon a weak commercial system, the continuing
vulnerability of much of the countryside to the vagaries of the weather, the weak
industrial base (despite decades of priority investment, particularly in heavy
industry) and the continued threat of overwhelming population increase.  Thus,
it must be asked whether the path of rural development through commodity
production and commercialisation proposed by the current regime can be
effective (ie maintain momentum and fulfil peasant expectations) in the long-
term, at the same time creating a markedly different rural economic system to
that which existed under the Maoists before 1978.

This question is a difficult and complex one.  The development path
espoused by the current regime is not without its own problems, some of which
are serious.  The changing relationships and emphases created by Dengist
policies and emerging in the current phase, relationships and emphases which
will no doubt determine the extent of rural prosperity as well as political stability
in the long-term, are the focus of this concluding chapter.

## Regional differentiation

Living standards have improved, but levels are low and uneven.2

In the regional chapters it has been argued that the impact of the post-1978
reforms and the ability of rural units to take advantage of them must vary
spatially.  Such variety, in the real world, translates into considerable differences
in the availability of production opportunities, and the ability to turn those
opportunities into higher incomes, real jobs, improved peasant livelihoods, and a
means to finance improvements in the local resource base and production
management systems.

There is considerable disagreement amongst both western and Chinese
commentators on this issue.  Some believe that in the new rural economic
climate, polarisation is necessary and unavoidable - at least in the short-term.[3]

Others take a different view, claiming that the Chinese countryside shows less sign of polarisation, and that on the contrary a levelling effect can be seen.[4]

That there is inequality within the Chinese countryside seems undeniable. Whether this inequality is widening or narrowing is a question which remains difficult, if not impossible, to answer. The lack of adequate low-level data and the immense diversity of local conditions makes a quantitative analysis of this question impossible. Certainly, the range of per capita incomes (admittedly an imperfect indicator of living standards) presented in the regional materials is sketchy, too often localised, and perhaps too often distorted to permit the drawing of real conclusions on the extent of inequality and future trends in the Chinese countryside.

Although the regional materials do not provide a wide-ranging database, they do provide for adequate qualitative - if also more tentative - conclusions about regional differentiation. More specifically, it is possible to make observations on the potential ability of rural production units to develop commodity production.

It has been demonstrated above that the state is unable or unwilling to make available the necessary investment capital for large-scale agricultural construction and development. The burden of responsibility for investment funds therefore falls upon the local production units and the peasant households themselves. Inevitably, the ability of local units and individual households to raise such funds varies considerably.

The state admits three broad regional classes of area within the Chinese countryside. The first region, including the periurban areas, has strong commodity economies, good transport facilities and a relatively good technical capacity. Links between city and rural industry are developing, often in terms of 'putting-out' relationships.

The third region is composed of the remote and poor areas. Inaccessible, economically backward, these areas still have problems meeting basic foodstuff and clothing needs. The second region is the remainder: areas with an intermediate level of development. Here, the problems of basic foodstuff and clothing supplies have been solved, but they lack the advantages to be found in the periurban areas. Development is possible but remains a struggle for most units.[5]

In numerical terms, 11.9% of the total rural population earn an annual net per capita income of more than 500 *yuan* and are considered advanced by the Chinese media. 7.6% earn less than 150 *yuan* and still have problems in finding adequate food and clothing. These are the backward areas. The bulk of the rural population, 80.5%, falls somewhere in between.

The significance of such broad statements depends on the level of resolution at which they are applied. At a meso-level this is important. All too often, by designating such large areas as 'developed', 'intermediate' or 'backward', as much can be hidden as revealed. In particular, the classification offered by incomes, in which 80% of China is considered intermediate, is not particularly revealing.

Such broad statements indicate, correctly, that the bulk of rural China seems to be enjoying a period of comparative prosperity but they do little to evaluate the basis for this progress, and more pointedly, the problems experienced by the local economies.[6]

Consider, for example, the following simple classification of the six example regions used in this book.

**Table 1 An example classification of six regions**

| Developed | Intermediate | Backward |
|---|---|---|
| Taihu agricultural district, Southern Jiangsu | Nenjiang prefecture, Heilongjiang | Mountains of Northern Guangdong |
| Suburban area of Nanjing city, Jiangsu | Xuhuai agricultural district, Northern Jiangsu | |
| | Yanbei prefecture, Shanxi | |

Although these six areas have markedly differing environments, at a general level this classification can perhaps be justified. Classifying spatially aggregate areas at the meso-level can avoid the worst excesses of generalisations at the national level, especially in a country as large and diverse as China, as well as those at the micro-level. Nevertheless, when contemplating such a classification it must be remembered that a wide range of development is possible within a given area.

In the mountains of Northern Guangdong for example, a backward area, some optimism is expressed in the media as to its development potential. Closer inspection, however, reveals that in actuality the development potential being discussed is concentrated on the relatively developed low-lying plains, for instance in Qingyuan county. Expressions of optimism for localities away from low-lying plains appear unfounded; certainly they are not being greatly illustrated. Still, it is also true, that the development potential of the Northern Guangdong mountains is far superior to that of other mountain areas, especially in the north, northeast and west.[7]

Of greatest interest are the intermediate areas in which the high-output-poor (or even low-output-poor) trap is most noticeable. Arguably the development of these areas in the long-term can have the greatest impact upon national economic development. The favourable characteristics which shape the wealth of developed areas and the problems which continue to beset backward areas will continue to act as constants unless rural policy alters dramatically. National development, traditionally, is most influenced by progress or otherwise in the key intermediate areas of the North China plain and its modern counterpart in the northeast.

The ability of these areas to finance long-term development becomes of increased importance. Variations in environment mean that for different intermediate areas the potential sources of necessary capital investment take on varying degrees of importance. In Yanbei prefecture, for example, the dominant source of capital is coal mining. Xuhuai agricultural district has a more broad-based potential to generate investment funds including numerous rural industrial enterprises (so important in the development of its southern neighbour Taihu), extraction industries and diversified undertakings.

On the ground these variations inevitably mean that some intermediate units will move out of the high-output-poor trap and become more advanced. However, a qualitative assessment of the production possibilities within a region is useful to distinguish between that improvement in rural units which is indicative of more widespread rural improvement and that which arises out of distinct local advantages (usually economic/geographic but also including political influences, past and present).

Whatever the merits or otherwise of a regional classification as illustrated in Table 1, it provides a framework around which materials can be usefully placed.

## 'State sponsored' differentiation

Two issues can be identified here, both concerned with state attitudes towards specialisation. First, the state's attitude towards specialised households. Secondly, state perceptions of areas as commodity grain producers.

The state admits that the introduction of specialised households into the Chinese countryside has inevitably led to inequalities and tensions.[8] Indeed, the regional materials have shown that such tensions can ignite bitter hostility. State officials at the highest level claim that this inequality need only be temporary with specialised households serving as models for others to aspire to. This claim represents little more than an attempt to hide the inevitable reality. That is, advanced, intermediate and backward households can be identified locally with advantages (or a combination of advantages) coming into play to offer a range of income and employment opportunities. In this way, some households - often under the guise of 'specialised households' - are able to profit greatly ahead of others. Given the difficulty (under current rural policies at least) of equalising income and employment opportunities among households in a given unit, inequalities will remain. Indeed, experience in other third world countries suggests that these inequalities will increase rather than diminish.

The inequality between grain specialists and non-specialists at household level is a situation the state must find most disquieting and of great immediate significance. Certainly the relative value of grain production remains significantly lower than that of other agricultural produce. It is interesting to note that when comparing the profits obtained by grain specialists with those for other agricultural produce the difference, though less obvious, is still real.

**Table 2 Net profits of crop production. Various crops; localities** (*yuan/mu*)

Grain:
| | |
|---|---|
| China | 11.16 |
| Shandong (wheat) | 10.17 |
| Datong county, Shanxi: | |
|    1 Non-specialised households | 29.07 |
|    2 Specialised households | 37.1 |
|    3 Luozhenying brigade: | |
|      - Non-specialised households | 51 |
|      - Fan Chengzhong (grain specialist) | 89.6 |
| Shanghai suburbs | 125 |
| Other crops: | |
| Shandong - peanuts | 68.54 |
| Shandong - cotton | 158.25 |
| Shanghai suburbs - cotton | 179 |
| Shanghai suburbs - oil-bearing crops | 266 |

Compiled from materials in Nong Yan, op cit; Datong county CPC and people's government, op cit; Hua Xicheng *et al*, op cit.

This material illustrates the continuing differentials between the profit which is possible from the production of grain and that of other agricultural produce, a differential likely to be greater if compared with other non-agricultural rural production. The availability of local subsidies/incentives in combination with the benefits (great or small) of specialisation is no doubt the reason why the grain specialists illustrated in Table 2 fare better than average, but as noted in the regional chapters, the ability of local units to provide subsidies/incentives and the large land-holdings from which grain specialists can and must benefit, varies and inevitably reinforces regional differentiation.

While grain specialists may be able to boost their incomes above the norm for grain production, locally they may still find themselves in a high-output-poor trap within their unit, with incomes below those earned by other peasants. Ironically, within these units the grain production of these specialists may be freeing - to whatever degree - local resources for other undertakings - undertakings from which other peasants reap large rewards. This point has been illustrated above but bears repeating.

Consider the following table comparing the production characteristics of four specialised households in Heilongjiang.

**Table 3  Guangrongliu brigade, Qianjin commune, Hailun county. Heilongjiang: four specialised households\*. Various indicators. 1984**

| | Head of Household | | | |
| --- | --- | --- | --- | --- |
| | Lu | Cao | Li | Wei |
| Household size | 6 | 9 | 10 | 5 |
| Labouring ability | 3 | 4 | 1 | 1 |
| Cultivable land: | | | | |
| 1 Total area (*mu*) | 36.48 | 65.84 | 49.22 | 31.94 |
| 2 *Mu*/capita | 6.08 | 7.3 | 4.92 | 6.38 |
| 3 *Mu*/labourer | 12.16 | 12.46 | 49.22 | 31.94 |
| 4 Grain (*mu*) | 31.95 | 57.055 | 38.21 | 24.665 |
| 5 Cash crops (*mu*) | 4.53 | 8.785 | 11.01 | 7.375 |
| Animal husbandry: | | | | |
| 1 Cows | 0 | 0 | 1 | 3 |
| 2 Marketed pigs | 3 | 10 | 15 | 0 |
| 3 Sows | 0 | 0 | 0 | 1 |
| 4 Hares/rabbits | 3 | 3 | 10 | 0 |
| 5 Oxen | 0 | 0 | 2 | 0 |
| 6 Goats | 2 | 0 | 0 | 0 |
| 7 Poultry | 10 | 20 | 40 | 0 |
| Incomes: | | | | |
| 1 *Yuan*/capita | 422 | 447 | 1083 | 1467 |
| 2 Gross household (*yuan*) | 2535 | 4025 | 10828 | 7811 |
| 3 From grain - *yuan* | 1319 | 2475 | 1498 | 1467 |
| - % | 52 | 61.5 | 13.8 | 20 |
| 4 From cash crops - *yuan* | 226 | 400 | 930 | 44 |
| - % | 10.5 | 9.9 | 8.6 | 0.6 |
| 5 From animals - *yuan* | 750 | 1100 | 5400 | 5600 |
| - % | 29.6 | 29.3 | 49.9 | 76.4 |
| 6 Other sources - *yuan* | 200 | 50 | 2000 | 700 |
| - % | 7.9 | 1.2 | 18.5 | 9.5 |
| Grain sales to the state (*jin*) | 10395 | 21330 | 9055 | 8181 |
| Commodity grain income (*yuan*/*jin*) | 0.13 | 0.12 | 0.17 | 0.18 |
| Per-unit yields of commodity grain (*jin*/*mu*) | 325.4 | 373.9 | 236.9 | 331.7 |

\*See text for definition of 'specialised household'.
Source: Heilongjiang social science research institute (b), op cit. Some figures deduced.

The four households in question are all designated as being 'specialised' according to different criteria: Lu's household by its total grain sales to the state being over 10,000 *jin*; Cao's household by the fact that its grain sales to the state are above 2000 *jin*/capita - both these households are grain-producing specialised households; Li's household by the fact that gross household income is above 10,000 *yuan*; and finally Wei's household as its per capita income levels are above 1000 *yuan*.[8]

What can be immediately drawn from Table 3 is the fact that the two grain specialists are considerably worse off. This has much to do with the importance of grain as an income source. Lu and Cao, the grain specialists, receive an average of only c 0.13 *yuan*/*jin* for commodity grain while Li and Wei receive c 0.18 *yuan*/*jin*. This difference presumably reflects contract requirements and agreements. The grain demands placed upon Lu and Cao allow some diversification, but the bulk of their income comes from grain farming. While it is not made clear in the materials if Lu and Cao receive any subsidies from the local production unit, it is clear from Table 3 that these subsidies would have to be substantial if the incomes of the four households were to be equalised. Indeed, the income figures may already include local subsidies which would point to even greater inequalities.

While it must be conceded that such factors as farming ability, machine availability and variable land quality may influence the production figures of the four households, there is little doubt that in this example grain production is the major cause of what is relative high-output-poverty for Lu and Cao (although it must be said that the level of per capita incomes demonstrated for Lu and Cao is high by Heilongjiang standards). This also perpetuates itself in that the higher incomes of Li and Wei can be reinvested in important producer goods promoting high grain yields and the possibility of furthering diversified undertakings - in particular, animal husbandry which, as noted above in Chapter Seven, is important in Heilongjiang. Certainly, it is noticeable that Li and Wei's grain productivity (using per-unit yields of commodity grain as a an indicator) is comparable to that of the grain specialists, Lu and Cao.

Grain production is also the focal point for potential disagreement between meso-level authorities and the state. While the state permits the payment of subsidies to grain specialists both within and outside the official contract system, it has to be aware that the underlying philosophy involved in such subsidies, if unchecked, will cause problems.

The ability of developed areas to subsidise grain production and thus free resources to develop the wider rural economy contrasts sharply with the inability of intermediate areas to do likewise. This regional divergence may ultimately prove intolerable. Intermediate areas, increasingly resentful of the ability of developed areas to stay within the system and still make money, may put pressure on the state to reduce their own grain burdens - especially if perceived by the state as a commodity grain producer - and pass them on to the developed (and usually more fertile) areas. However, the state appears more likely to prefer the continuing delivery of (more lucrative) diversified commodities from the developed areas.

Certainly, areas such as Taihu, mindful of the years when they had to subsist on low grain rations and disproportionately contributed to state procurement quotas, are eager to make the most of current state attitudes.[9] In Taihu, while basic grain contracts are fulfilled, total grain sales to the state have fallen considerably in recent years, in part because the peasants understand and take advantage of the greater benefits that can be gained from developing other rural production undertakings and also because the state has allowed them to do so.[10]

If the state allows this situation to continue, and there are no indications that it will do otherwise, the burden of responsibility for grain production will rest even more heavily on the traditional granaries. These are the areas which struggle to diversify beyond grain: the high-output-poor areas. This can only serve to further regional differentiation and tensions.

## The emergence of the household as the basic production unit

When the immediate gains of the post-1978 reforms have been exhausted and the Chinese countryside is forced - stability of regime permitting - to face up to the reality of long-term needs, the most striking legacy likely to be bequeathed to a long-term development programme is that of the increased importance of the individual household as the basic production unit in the rural economy.

A great degree of decentralisation in the agricultural production decision-making process has occurred. The result is that the individual peasant household is in a far stronger position than before the 1978 agricultural reforms. While this decentralisation is in itself a significant factor in the recent improvement of the rural economic sector, as a foundation for long-term development it will surely have interesting repercussions.

Two points seem to be most significant: first, the emergence of individual households as the basic production unit relates well to the state's call to improve specialisation in agricultural production. Specialisation of production, amongst other things, requires that skills at the household level be allowed to blossom.

The second point of interest is that arguably the way out of the high-output-poor trap is made even more difficult by the emergence of the individual household as the basic production unit in the countryside. The problems of the high-output-poor areas, (further emphasised in the low-output-poor areas), appear soluble only through high-cost incentives or similarly costly long-term development measures. However, high-output-poor areas, and even more so low-output-poor areas, by their very nature often do not have the necessary capital and find it difficult to accumulate. There are two ways in which the emergence of household production has done little to improve this situation. First, any gains made by households in high-output-poor or low-output-poor areas have predominantly accrued directly to the individual households and more often than not have resulted in spending on consumer goods rather than on producer goods. Secondly, it has made the maintenance of existing capital construction projects and the execution of any new capital construction plans more difficult.

In other words, in those weaker areas where the strengths of the collective system might improve agricultural production and peasant livelihoods in the long-term, the rise of the individual household can be seen in a negative light. Conversely, in long-established, commercially developed rural areas, the emergence of individual households, facilitating as it does specialised production, can only further encourage their relative wealth provided that measures can be taken to maintain and expand upon capital construction projects which benefit the local resource base.

It is difficult to see where the break-point is, that is, how intermediate areas might usefully utilise the advantages of the household while also maintaining collective benefits, potential and real.

It has been intimated in the regional materials above that specialised service companies - a collection of households, both specialised and non-specialised, which provide production services to producers - may be the way to combine the benefits of household production with a collective structure. These service companies, or others like them, have conspicuously developed to support commodity production. As one commentator notes, emerging to 'function as one level of the collective economy', yet ostensibly being an organisation controlled by the local peasants and not the state organs.[11]

However, many peasants view them as essentially adjuncts of the collective system which did so much to limit rural production under the Maoists. Consequently, the localities cannot expect enthusiastic support - at least not initially. If local economies cannot encourage sophisticated production then what is left will be little more than family farming.

In areas of intermediate resource, development will thus follow the path outlined above, that is specific local advantages helping some units to prosper ahead of others. Because such development is concentrated at the micro-level, it is not easy to see how significant capital construction projects (for example, irrigation-and-drainage projects) can be administered with any effectiveness. Such projects, financially burdensome, are exactly those which rural China must be able to fund in the future. But there is little 'collective spirit' being displayed at the meso-level. Households want independence without conditions.

The temptation for conspicuous consumption by the local authorities has similarly proved hard to resist. Many commune and brigade authorities seem unconcerned about human and financial resources as they blindly expand non-productive capital construction - movie houses, theatres and office buildings. In this way, local authorities are spending millions of *yuan*, and yet at the same time complain that they are unable to support grain-contracting specialised households. Support for these households may often be nothing more than hollow rhetoric.[12]

Undoubtedly, many households have grasped the opportunity to work for themselves firmly in both hands. In the intermediate areas this can only make

222

long-term development more difficult unless rural production can develop the means to combine the freedoms offered to the households by *baogan daohu* with the advantages claimed for, if not always realised by, the collective structure.

## State influence in the Chinese countryside

Any distinct change in the relationship between the state, collective and individual can have profound implications for future production environments. Thus, it would seem appropriate to follow comments on the emergence of the household with some points about the state's position in the Chinese countryside

Before 1978 the state's position was very strong. It had strict control over production and the state monopoly on marketing and purchasing was rigorously enforced. The collective too had strong control over production, output, finances and the peasants themselves. Indeed, after 1978, commentators criticised the collective authorities of the mid-1970s as having extracted too large a share of gross output and income so that they 'squeezed the state above and the commune members below'.[13]

In reality the state was probably little squeezed. However, the individual peasants unquestionably suffered from the strength of the collective, in addition to that of the state. Individual peasants had little control over land, labour or capital and even the extent of their private plots was severely curtailed by the Maoists. Even if the peasants could engage in sideline production, they had little access to markets. The official commercial channels were strongly controlled and often severely impeded and rural markets and fairs had virtually disappeared.

Since 1978, there has been a new emphasis in the state, collective and individual relations; one of 'pressing the centre (the collective) and guaranteeing the two ends (the household and the state)'.[14] More correctly perhaps, the emphasis was firmly put on assuring supremacy of the state in dealings with both the collective and the peasants:

> The state is a tool for the people to exercise their power and realise their economic interests. It represents and protects the fundamental interests of the people ... Therefore, compared with the interests of the collective and the interests of the individual, the interests of the state cannot help but have first priority.[15]

The introduction of household responsibility systems must be interpreted as giving more initiative in production decision-making to the individual. However, the state has achieved this largely at the expense of the collective. The state appears to have forced the collective (at whatever level) to adopt a role of implementing state plan production targets through production contracts. This represents a considerable loss of autonomy and power in comparison to the pre-1978 period. Certainly the state remains determined, through its dominant position when concluding contracts, to retain strong control over agricultural production.[16]

Yet, because of its determination to maintain authority and control in the rural sector, the state increasingly finds itself under pressure from the peasants to improve its performance. Despite the fact that in much of the Chinese countryside development remains limited and uneven, the scale of the agricultural sector is sufficient to ensure that even limited and uneven development creates a large demand for agricultural producer goods for example. It is thus vital that the state be able, both in terms of availability of producer goods and their distribution to and within the countryside, to meet such demands. If supplies fail to meet demand, development will be greatly hindered resulting in severe damage to peasant enthusiasm for production and an increase in corruption and illegal activities in order to obtain the necessary producer goods. Thus, the state is under increasing pressure to actively reform both the official commercial channels and also the nation's industry. Both are difficult tasks.

A further challenge to the state may come from the more wealthy peasants within a local unit. Under the current policies such peasants find it possible to accumulate significant parcels of cultivable land. With long-term contract periods currently being encapsulated within production contracts, it is not difficult to envisage 'landowner-labourer' relationships developing in some units. This is especially true where specialisation of agricultural production takes place. The incidence of wage-labour, illegal rent payments and other 'unwelcome tendencies' will inevitably increase because specialisation tends towards very uneven distribution of land holdings, and the same is true of optimal use of land resources.

These actions, and others like them, may or may not be unacceptable to the state. At present it seems that the state is effectively willing to ignore such actions in order to maintain peasant enthusiasm for production - especially commodity production - and to see rural economic development proceed as far as current policies will allow.

The state's attitude here reflects the importance of peasant enthusiasm to the development of rural production in the current phase. It is a concern which is markedly different from that exhibited by the Maoists. However, the current regime must be painfully aware that once this enthusiasm diminishes in the face of the continuing high-output-poor trap or other kinds of discouragement, rural economic growth will likewise stagnate.

For the moment, the state retains its pre-eminent position, undoubtedly bolstered by the success - albeit perhaps short-term - of its rural economic policies. This success has been at some considerable cost to the power and influence of the collective which increasingly appears to be an auxiliary state organ with little local autonomy. Similarly, the success of current policies has brought the state fresh challenges and demands, especially with the emergence of the household as the basic production unit in the countryside. These challenges and demands are serious and will become increasingly acute as the initial wave of enthusiasm for the post-1978 reforms has passed and the state and peasants alike have to face continuing long-term problems - for example in commerce, industry, the environment and population growth - which have no easy solutions.

Finally, while the state retains pre-eminence in economic affairs through production contracts administered by the collective and signed by individual peasants, it is perhaps losing some grip on its social control of the countryside. Whilst not arguing that this loss is a substantial one, it is nonetheless evident. The upsurge in corruption, at all levels, flagrant breaches of state regulations and contracts are all indicative of a loss in the state's social control. This loss could have serious implications for the state in its ability to implement policy, especially unpopular policy.

## Stability and flexibility

The post-1978 reforms contain within them measures to satisfy conflicting demands for stability and flexibility in the rural economy. Inevitably this has led to troublesome contradictions. In some senses this issue has already been raised in another context. The emergence of the household, for example, promotes the flexibility in production sought by the peasants but which at the same time could deprive them of the production stability (in terms of the creation of a high stable-yield agricultural resource base) that the collective might provide.

The contradiction is more noticeable on the issue of land contracts and land transfer. The introduction of long-term production contracts was a significant measure attempting to provide peasants with some stability and continuity in landholdings so that they might feel more inclined to invest in that land. However, problems arise with this, most obviously with production specialisation where the transfer and consolidation of landholdings is important. Again, production conditions may change dramatically in the lifetime of a contract. Even more, household conditions may also change dramatically in such a space of time. How easy will it be to change these contracts under these changing circumstances? If it is too difficult, the state may find itself saddled with very unrealistic rigidities; if it is too easy, then it is also easy to understand peasant wariness. Similar questions arise about the strictness of contracts in times of natural disasters for example. The media materials are noticeably weak on this issue and it seems inevitable that this silence itself could promote wariness and unease.

Certainly, the contradiction between the need for flexibility and the need for stability in the rural economy is one which seems unlikely to go away in the near future. It is an area of policy which may present the state with difficult choices. On the one hand the state is concerned that peasants should take responsibility for investment in the land, on the other it seeks to increase specialisation in agricultural production. To achieve both appears to involve contradictions in policy which the state must convince peasants need not necessarily be so.


## Rural industry and diversification

> At present, rural commodity production marches forward on `two legs', so to speak. One is the specialised households, which should focus on production based on local resources, while the other is the commune- and brigade-run enterprises which should concentrate on processing farm and sideline products, and on producing daily necessities as well as equipment and implements for the countryside.[17]

Rural industry and diversified undertakings are crucial to the future of China's rural economy. Important sources of income and employment opportunities, it has been demonstrated in the regional materials that the range and depth of rural industrial and diversified undertakings very much dictate the extent of economic development in a given area.

However, perhaps the state expects too much from rural industry and diversification. On the question of land redistribution, for example, the state acknowledges that constantly redistributing the land amongst rural households in response to changed domestic circumstances is not beneficial to stability in farming or economic development. New labour forces, it argues, must be gradually shifted to non-farming trades so as to limit the constant division and redistribution of land resources.[18]

However, given the pre-existing levels of rural surplus labour, it is unrealistic to expect rural industrial and diversified undertakings to provide more than a fraction of the necessary income and employment opportunities. The state concedes that for the immediate future, this must be the case. The truth is that this must be the case for many years to come.

It could also be argued that fairly frequent land redistributions are a political end in themselves intended to prevent the growth of 'estates' and a landowner class and hence, to some, more desirable than economic growth. This is, however, perhaps a somewhat cynical view. More likely, the frequent distributions relate to genuine peasant concerns about having equal opportunities for wealth creation, and the traditional attachment to the land.

The problem of surplus labour will of course continue to be an important one in rural China. It can be seen that if rural industry and diversification is to be important in the solution of this problem, as it seems likely to be, then it will be areas such as Taihu, Southern Guangdong and the periurban locales which can develop such undertakings and provide income and employment opportunities. The intermediate and backward areas cannot anticipate similar development and underemployment will remain a major problem.

Conclusions

Nevertheless, it must also be pointed out that even in areas such as Taihu and Southern Guangdong, competition between rural production units for both resources and markets is acute. Although the Chinese media is happy to present the Chinese countryside as a seemingly perpetual source of income and employment opportunities for those who wish to develop rural industrial and diversified undertakings, inevitably this is not the case. Without some form of control, rural industrial and diversified concerns may spend too much of their time in unprofitable, wasteful and harmful competition thereby severely limiting rural economic growth.

Further, while it is true that profits from rural industry remain an important source of investment funds for agriculture, it is less clear that such subsequent investment in agriculture has top priority. Evidence for 1985, for example, suggests that localities are more concerned with expanding rural industrial capacity than that of farming. Investment in rural industry is growing much quicker than that in farming (which actually fell from 1984 in part due to the poorer rural performance in that year).[19] Data from 1988 and 1989 would seem to confirm this trend.[20] On the one hand, this makes economic sense, on the other hand, it may preclude much-needed investment in farming. This is just another hard choice which the localities now face.

## New China, old China

There has been, undeniably, enormous upheaval in China and the Chinese countryside in the past decade. The China of the open door is a much different place from the China of Mao: the dominant collective structure has been usurped by the household and family farming; 'small and complete' models of commodity self-sufficiency have been replaced by calls for inter-dependence and commodity specialisation; egalitarian distribution of income replaced by slogans urging peasants that 'to get rich is glorious'; and politics in command of the economy is being replaced by a combination of the market-place and the planning system.

Yet, there is a China - old China if you will - that current policy has done little, if anything, to change. The rural economic reforms introduced in 1978 will do little to profoundly alter the traditional geography of China: the essential difference between the production conditions of North and South China, and the resultant tendency of the South to reluctantly 'feed' the North; the continued development of the coastal provinces at the expense of the interior - with the notable exception of Sichuan, an area of long-standing natural fertility; the inability of mountain communities to effectively utilise their environments to generate wealth and achieve the levels of prosperity attained on the plains; and the continued neglect of the 'peripheries', in particular the provinces of Xinjiang, Qinghai, Tibet, Gansu, Ningxia and Inner Mongolia, where the bulk of China's minority population is found.

227

The prescriptions for rural economic development proffered by the Dengist regime seem to ignore the traditional geography of China, ironically in the same way as the Maoists were accused of doing. Current policy, which on the one hand represents a move towards a more sophisticated, complex and 'modern' market economy, on the other hand does little except compound natural and historical distinctions.

The policies of 'New China' essentially 'institutionalise' these distinctions. Wealth creation through commercialisation heavily favours the rural economies of the coastal areas (with their relatively convenient infrastructure) over the interior; and the fertile areas of southern Jiangsu and southern Guangdong over the traditional granaries of the North China plain. Furthermore, in the current phase, the state has chosen to emphasise the development of the coastal areas over the interior. In theory, these developed areas become an 'open door' for the interior. But in effect the state has chosen to consolidate the advantages of the coastal as the best way to maximise economic returns on its limited investment funds, consigning the interior and the peripheries to internally generate income and employment opportunities. That is, compounding the traditional regional differentiation within China: 'Old China'.

## Concluding remarks

Since liberation, the Chinese countryside has endured many attempts by various factions within the Chinese Communist Party to speed up rural economic development. These attempts have utilised a variety of normative, coercive and remunerative appeals ranging from the 'socialist impatience' exhibited in the Great Leap Forward and Cultural Revolution to the neo-market socialism of the current regime.

It remains to be seen of course, if the policies of the current regime will prove resilient to criticism. The experience of the past 40 years in China would make it foolhardy to assume that they definitely will. However, it must be said that these policies may prove durable because of their popularity with the rank and file - especially after the excesses of Maoism. It will also help that Deng Xiaoping has been active in placing his supporters at the highest levels of the party bureaucracy to ensure their longevity. Also, increasingly few of China's population remembers China before liberation, and so more and more Chinese judge the successes of current policy against the performance of post-liberation rather than pre-liberation regimes. In this regard, these reforms are welcome.

Contemporary Chinese rural economic history must be seen as a series of short-term policy proposals and counter-proposals as different factions held sway in Beijing. Interestingly, many long-term development proposals change little from one regime to the next. This is perhaps due to the standard nature of many of these proposals, their apolitical nature or perhaps simply a lack of interest in long-term measures in a period of China's history when change seems to be endemic. Yet important ecological and technical problems will have to be tackled if the Chinese rural economy is going to be able to sustain its growing population and develop beyond grain production.

China's environmental problems must not be underestimated. Too many local economies have fallen into a trap of expanding agricultural production at the margin to meet increasing needs, only to see outputs fall and costs rise - 'more poverty means more cultivation, more cultivation means more poverty'.[21] Local ecological systems are undermined and the incidence of natural disaster (with a greater than 30% drop in production over the previous year used as a baseline) is increasing. In the long-term, this issue must be confronted.

Finally, there is no doubt that the stable supply of grain remains at the heart of Chinese rural study. Until the Chinese are able to consistently produce sufficient supplies of grain to satisfy consumer demands fully, and to do so without excessive demands upon land, labour and capital, research upon rural China must continue to emphasise grain production. This is even more certain given the fact that even optimistic accounts of China's population growth indicate no significant decline in numbers until well into the next century.

The Chinese rural economy appears to be reaching, or in some places to have reached, the point in its current development where short-term stimulation can no longer sustain the rapid improvement witnessed since 1978. The state is unable to guarantee continued improvement, perhaps not surprisingly given the many and varied demands on its limited resources, demands which are likely to get heavier. With such tight economic constraints - as well as long-standing geographic and historical influences - limiting the state's action, it is difficult to propose policies for the bulk of the countryside which go far beyond the acceptance of present realities.

# Notes to Chapter Ten

1   Ningbo agricultural committee, op cit.
2   Li Chengrui *et al*, op cit.
3   Du Runsheng (b), op cit.  Wang Shuheng, 'A second "golden age" in Yichun', *Beijing Review*, 17.9.1981 24 (33) pp 22-5.  E B Vermeer, 'Income differentials in rural China', *China Quarterly*, 1982 (89) pp 1-33.
4   He Rongfei, 'Agricultural production responsibility systems and the problems of impoverished households', *Guangming Ribao*, 5.10.1982 tr FBIS/DR/PRC 5.10.1982, K11-13.   K Griffin, 'Comment: income differentials in rural China', *China Quarterly*, 1982 (92) pp 706-11.
5   *People's Daily*, 'Enlightenment gained from Haian', 29.11.1984 tr FBIS/DR/PRC 5.12.1984, K3-4.
6   Gao Chilian, 'Do not compare in this way', *Beijing Ribao*, 26.2.1985 tr FBIS/DR/PRC 8.3.1985, K17-20.
7   Song Linfei (b), op cit.
8   Heilongjiang social science research institute (a), 'Important avenues in the building of commodity grain base counties - a probe into questions about grain-producing specialised households', *Xuexi Yu Tansuo* (*Study and Discussion*), 1984 (2) pp 35-42.
9   T P Bernstein, 'Stalinism, famine and Chinese peasants: Grain procurement during the Great Leap Forward', *Theory and Society*, 1984 13 (3) pp 339-57.
10  Zhao Ziyang, op cit.
11  Baoding prefecture, op cit.
12  Ningbo agricultural committee, op cit.
13  *People's Daily*, 'The key to bringing into full play the peasants' socialist enthusiasm lies in implementing the party's rural policies', 15.2.1978 tr FBIS/DR/PRC 17.2.1978, E12-14.
14  *Sichuan radio*, untitled, 22.12.1977 tr FBIS/DR/PRC 4.1.1978, J2-3.
15  Xue Xi, 'Put right the relationship between the state interests and individual interests', *Beijing Ribao*, 13.2.1982 tr FBIS/DR/PRC 22.2.1982, R1-3.
16  *People's Daily*, 'Establish the concept of co-ordinating all the activities of a nation like pieces in a chess game', 24.2.1982 tr FBIS/DR/PRC 26.2.1982, K1-2.
17  Song Linfei (b), op cit.
18  *People's Daily*, 3.7.1984, op cit.
19  *Statistical Yearbook of China, 1986*, op cit.
20  *China Statistical Abstract, 1990*, (Praeger).
21  Shi Shan, Yang Hanxi, Yang Tingxiu & Shen Changjiang, 'Ecological problems and the creation of a new situation in agriculture', *Red Flag*, 1.9.1981 tr JPRS/CR/RF No 17, pp 32-41.

# Bibliography

## Selected Readings

This list is not to be considered in any way comprehensive, but rather as a selection of work both on rural China specifically, and China in general. Some of the work is quite general in nature, some is more academic. Further, the readings cover China's development both before and after 1978.

R Barker, R Sinha and B Rose (eds), *The Chinese Agricultural Economy*, (Westview, 1982)

C Blundin and M Elvin, *Cultural Atlas of China*, (Equinox, 1983)

T Cannon and A Jenkins (eds), *The Geography of Contemporary China: The Impact of Deng Xiaoping's Decade*, (Routledge, 1990)

*China Quarterly*, (Special Issue) *The Readjustment in the Chinese Economy*, December 1984

A Eckstein, *China's Economic Revolution*, (Cambridge University Press, 1977)

S Feuchtwang and A Hussain (eds), *The Chinese Economic Reforms*, (Croom Helm, 1983)

W Hinton, *Fanshen*, (Vintage Books, 1968)

F Leeming, *Rural China Today*, (Longman, 1985)

C W Pannell and L J C Ma, *China, the geography of development and modernization*, (Edward Arnold, 1983)

A Rabushka, *The New China: Comparative Economic Development in Mainland China, Taiwan and Hong Kong*, (Westview, 1987)

Ren Mei'e, Yang Renzhang and Bao Haosheng, *An Outline of China's Physical Geography*, (Foreign Languages Press, 1985)

V Smil, *The Bad Earth: Environmental Degradation in China*, (M E Sharpe, 1984)

Xue Muqiao, *China's Socialist Economy*, (Foreign Languages Press, 1981)